PENGUIN BOOKS

FROM EROS TO GAIA

Freeman Dyson is a professional scientist who has made a second career writing books for non-scientists. He likes to vary his scientific activities with forays into engineering, politics, arms-control, history and literature. He writes mostly about people and things he has seen, sometimes about people and things he has imagined. He was born and raised in England, worked during the Second World War as a boffin for Royal Air Force Bomber Command, emigrated after the war to America, and became famous by solving some esoteric mathematical problems in the theory of atoms and radiation. Since 1953 he has been a Professor of Physics at the Institute for Advanced Study in Princeton, New Jersey. The main theme of his life is the pursuit of variety. This includes variety of people, variety of scientific theories, variety of technical tricks, variety of cultures and languages. It also includes the variety of chapters and topics to be found in this book.

S0-BNB-406

FREEMAN DYSON

FROM EROS TO GAIA

PENGUIN BOOKS

PENGUIN BOOKS

Published by the Penguin Group
Penguin Books Ltd, 27 Wrights Lane, London W8 5TZ, England
Penguin Books USA Inc., 375 Hudson Street, New York, New York 10014, USA
Penguin Books Australia Ltd, Ringwood, Victoria, Australia
Penguin Books Canada Ltd, 10 Alcorn Avenue, Toronto, Ontario, Canada M4V 3B2
Penguin Books (NZ) Ltd, 182–190 Wairau Road, Auckland 10, New Zealand

Penguin Books Ltd, Registered Offices: Harmondsworth, Middlesex, England

First published in the USA by Pantheon Books 1992
First published in Great Britain in Penguin Books 1993
3 5 7 9 10 8 6 4

Printed in England by Clays Ltd, St Ives plc

Contents

CONTENTS

Preface

The world of science and the world of literature have much in common. Each is an international club, helping to tie mankind together across barriers of nationality, race, and language. I have been doubly lucky, being accepted as a member of both. As a scientist, I have professional friends and colleagues, people I know and feel at home with, in thirty countries around the Earth. As a writer, I have pen friends, people who write me eloquent and personal letters, spread over an equally wide range. It is wonderful to discover that, in this age which is supposed to be dominated by television and computers, people still read books and write letters.

My mother used to say that life begins at forty. That was her age when she had her first baby. I say, on the contrary, that life begins at fifty-five, the age at which I published my first book. So long as you have courage and a sense of humor, it is never too late to start life afresh. A book is in many ways like a baby. While you are writing, it is curled up in your belly. You cannot get a clear view of it. As soon as it is born, it goes out into the world and develops a character of its own. Like a daughter coming home from school, it surprises you with unexpected flashes of wisdom. The same thing happens with scientific theories. You sit quietly gestating them, for nine months or whatever the required time may be, and then one day they are out on their own, not belonging to you anymore but to the whole community of scientists. Whatever it is that you produce—a baby, a book, or a theory—it is a piece of the magic of creation. You are producing something that you do not fully understand. As you watch it grow, it becomes part of a larger world, and fits itself into a larger design than you imagined. You belong to the company of those medieval craftsmen who added a carved stone here or a piece of scaffolding there, and together built Chartres Cathedral.

I was born in 1923 in Crowthorne, a village in the south of England without pretensions to scientific fame. My parents' interests were artistic and literary rather than scientific. My mother was a lawyer, my father a musician. Our only connection with professional science was Sir Frank Dyson, who held the exalted position of Astronomer Royal. Sir Frank was not related to us, but he came from the same part of Yorkshire as my father. We were proud to share his name. His glory helped to turn my infant thoughts toward astronomy.

When my mother died at the age of ninety-four, I found among her papers a long-forgotten manuscript, an unfinished novel with the title *Sir Phillip Roberts's Erolunar Collision,* which she had preserved among the relics of my childhood. I wrote it at the age of nine. My hero Sir Phillip is clearly based on Sir Frank Dyson, the literary style is borrowed from Jules Verne's story *From the Earth to the Moon and a Trip Around It,* and the theme of a collision between the asteroid Eros and the Moon must have been suggested by the close approach of Eros to the Earth in the year 1931. The Eros encounter was in fact an important opportunity for the professional astronomers of that era, who used it to obtain an accurate determination of the distance between the Earth and the Sun. It is likely that Sir Frank was involved in organizing the observation and analysis of Eros's movement across the sky. In 1931 he was not only Astronomer Royal but also President of the International Astronomical Union. No doubt, as a seven-year-old, I heard his activities discussed daily by my elders at the breakfast table. In my story Sir Phillip successfully predicts the Erolunar collision by calculating the orbit of Eros ten years in advance, and then organizes an expedition to the Moon to observe the event in detail, just as Sir Frank had organized the expeditions to Africa and Brazil to test Einstein's theory of general relativity by measuring the bending of light by the Sun's gravity during the solar eclipse of 1919. Unfortunately, the narrative stops abruptly before Sir Phillip's expedition has left Earth. When I rediscovered this fragment forty-two years later, I was amused to see how little I had changed. I was a writer long before I became a scientist. And I was always in love with spaceships. In all my writing, the aim is to open windows, to let the experts inside the temple of science see out, and to let the ordinary citizens outside see in.

The kernel of this book is a set of three Danz Lectures given at the University of Washington in 1988 with the title "On Being the Right Size: Reflections on the Ecology of Scientific Projects." I am grateful to the Jessie and John Danz Fund and to the regents of the University of Washington for sponsoring the lectures. They gave me the opportunity to collect stories about projects that failed and projects that succeeded, and to speculate about the causes of success and failure. The lectures appear here as chapters 2–5. At the instigation of my editors, Cornelia and Michael Bessie, I decided to incorporate the Danz Lectures into an anthology of other non-technical writings, published and unpublished, extending over six decades from 1933 to 1990.

The title *From Eros to Gaia* defines the beginning and the end. By a happy coincidence, the names of two Greek gods have become attached to two astronomical objects, the errant minor planet Eros and the fertile life-giving mother-planet Earth. Eros is the god of youthful passion, Gaia the goddess of motherhood and of caring for all life's creatures. Eros is a swift-moving and potentially destructive hunk of rock; Gaia is the guardian of trees and fish and bacteria and humans. The pilgrimage from Eros to Gaia is a good metaphor for the life of a writer, beginning with a joyful fantasy of interplanetary fireworks and ending with a serene fantasy of green leaves and peaceful death.

I included the juvenile Eros fragment in this book with some hesitation, knowing that it is vastly inferior as a work of literature to the incomparable classic *The Young Visiters,* written by the nine-year-old Daisy Ashford. Ashford wrote a complete novel, with a sophistication of plot and characterization far beyond my reach. My fragment is not presented here as a rival to Ashford's novel, but merely as evidence of how the world of science appeared to an attentive nine-year-old in the 1930s. Two features of the narrative strike me now as noteworthy. First, the chief character, who is supposed to be a professional astronomer, spends his time fund-raising and doing calculations at his desk, rather than observing the sky. Second, the driving force of a scientific project is institutional self-aggrandizement rather than intellectual curiosity. These two insights show that the practice of science has changed less than one might have expected between 1933 and 1991.

The concluding Gaia story was written for an anthology with

the title *Living Philosophies,* edited by Clifton Fadiman and published in 1990. I am grateful to Doubleday for permission to reprint it here. Between Eros and Gaia come thirty-three other pieces classified in six categories: Stories, Things, Institutions, Politics, Books, and People. The pieces within each section are arranged chronologically. "Stories," beginning with Eros and the Danz Lectures, are mainly anecdotal history. "Things" are expository popular-science articles, mostly written for *Scientific American.* "Institutions" are lectures given on various occasions, discussing questions of public policy related to the support and administration of science. "Politics" are lectures and articles going beyond science into the human problems that science and technology have created. "Books" is a sample of book reviews, chosen in the hope that they have something to say beyond the ephemeral. "People" is a gallery of portraits, mostly of people I have known personally, ending with the invocation to Gaia. The bibliographical notes at the end of the book contain detailed references to the sources from which each of the previously published items were taken.

The chapters are not intended to be read consecutively. As a guide to readers who have time only for the highlights, here is a list of my favorite pieces, one from each section. "Six Cautionary Tales for Scientists," the first of the three Danz Lectures, is a collection of stories illustrating the human frailties that scientists share with other mortals. "Energy in the Universe" tries to put the problems of our use of energy on Earth into a larger and longer perspective. "Astronomy in a Private Sphere" is a historical essay, celebrating the triumph of human idiosyncrasy over bureaucratic organization. "Pugwash 1962" is a sketch of scientists discussing disarmament, with a brief glimpse of Leo Szilard, the legendary figure who otherwise appears in this book only in the section headings. "Manin and Forman" is a review of two superb little books, by the Russian mathematician Yury Manin and the American historian Paul Forman, which gave me an excuse to trace connections between the gloom-and-doom prognostications of Oswald Spengler and the revolutionary discoveries of modern science. Finally, "Feynman in 1948" is a reminiscence of the wonder-year in the life of Richard Feynman, the year in which I had the luck to watch an indubitable genius at work and at play.

When I read the older pieces today, I am struck, as my readers will be struck, by the frequent use of the masculine pronoun referring to students or scientists in general. In the more recent pieces this usage is avoided. I decided not to change every "he" in the older pieces to "he or she," but to let the pronouns stand as they are. I hope that younger readers will understand that the old usage of the masculine pronoun does not mean that we were all male chauvinists in those days. On the contrary, it never occurred to us then that our female colleagues such as Chien Shiung Wu and Cécile DeWitt were not in every respect our equals, or that the habit of using a masculine pronoun to include the feminine could be interpreted as implying a lack of respect for their achievements as women and as scientists.

I am grateful to the audiences at many times and places who listened to my lectures, corrected my mistakes and sharpened my judgments. I am grateful to the many readers of my books who have written thoughtful letters in response, sometimes in anger but more often in friendship. Most of them were answered. I apologize here to those who were not. Finally, I am grateful to Cornelia and Michael Bessie for their unfailing help and encouragement. If my books are babies, they are the midwives.

Stories

○○○○

DO YOUR WORK FOR SIX YEARS; BUT IN THE SEVENTH,

GO INTO SOLITUDE OR AMONG STRANGERS, SO THAT

THE MEMORY OF YOUR FRIENDS DOES NOT HINDER YOU

FROM BEING WHAT YOU HAVE BECOME.

—LEO SZILARD,
"TEN COMMANDMENTS"

CHAPTER I

Sir Phillip Roberts's Erolunar Collision

.....

1 9 3 3

I. THE GREAT DISCOVERY

Sir Phillip Roberts, director of the British South-African Astronomical Society, was sitting in his study, calculating facts about Eros, the minor planet which revolves at between 100,000,000 and 180,000,000 miles from the sun, and which sometimes approaches within 13,000,000 miles of the Earth. He had just discovered that Eros was going to come exceptionally near to the Earth in 10 years and 291 days, and might, by some luck, be caught within the Earth's attraction. He quickly went off and told one of the members of the society, Major Forbes, who was rather a friend of his, the good news. At first, Major Forbes would not believe it, and said that it was impossible, but, after looking at Sir Phillip's calculations, he admitted that it was very likely to happen.

After rechecking the calculations, and finding that they were true without doubt, Sir Phillip called all the members of the Society together in they meeting-place, and he began a speech:

"I, Sir Phillip Roberts, and my friend, Major Forbes," he began, "have just unravelled an important secret of nature; that Eros, that minor planet that is so well-known on account of its occasional proximity with the Earth, Eros, will approach within 3,000,000 miles of the Earth in 10 years 287 days hence, instead of

3

the usual 13,000,000 miles every 37 years; and, therefore it may, by some great chance, fall upon the Earth. Therefore I advise you to calculate the details of this happening!"

"Three cheers for Eros!" said a certain member, "Hip, Hip!"; "Hurrah!" they all shouted; "Hip, Hip!" said he; "Hurrah!" bellowed everybody; "Hip, Hip!" said he, a third time; "Hurrrraaaaaaaah!!!" bellowed everybody once more!

II. MORE DISCOVERIES

When the cheers were over, and everybody had gone home, it did not mean that the excitement was over; no, not at all; everybody was making the wildest calculations; some reasonable, some not; but Sir Phillip only wrote coolly in his study rather more than usual; nobody could tell what his thoughts were.

After a few days, one of the members of the society found out that Eros would approach within rather more than 240,000 miles of the Earth, or about the Moon's distance from the Earth when the Moon is at its aphelia, or its farthest point from the Earth; this was checked by Sir Phillip, and proved true.

This set everybody calculating exactly where the Moon would be at that time; and, wonder of wonders!, the Moon was found to be due at the exact spot where Eros would be in 10 years, 285 days' time; or, to put it more shortly, Eros would collide with the Moon.

III. THE GREAT IDEA

Of course, this was a great opportunity for the B.S-A.A.S. to become important; so all the members did all they could with the opportunity. They tried to think of something great to do, but nobody could for some days.

One day, another member, Brig.-General Mason, thought of the thing that this book is about; in fact, he proposed to reorganize that daring expedition of Barbicane, Nicholl and Michel Ardan to the Moon, to witness the collision.

The expedition which Michel Ardan made so world-famous,

and in which President Barbicane, Captain Nichol, and Michel Ardan ascended beyond the Moon in trying to reach it, is fully told in Jules Verne's "From Earth to Moon and a Trip Round It."

General Mason went and told Sir Phillip his idea at once. "Accounting for delays," said Sir Phillip, when General Mason had told him his idea, "and the journey, and preparations on the Moon, we will still have well over ten years to make our canon, projectile, and gun-cotton, we will use gun-cotton, it is much better than ordinary powder, therefore we can make our expedition much larger than Barbicane's; don't worry about money, subscripsions will be almost infinite. We will hold a meeting soon; au revoir for the time being." With this, he and General Mason left the room.

Sir Phillip wrote a letter, and then type-wrote it some few times, and adressed the copies to various astronomical observitaries and newspapers; this was the letter:—

"I, Sir Phillip Robertson, head of the British South-African Astronomical Society, and my followers, or rather the other members of the B.S-A.A.S., have dicovered that Eros, that minor planet about which you all know, will collide with the Moon, our only visable sattelite, 10 years, 283 days hence; and the B.S-A.A.S. have discided to reorganise Barbicane's expedition to the Moon on a larger scale; and we will witness the collision ourselves with the naked eye, instead of through a telescope. If you can provide them, we would not mind a few million pounds' worth of subscripsions.

> Yours:—Sir Phillip Roberts"
> Director of the B.S-A.A.S."
> Dombardy Observertary"
> Nr: Kimberly"
> Brit. S. Africa."

He then retired, with a lot to thing about; after all, he had been daring enough to disclose to the public that he would send a large expedition to the Moon, spinning 220,000 odd miles away, with only a few pounds in his pocket, at least, only a very very few compared with the amount he would want.

IV. THE QUALITIES OF THE PROJECTILE

Now, the size and shape of the projectile, cannon, and powders had to be discussed; the first meeting was about the future projectile.

The next day, the first meeting was held.

"Well," said Sir Phillip, "we are here to converse about our projectile inside which we are to ascend to our only satellite; what size do you prepose?"

"It is to be much larger than Barbicane's?" said Mr. Morgan, seceratry of the Society.

"Yes, certainly," said Sir Phillip.

"It really depends on the size of the party inside it," said G. H. I. Hurst. "How large will that be?"

"We will need about half a dozen at the place where the great collision will take place, another half dozen at the other side of the Moon to witness white-hot Eros emerging from the Moon at the other end, and three to guard the projectile from Selenite storms and animals; fifteen in all," said Sir Phillip.

"Will Eros really go right through our sattelite?" said Major Forbes.

"Yes," said Sir Phillip, "Its speed, and its small weight and resistance, will bring it through our sattelite, it will be a picture, suddenly rising white-hot from the Moon's internal fires, followed by a stream of liquid lava."

"Well," said somebody, "Fifteen men, five times as many as Barbicane crew, will need five times as much stores, air, and heat than Barbicane's expedition."

"Do you prepose to carry a columbiad and projectile and powders for our return?"!!! The proposer of this mad idea, even of launching a second columbiad into space with its projectile, was thought by each member of the Society to be killed at least by all the others, except Sir Phillip, but nothing happened!

"Well," said Sir Phillip, much to everyone's amazement, "what about the idea, it is very daring, but worth thinking about. "It will need an enormous projectile to hold, and therefore an unbelievable columbiad to launch it into space, with the columbiad, and the rest, the projectile will be like this," and he drew this:

[Here follows a diagram of the projectile with its internal compartments]

"We will carry a telescope, in order to see Eros coming; it, of course, and the columbiad, will be left on our sattelite for further crossing to the Moon."

"But what tremendous projectile will carry the lunar columbiad?" asked somebody.

"I have worked out that the lunar columbiad need not exeed in length 25 feet, and in diameter 10 feet; so the projectile, with rooms and telescope, need not exeed 32 ft. in length, and 15 ft. in diameter. And the celestial columbiat need not exeed two miles in length."

[At this point the narrative stops]

CHAPTER 2

On Being the Right Size

Reflections on the Ecology of Scientific Projects

.....

1 9 8 8

J. B. S. Haldane published his essay "On Being the Right Size" in a book, *Possible Worlds,* which I read as a teenager about fifty years ago. *Possible Worlds* was published in 1927 but has much to say that is still relevant in 1988. Here, for example, is Haldane describing the effects of gravity and air resistance on animals of various sizes:

> You can drop a mouse down a thousand-yard mine shaft; and, on arriving at the bottom, it gets a slight shock and walks away. A rat is killed, a man is broken, a horse splashes.

Haldane was a physiologist who did important work investigating physical and chemical hazards to which miners were exposed in English coal mines. One can be sure that his remarks about the behavior of mice and horses falling down mine shafts were based on precise observation. He was also a socialist, and did not hesitate to extrapolate his physiological observations to the domain of social theory. I quote again:

> To the biologist the problem of socialism appears largely as a problem of size. The extreme socialists desire to run

every nation as a single business concern. I do not suppose Henry Ford would find much difficulty in running Andorra or Luxembourg on a socialistic basis. He has already more men on his pay-roll than their population. . . . But while nationalization of certain industries is an obvious possibility in the largest of states, I find it no easier to picture a completely socialized British Empire or United States than an elephant turning somersaults or a hippopotamus jumping a hedge.

Following Haldane's lead, I try in the next three chapters to explore the effects of size on the health and pathology of scientific enterprises. As Haldane knew, the survival of animals of various sizes depends not only on their physiology but on their ecology. To survive, an animal has not only to be of the right size for the functioning of its internal anatomy. It has also to be of the right size to form a stable community with the bigger and smaller creatures on which it is dependent. In the natural ecology of living creatures, the overwhelming majority of successful animals are small, but the few large animals tend to dominate the landscape. The large animals have an ecological importance that is out of proportion to their numbers. And so it is also in science. The vast majority of successful scientific enterprises are small, but the big enterprises also have an essential role to play. And the big enterprises tend to dominate the political and educational milieu within which the small enterprises must learn to survive. Out of this dominance of the big enterprises arise the central questions of scientific ecology. How should the balance between big and small be maintained? How big is too big and how small is too small? How can we launch large projects without creating political pressures that endanger the integrity of science?

I shall not try to give general answers to these questions. We cannot calculate from general principles the optimal size of a scientific project, any more than we can calculate from general principles the optimal size of an elephant or a whale. Every scientific project is unique, just as every species of animal is unique. The purpose of the science of ecology is not to calculate the sizes of elephants and whales but to understand the conditions under which elephants and whales can flourish. Instead of discussing scientific enterprises in the abstract, I shall examine particular examples and see whether they suggest any general rules of behavior. Examples of successful and unsuccessful projects may give us some useful guidance when we make our plans for the future.

The science of ecology has made its major impacts on society in the form of warnings of disaster. Ecologists have not been shy to issue such warnings, even when the evidence of imminent disaster was controversial. If you wait to take action against acid rain until the evidence for its ecological effects is unambiguous, you have waited too long. The ecologists have learned by hard experience to speak promptly and loudly when they see disasters coming. I follow their good example. When I think that a project is likely to turn into an ecological disaster for science, I say so. I do not expect everybody to agree with my judgments. After all, ecologists are often useful even when you do not agree with them. My purpose is not to compel agreement but to provoke discussion.

CHAPTER 3

Six Cautionary Tales
for Scientists

.....

1988

I. THE THIRD WORLD

I begin with three cautionary tales, one from each of the three worlds into which our planet is divided. These tales will have various morals. One of the morals is that human nature is the same in all three worlds. We are the same people making the same mistakes, whether we happen to belong to the third world, the second world, or the first world. But let me tell you the stories first. The stories should speak for themselves. After you hear the stories you can decide what the morals ought to be.

To represent the third world I choose the village of Ngon, a village in Central Africa where my daughter Mia spent some time as a Peace Corps volunteer. My information comes from an unpublished report which Mia wrote after she came home. Mia visited Ngon as an employee of the Office of Community Development of the Republic of Cameroon. Her official function was to assist and encourage local initiatives leading to the improvement of public health and education.

The main problem in Ngon is water. The village is several kilometers away from the nearest source of potable water. Night and morning, the women of the village must walk to the spring and back, with heavy waterpots balanced on their heads. During

Freeman Dyson

the dry season the spring degenerates into a muddy swamp. In 1985 the official Committee of Village Development, composed of prominent residents of Ngon and three neighboring villages, met to consider the problem of water supply. The meetings were conducted according to the traditional rules of African hospitality, the village chiefs presiding, their wives keeping the delegates supplied with food and drink, my daughter as an honored guest seated among the chiefs. The villagers mostly belong to the Boulou tribe and have their own Boulou language, but they have been educated for three generations in French bureaucratic jargon. The Committee of Village Development, in keeping with its official status, conducted its deliberations in French.

Two courses of action were available. I will call them Plan A and Plan B. Plan A was to engage the services of a professional well digger who happened to live nearby. The fee he charged was high by village standards, but not prohibitive. He would design and direct the construction of an adequate well, including a bathhouse and laundry, using the villagers as his work force. My daughter had made enquiries about his work in other villages and found that the results were generally satisfactory. Plan B was to write a formal proposal to the central government in Yaoundé, three hundred kilometers away over very bad roads, for a massive water adduction system using urban technology. The chance that the proposal would be accepted was small. Many hundreds of villages were competing for the central government's limited resources. But if Ngon should happen to be the lucky winner, the rewards would be great, especially for the members of the Committee of Village Development. The decision was made unanimously to proceed with Plan B. As a result, at least up to the time when my daughter left the country, Ngon still had no water supply.

After the meetings were over, my daughter went back to the village and spoke privately with the villagers, trying to understand why they had made what seemed to her a clearly wrong decision. She found that everybody, including the women who carry the waterpots to and from the spring, was in favor of Plan B. In the end, they almost convinced my daughter that Plan B made sense. After all, as one of the women said to my daughter, nobody in Ngon ever dies of thirst. The problem of the water

12

supply is not a matter of life and death. The problem is a matter of status. On the one hand, the act of writing an official proposal to the government would enhance the status of the village and of the Committee of Village Development, even if nothing ever came of it. It would open a channel of communication and create contacts between the villagers and the political authorities in Yaoundé. In the long run, such contacts are more important to the life of the village than a communal bathhouse. On the other hand, the act of making a deal with a backwoods well digger would be unworthy of the dignity of an official Committee of Village Development. If these arguments had not been sufficient, there was an even more cogent reason for rejecting Plan A. The well digger is a Fulani. He belongs to the wrong tribe. The Boulous of Ngon are a settled agricultural people. They have lived from time immemorial in villages and consider themselves civilized. The Fulanis are northerners, nomads, and cowherds. No self-respecting Boulou would want to take orders from a Fulani.

So I leave the villagers of Ngon, on the whole a happy and contented people. They were always friendly and hospitable to my daughter, even when they found her ideas a little strange. I pass on now from the third to the second world.

2. THE SECOND WORLD

To represent the second world I choose the great Soviet astronomical observatory at Zelenchukskaya in the Caucasus Mountains. I visited the observatory in 1977. The six-meter telescope, the largest optical telescope in the world, was then brand-new and just beginning to go into operation. I spent three days and nights on the mountain and enjoyed my stay very much. The astronomers at Zelenchukskaya were as friendly to me as the villagers of Ngon were to my daughter. They talked frankly about the six-meter telescope and its history.

Twenty years earlier a committee of the Soviet Academy had met to discuss with the political authorities the facilities for optical astronomy in the Soviet Union. The six-meter telescope was their Plan B. Plan A was to construct four or five modern observatories of modest size at optically excellent sites in Central Asia. One example of a Plan A observatory already existed at Byurakan in Soviet Armenia. The Armenians are the Fulanis of the Soviet Union. I also visited Byurakan and saw there a two-meter telescope with a Fulani by the name of Markaryan in charge. Markaryan was using his telescope to great effect, taking pictures of the sky with an objective grating and picking out objects that have strong emission in the blue and violet parts of the spectrum. Many of the most interesting objects in the universe were first identified by Markaryan and still carry Markaryan's catalog numbers. Byurakan has been for thirty years in the hands of Fulanis who know how to do important science with limited means.

Unfortunately, there are no other observatories like Byurakan in the Soviet Union. Instead, Plan B prevailed. The committee of academicians decided to build the biggest telescope in the world. Six meters was chosen as the mirror diameter because it had to be decisively bigger than the five-meter telescope at Palomar. The manufacture of the telescope was entrusted to a heavy industrial outfit in Leningrad which had little previous experience with astronomy. The observatory was under construction for twenty years. When I visited it in 1977, one of the Soviet astronomers remarked that the structure was built out of leftover pieces from dismantled battleships. Another Soviet astronomer told me that this one instrument had set back the progress of optical astronomy in the Soviet Union by twenty years. It had absorbed for twenty years the major part of the funds assigned to telescope building, and it was in many ways already obsolete before it began to operate. It deprived a generation of young astronomers of the opportunity to put their skills to use. Now another thirteen years have gone by and the telescope has set back the progress of astronomy in the Soviet Union by thirty-three years.

One of the factors which the committee planning the observatory did not worry about was the Zelenchukskaya weather. I was on the mountain for three nights and did not see the sky. Even at Mount Palomar one may be unlucky and run into a string of cloudy nights. But at Zelenchukskaya the weather is consistently bad for the greater part of each year. The site is far too close to the high Caucasus peaks which are regularly stirring up storms and clouds. The committee probably chose this site because it is easily accessible by rail and road. The sites with good astronomical

seeing in Central Asia may have been excluded because they have
no roads suitable for the transport of a supermassive structure. At
Zelenchukskaya the roads are good because there is a skiing resort
in the same valley. Of course, the snow which makes the area
good for skiing also causes problems for the telescope. When I
was there, a great mass of accumulated ice had blocked the action
of the dome so that the slit could not be opened. Even if the sky
had been clear, the telescope would not have been able to see it. I
gave a theoretical seminar to the astronomers in a lecture room
where the temperature was minus ten Celsius. The situation did
not look good for anybody who wanted to do serious work in
astronomy.

During my stay at Zelenchukskaya, I looked for clues which
might explain how this scientific disaster had happened. I found
the essential clue in the visitors' gallery. Some of you may have
gone as tourists to visit the 5-meter telescope at Palomar. Palomar
has a visitors' gallery, a glass-enclosed area inside the dome where
tourists can see the telescope but cannot pollute the air around it
with the heat and humidity of their breathing. At Zelenchukskaya
they have a visitors' gallery, like the one at Palomar, only about
ten times as big. And behind the visitors' gallery at Zelenchukskaya they have a white wall for visitors to write their names on.
Instead of a visitors' book they have a wall, and they invited me to
write my name on the wall. The wall is huge, about a hundred
feet long, and still I had a hard time finding an empty space large
enough to write my name on. Every square inch of the wall was
tightly packed with names.

When I saw that wall, I understood for the first time what the
Zelenchukskaya observatory was for. The government officials
who decided to build the observatory twenty years earlier did not
care much about astronomy. They did not mind keeping the astronomers waiting for twenty years while the telescope was being
built. Even when the telescope was finished, they were not in any
hurry to get the dome unstuck so that the astronomers could get
to work. For those government officials the things that mattered
were the visitors' gallery and the wall. The visitors' gallery and
the wall must have been given high priority. They were in full
swing for many years before the telescope was ready. For years
and years before my visit, busloads of schoolteachers and factory

workers and party chairmen were trooping through the visitors' gallery, admiring this latest triumph of Soviet science, and writing their names on the wall.

Plan B gave the political authorities in Moscow what they wanted, a tangible symbol of Soviet greatness. Plan A might have been better for science. Plan A might have saved a whole generation of astronomers from frustration. But with plan A, the political authorities would not have had the satisfaction of building the biggest telescope in the world, and there would have been no hundred-foot wall for the visitors to write their names on.

3. THE FIRST WORLD

My third cautionary tale concerns our own world, the so-called first world. The astronomers of the United States have made a habit of setting up a committee at the beginning of each decade to plan the facilities to be built in the subsequent ten years. The committees are called by the names of their chairmen, all of them distinguished astronomers. The first was the Whitford Committee which made plans for the 1960s. Next came the Greenstein Committee which dealt with the 1970s. I shall talk about the third committee, the Field Committee, which dealt with the 1980s and published its report in 1982. The Field Committee had a number of sensible recommendations for ground-based astronomy which I shall not discuss. I shall talk only about the problems of space-based astronomy, the launching and operation of astronomical telescopes in orbit.

While the Field Committee was meeting from 1978 to 1980, the situation of American space-based astronomy was roughly as follows. We had two active space telescope projects with very different characteristics. We had one Boulou space telescope and one Fulani space telescope. The Boulou telescope was the Hubble Space Telescope, a grand and elaborate instrument which had already been recommended by the Greenstein Committee ten years earlier and was supposed to be launched by the shuttle, if all went well, in 1985. The Fulani telescope was a small and comparatively cheap instrument called the International Ultraviolet Explorer, or the IUE, which had not been recommended by the Greenstein

Committee or by any other prestigious committee of experts. I will have more to say about the IUE in chapter 5. The IUE was launched in January 1978, before the Field Committee started work, and has been from the beginning, like Markaryan's telescope in Armenia, a brilliant scientific success. It is still going strong and still doing excellent science after twelve years in space.

The Field Committee considered two programs of space-based astronomy which I will call Plan A and Plan B. I am here interpreting the committee's discussions in my own way. You won't find any explicit mention of Plan A and Plan B in the committee report. Plan A was a series of Explorer missions following the pattern of the IUE. An Explorer mission means a mission small enough and cheap enough to be paid for out of the NASA space science budget without special exertions. Roughly speaking, each Explorer mission costs about one-fifth of the annual space science budget. If Explorer missions were given the highest priority, it would be possible for NASA to sustain a launch rate of one astronomical Explorer per year in addition to the Explorers concerned with other things such as earth-science and plasma physics. There are many important things for astronomical Explorers to do. If we had one Explorer mission in X-ray astronomy, one in infrared, one in extreme ultraviolet, one in astrometry, and one in radio interferometry, the scientific harvest would be enormous. If Plan A had been adopted, we could have had all of these flying in the 1980s without any stretching of the NASA space-science budget.

The Field Committee, however, like the committees in Ngon and in Moscow, preferred Plan B. Plan B consisted of a series of space missions known collectively as Great Observatories. The Hubble Space Telescope was the first Great Observatory. After that would come the Gamma-Ray Observatory, also dependent on the shuttle for its launch and scheduled to go up in 1987. Next would be the Advanced X-ray Astrophysics Facility, familiarly known as AXAF. AXAF was the highest-priority item on the Field Committee list of new missions, since the committee assumed the first two Great Observatories, the Hubble Telescope and the Gamma-Ray Observatory, to be already in the bag. After AXAF would come a fourth Great Observatory called LDR, or Large Deployable Reflector, a far-infrared telescope with mirror diameter in the ten-meter class. Plan B began with these four

17

Great Observatory missions, plus a number of smaller missions left over from earlier committee reports. To be fair I should mention that Plan B included an Explorer mission called IRAS or Infrared Astronomy Satellite which flew in 1983 and gave us our first comprehensive view of the infrared universe. IRAS was, like the earlier Explorer mission IUE, an international venture and an enormous scientific success.

The main emphasis in the Field Committee report was on the Great Observatories. Each Great Observatory costs as much as five or ten Explorers. Each requires protracted and difficult negotiations between NASA and various committees of Congress to obtain the necessary funds. Each requires about a decade to complete its engineering development and construction after its funding has been authorized. And each requires a shuttle launch to put it into orbit. As a consequence of the *Challenger* disaster of January 1986, the Great Observatories have been delayed by an additional three or four years. The scientific return from the entire Plan B program, apart from IRAS and some ground-based activities which I am not discussing here, has been in no way commensurate with its cost. Just like in Ngon. Just like in Zelenchukskaya.

It is important to understand that the debacle of the Great Observatory program is not simply a consequence of the shuttle accident. The Great Observatories were in deep trouble long before the *Challenger* crashed. Their troubles were technical as well as political. The Hubble Telescope, the only Great Observatory yet built, had a long history of engineering difficulties, delays, and cost overruns. Even if the shuttle had remained alive and well, none of the missions recommended by the Field Committee and not already recommended by earlier committees could possibly have been launched in the 1980s. The Field Committee report was entitled *Astronomy and Astrophysics for the 1980s*. The title shows that the members of the committee were deluding themselves. So far as the 1980s were concerned, their program was a mirage.

The fundamental flaw in the Great Observatory program is ecological. The Great Observatories are too big and too slow and too expensive to fit comfortably into the ecology of science. They take so long to fund, to build and to launch that they are unable to keep pace with the rapid growth of science. Scientific discoveries emerge, scientific ideas change, and scientific tools develop, all within a year or two. A Great Observatory which takes ten years to build is always in danger of being left behind. The ecology of science needs missions that are small, cheap, and quick enough to respond to new ideas and new questions. This is true, whether or not the shuttle crashes.

That is the end of my third tale. One moral of these tales is clear. The nature of committees is the same, whether it is revealed in an African village assembly or in the academic politics of Moscow and Washington. The same drama is played, whether it is the Committee of Village Development, the Soviet Academy of Sciences, or the Field Committee that takes the leading role. The ascendancy of the committeemen began early in the history of science. One of the decisive steps in their upward progress in the United States occurred in 1906, when the administrators of the newly established Carnegie Institution, at that time the largest source of money for scientific research, announced that funding would be denied for "the amateur, the dilettante and the tyro." In other words, to qualify for funding you had better have a Ph.D., a certificate of academic respectability. Well diggers need not apply.

The game of status seeking, organized around committees, is played in roughly the same fashion in Africa and in America and in the Soviet Union. Perhaps the aptitude for this game is a part of our genetic inheritance, like the aptitude for speech and for music. The game has had profound consequences for science. In science, as in the quest for a village water supply, big projects bring enhanced status; small projects do not. In the competition for status, big projects usually win, whether or not they are scientifically justified. As the committees of academic professionals compete for power and influence, big science becomes more and more preponderant over small science. The large and fashionable squeezes out the small and unfashionable. The space shuttle squeezes out the modest and scientifically more useful expendable launcher. The Great Observatory squeezes out the Explorer. The centralized adduction system squeezes out the village well. Fortunately, the American academic system is pluralistic and chaotic enough that first-rate small science can still be done in spite of the committees. In odd corners, in out-of-the-way universities, and in obscure industrial laboratories, our Fulanis are still at work.

Freeman Dyson

4. TWO SUCCESS STORIES

I am tempted to say that the moral of these stories is that committees are the root of all evil. Let us abolish committees and see how science will flourish. But life is not so simple. My stories were chosen with a certain bias. I could tell some other stories about committees which did not do so badly. In the ecology of science, as in the ecology of nature, there must be a balance between big and small enterprises. We cannot all be Fulanis. Even committees have a place in the ecology.

To be fair, let me tell next a story in which Plan B turned out to be right. I go back to the Greenstein report of 1972, the predecessor of the Field report. Like other committees, the Greenstein Committee recommended a Plan B in which the highest-priority item was also the biggest. The highest priority was given to the Very Large Array, or VLA, a huge Y-shaped array of radio telescopes to be constructed in the New Mexico desert near Socorro. The scientific purpose of the VLA was to provide pictures of remote and complex radio sources with an angular resolution surpassing the best optical telescopes. The beautiful multicolored VLA pictures of radio galaxies and supernova remnants on the covers of magazines such as *Scientific American* and *Sky and Telescope* are sufficient proof that the VLA has been an outstanding success. It is the finest general-purpose radio telescope in the world. It has fulfilled abundantly the Greenstein Committee's expectations. Even more remarkably, in comparison with other large projects, the VLA is cost-effective. After the Greenstein Committee recommended it in 1972, it was built for a total cost of $78 million and finished in 1980, on schedule and within budget. In performance it is comparable with a Great Observatory, but in cost it is comparable with an Explorer.

There are many reasons for the success of the VLA. First of all, it is large but not disproportionately large. It forms part of a worldwide community of instruments, some large and some small, which conveniently share the work of exploring the radio sky. The VLA did not absorb the lion's share of the funds spent on astronomy in the 1970s. It did not squeeze out smaller enterprises. In other words, it found its niche at the top of the food chain in a well-balanced ecology.

Another reason for the VLA's success is that it was built quickly

20

enough so that it was not overtaken by newer technologies. A
third reason is that Jesse Greenstein himself was acutely aware of
the danger of big projects squeezing out small ones. He is, in his
own professional life, a Fulani. He likes to study small, dim, peculiar stars that nobody else is interested in. He made sure that, in
spite of the VLA, small-scale science got its fair share of emphasis
in the Greenstein report. To achieve this balance between big and
small, he had to threaten to quit as committee chairman. I quote
now a few sentences from a personal account which he wrote
twelve years later:

> The VLA is successful. Its story is a useful one for aspir-
> ing promoters of further large projects. The issue of bal-
> ance between individual and national goals is indirectly
> addressed in the [Greenstein] report. During our final dis-
> cussions, it caused me intense discomfort. I resigned for a
> brief time as chairman, since I was uncertain that I could
> fully support all the recommendations. That survey report
> is schizoid as published. It says, build large new national
> instruments, but [in brackets] please do not neglect to sup-
> port university scientists and their new instruments. The
> parenthetical phrase may be intellectually correct but it is
> impotent, with no political or budgetary clout. The indi-
> vidualistic style of my own research was possible at insti-
> tutions founded to pursue new, unplanned and often
> changing goals. That system was good. I remain skeptical
> that it is completely outmoded.

So I leave Jesse Greenstein, musing over the possibly destructive
effects of the juggernaut which he helped to set in motion. The
moral of this story is, if you have to have a committee to apportion
resources between large and small projects, make sure that the
chairman is as wise and as sensitive as Jesse Greenstein.

My next story is a more recent one. During the last few years
the community of molecular biologists in the United States has
been struggling with the question of whether to set up a large
project to map and sequence the human genome, the set of 3 billion base pairs in the genes of a human being. To map means to
find out roughly where each of the genes is sitting; to sequence
means to find out exactly where each base pair in the whole ge-

nome is sitting. Following the example of the astronomers, they appointed a committee. The chairman of the committee was Bruce Alberts, a microbiologist at the University of California at San Francisco. The committee published its report in 1988. The report marked a turning point in the history of biology. It was the first time that biologists had to face the possibility that Big Science might come to dominate their activities as it has dominated astronomy and physics.

The Alberts Committee, like other committees, had its Plan A and Plan B. Plan A was to continue unchanged so far as possible the existing way of doing things, with mapping and sequencing activities carried on in decentralized fashion by many groups of scientists investigating particular problems of human genetics. In Plan A there would be no centralized big project, and no drive to sequence the 3 billion bases of the human genome in their entirety irrespective of their genetic significance. Plan B would be the opposite. Plan B would establish an industrial-scale facility for sequencing, and would aim to have the whole job done by an army of technicians within a few years. In conjunction with the sequencing project there would also be a large centralized mapping project, using the sequence data to identify all known and unknown human genes with precisely known places in the genome. Plan B would require a large new expenditure of public funds, with the usual attendant problems of deciding who should administer the funds and who should receive them.

According to Bruce Alberts, the members of his committee were at the beginning sharply split, with some favoring Plan A and some Plan B. He himself claimed to be neutral, but he is, like Jesse Greenstein, a strong defender of the importance of small science. In his own laboratory he studies with a team of colleagues and students the details of the machinery of DNA replication. He is by temperament closer to Plan A than to Plan B. Nevertheless, he observed, during the year that his committee was meeting, that the opinions of the members converged upon a plan that was neither A nor B but a compromise somewhere in between. The compromise plan was recommended unanimously in the committee's report, after Walter Gilbert, the only irreconcilable advocate of Plan B, had resigned. Roughly speaking, the recommended compromise plan is three-quarters A and one-quarter B.

The Alberts Committee recommendations are as follows. First, no crash program to sequence the genome. Second, mapping and sequencing activities continue to be conducted by local groups as before, with an informal international division of labor. Third, mapping and sequencing to be driven by the needs of genetic science and medicine, with nonhuman and human genomes treated alike. Fourth, mapping to have higher priority than sequencing. So far, the recommendations are pure Plan A, but now comes a little of Plan B. Fifth, substantial new money, estimated at $200 million a year for fifteen years, to be spent in support of mapping and sequencing. Sixth, a substantial fraction of this money to be spent on development of new technology for radically cheaper and faster sequencing. Seventh, centralized facilities to be set up for the two services which require them, a data bank of DNA sequences to be collected from all over the world and stored on computers, and a clone bank of actual pieces of DNA that have been mapped or sequenced. The data-bank and the clone-bank should be fully documented and accessible to the world community of scientists.

In my opinion, these recommendations embody considerable wisdom. They are politically and technically feasible. The new money that they require is only 3 percent of the annual National Institutes of Health budget for biology and medical research. Of this 3 percent, only a fraction will go into centralized facilities. The new facilities are not on such a scale as to squeeze out the small teams of scientists who will be doing the bulk of the work in human genetics. In spite of my bias against committees, I have to admit that the Alberts Committee, like the Greenstein Committee, made the right choices.

The Alberts Committee is noncommittal about the main question it was originally asked to decide, whether and when the entire human genome should be sequenced. The committee says the complete sequence should not be a primary objective. The complete sequence should be done when, and only when, we have developed the technology to do the job cheaply and quickly. When it can be done cheaply, go ahead and do it. But don't waste large quantities of money and manpower on an objective that is not scientifically essential.

The complete human genome sequence in biology is like the

Palomar Sky Survey in astronomy. The Palomar Sky Survey is a complete set of photographs of the northern half of the sky, taken with the 48-inch Schmidt telescope on Mount Palomar during the years 1949 to 1956. It was later extended to the Southern Hemisphere, using a similar Schmidt telescope in Australia. At every major observatory in the world, there is a set of Palomar Sky Survey plates, copied from the original plates at Palomar. The Palomar plates are enormously useful to astronomers. Before you decide to point a telescope at something interesting in the sky, you have a look at the Palomar plate to see what that piece of the sky looks like. The plates are also used by many astronomers for statistical work, for counting stars and galaxies and clusters and measuring their distributions on the sky. When we have a complete human genome sequence, it will be used in the same way. Every microbiological or medical research laboratory will have a copy of it handy. When you want to study any particular gene, you will look first at the genome sequence to see what the neighboring DNA looks like. And the sequence as a whole will be a primary tool for statistical studies of human genetics and evolution.

The Palomar Sky Survey was remarkably cheap. The entire project was funded privately by the National Geographic Society, without any government money. It cost altogether about a million dollars. In 1956 you could buy a complete set of Sky Survey plates for about $2,000. The invention of the Schmidt camera reduced the cost of photographing large areas of sky by a factor of a hundred. Before the Schmidt telescope was invented in 1930, there had been an international project with the name Carte du Ciel, which tried to make a complete sky survey with ordinary telescopes. The Carte du Ciel languished because the work was tedious and no end was in sight. After the Schmidt camera came along, a small group of dedicated and hardworking people could finish the job in seven years. The project became so obviously cost-effective that the necessary funds could be raised without much difficulty.

It is likely that the human-genome-sequencing project will have a similar history. At present, the cost of sequencing is about one dollar per base. Since the genome has 3 billion bases, the entire sequence using present-day technology would cost $3 billion. At that price it makes no sense to do it. But one day some clever inventor will find the equivalent of the Schmidt camera. When the cost of sequencing comes down to one cent per base, the whole sequence will cost $30 million, roughly five times the cost of the Palomar Sky Survey in 1990 dollars. Then we will be able to do not just a single human genome but complete sequences of genomes of men and women with a variety of medical histories, not to mention chimpanzees, mice, fruit flies, frogs, and bacteria. In the end, the limit to the sequencing of genomes will probably be set, not by the cost of sequencing, but by our ability to digest and use the vast amount of information that the sequences contain.

The Alberts Committee wisely refrained from recommending a fixed timetable for the mapping and sequencing program. How fast it goes will depend on discoveries and inventions still to be made. Their essential recommendation, for dealing with a situation of immense promise and immense uncertainty, was to stay flexible and avoid premature commitment to rigid programs. This is a recommendation that ought to apply just as well to physics and astronomy as it does to biology. Unfortunately, in the history of committees planning scientific programs, such wisdom is rare.

5. THE SUPERCONDUCTING SUPERCOLLIDER

My final story is the Superconducting Supercollider or SSC. This story is still unfinished. The SSC is a proposed machine for doing high-energy physics. It was recommended to the United States government in 1984 by a committee of famous particle physicists. The committee is called HEPAP, High-Energy Physics Advisory Panel. The SSC was formally approved by President Reagan in 1987. It is a ring-shaped proton accelerator of stupendous size. It will be the biggest accelerator in the world and will reach the highest energy. It will cost about $8 billion and will take about ten years to build, if the remaining financial and technical uncertainties can be overcome.

The SSC is an extreme example of Plan B. The question we have to address is whether SSC is a good Plan B like the Very Large Array or a disastrous Plan B like Zelenchukskaya. Nobody can be sure of the answer to this question. I do not claim to be infallible when I make guesses about the future. But the SSC shows all the characteristic symptoms of a bad Plan B. It is bad politically because it is being pushed by economic interests and by considerations of national prestige having little to do with scientific merit. It is bad educationally because it pours money into a project which offers little opportunity for creative involvement of students. It is bad scientifically because the proton-proton collisions which it produces are peculiarly difficult to interpret. It is bad ecologically because it squeezes out other avenues of research which are likely to lead to more cost-effective high-energy accelerators. None of these arguments by itself is conclusive, but together they make a strong case against the SSC. There is a serious risk that the SSC will be as great a setback to particle physics as the Zelenchukskaya Observatory has been to astronomy.

When I discuss these misgivings with my particle physicist friends, some who belong to HEPAP and some who don't, they usually say things like this: "But look, we have no alternative. If we want to see the Higgs boson, or the top quark, or the photino, or any other new particles going beyond the standard model, we have to go to higher energy. It is either the SSC or nothing." This is the same kind of talk you always hear when people are arguing for Plan B. It is either Plan B or nothing. This argument usually prevails because Plan B is one big thing and Plan A is a lot of little things. When your eyes are blinded by the glitter of something big, all the little things look like nothing. Fortunately, this argument did not prevail on the Alberts Committee. The biologists on the committee knew that the small items of genome mapping in Plan A add up to more scientific knowledge than one big sequence.

But to answer the physicists who say "SSC or nothing," we must produce a practical alternative to the SSC. We must have a Plan A. Plan A does not mean giving up on high-energy physics. It does not mean that we stop building big accelerators. It does not mean that we lose interest in Higgs bosons and top quarks. My Plan A is rather like the plan recommended by the Alberts Committee. It says, let us put more money into exploring new ideas for building cost-effective accelerators. Let us build several clever accelerators instead of one dumb accelerator. Let us measure the value of an accelerator by its scientific output rather than by its energy input. And meanwhile, while the technology for cheaper and better accelerators is being developed, let us put more money into using effectively the accelerators we already have.

The advocates of the SSC often talk as if the universe were one-dimensional, with energy as the only dimension. Either you have the highest energy or you have nothing. But in fact the world of particle physics is three-dimensional. The three dimensions in a particle physics experiment are energy, accuracy, and rarity. Energy and accuracy have obvious meanings. Energy is determined mainly by the accelerator, accuracy by the detection equipment. Rarity means the fraction of particle collisions that produce the particular process that the experiment is designed to study. To observe events of high rarity, we need an accelerator with high intensity to make a large number of collisions, and we also need a detector with good diagnostics to discriminate rare events from background.

I am not denying that energy is important. Let us by all means build accelerators of higher energy when we can do so cost-effectively. But energy is not the only important variable. If we look back over the history of particle physics for the last forty years, we can identify nine experimental discoveries that were of preeminent scientific importance. My list agrees with the judgments expressed by the Nobel Prize Committee in their awards. By and large, the Nobel Committee has done an excellent job in picking out the contributions that everybody agrees are important.

Each of the big experimental discoveries happens on some frontier between known and unknown territory. If a discovery results from observing things at higher energy than anybody has done before, then I say it is on the energy frontier. If a discovery results from measuring things with higher accuracy than has been done before, then I say it is on the accuracy frontier. If a discovery results from observing events that are rarer than anybody has seen before, then I say it is on the rarity frontier. When you look at the list of nine crucial experiments, you find three experiments on the energy frontier, three on the accuracy frontier, and three on the rarity frontier. The fact that the numbers come out exactly equal is not important. You could choose different criteria and come out with different numbers. The important point is that the numbers of discoveries on the three frontiers are comparable. In some rough sense the three frontiers are equally promising places to look for new laws of nature. This is what I mean when I say that the world of particle physics is three-dimensional and not one-dimensional. Only one-third of the frontier lies in the direction of higher energy.

My Plan A for the future of particle physics is a program giving roughly equal emphasis to the three frontiers. Plan A should be a program of maximum flexibility, encouraging the exploitation of new tools and new discoveries wherever they may occur. To encourage work on the accuracy frontier means continuing to put major effort into new detectors to be used with existing accelerators. To encourage work on the rarity frontier means building some new accelerators which give high intensity of particles with moderate energy. After these needs are taken care of, Plan A will still include big efforts to move ahead on the energy frontier. But the guiding principle should be: more money for experiments and less for construction. Let us find out how to explore the energy frontier cheaply before we get ourselves locked into a huge construction project. Let us follow the good example of the Alberts Committee when they say: "Because the technology required to meet most of the project's goals needs major improvement, the committee specifically recommends against establishing one or a few large sequencing centers at present."

Plan A consists of a mixture of many different programs, looking for opportunities to do great science on all three frontiers. Plan A lacks the grand simplicity and predictability of the SSC. And that is to my mind the main reason for preferring Plan A. There is no illusion more dangerous than the belief that the progress of science is predictable. If you look for nature's secrets in only one direction, you are likely to miss the most important secrets, those which you did not have enough imagination to predict.

CHAPTER 4

Telescopes and Accelerators

.....

1 9 8 8

I. FRITZ ZWICKY

This chapter contains another batch of cautionary tales, half concerned with astronomy and half with physics. The focus of the stories now shifts from committees to individuals. I trace the history of various discoveries and examine the character of the discoverers and their instruments. The successful discoverers are about equally divided between mainstream scientists and outsiders, or, according to the ethnographic metaphor of chapter 3, between Boulous and Fulanis.

In chapter 3, I mentioned the International Ultraviolet Explorer, or IUE, the little 18-inch space telescope which gave us our first comprehensive view of the universe in ultraviolet light. Before the IUE, there was another little 18-inch telescope that stayed on the ground, the 18-inch Schmidt on Mount Palomar. The 18-inch Schmidt has been even more cost-effective than the IUE. The Schmidt telescope is named after Bernhard Schmidt, the one-armed lens-grinder without any academic qualifications who worked as an unpaid volunteer at the Hamburg Observatory in the 1920s and there invented his telescope. The first Schmidt telescope, which Schmidt himself built at Hamburg with his left hand, had a 14-inch mirror. The 18-inch Schmidt at Palomar was operating only six years later. It was the first Schmidt to look at the sky from a first-rate astronomical site.

The Schmidt telescope caused a revolution in astronomy. Before Schmidt, astronomical photographs could be sharp only in a small area around the center of the field. Schmidt's invention made it possible for the first time to obtain high-quality pictures covering the entire sky on a reasonable number of plates. Once you have the idea, Schmidt telescopes are not particularly expensive or hard to build. Nowadays an amateur can buy a mass-produced eight-inch Schmidt for under a thousand dollars.

The 18-inch Schmidt was the first telescope to be put on Mount Palomar. It was working there for twelve years before the 200-inch Hale telescope and the big 48-inch Schmidt which did the Palomar Sky Survey. It was there because the Swiss astronomer Fritz Zwicky was interested in supernovas, the rare events in which an entire star explodes and the debris shines briefly as bright as a billion suns. Zwicky was the first astronomer to observe supernovas systematically. Supernovas appear randomly in galaxies all over the sky at a rate of roughly one per galaxy every three hundred years. Each supernova in a distant galaxy is visible for a few weeks before it fades out. To observe a significant number of supernovas, Zwicky needed a telescope that he could have all to himself, taking pictures of galaxies night after night. So he organized the building of the 18-inch Schmidt on Palomar and made sure that he would be in charge. As often happens in astronomy, to have unlimited observing time is more important than to have a big mirror. Zwicky made good use of his time. Here is his own account written thirty years later:

I put this instrument into operation on the night of September 5, 1936, and immediately started a survey of several thousand galaxies. This proved to be a most rewarding project, inasmuch as twenty of the very elusive supernovae were discovered by my assistant J. J. Johnson and myself in the period from 1936 until 1941. As gratuities, so to speak, many new clusters of galaxies, variable stars, common novae and flare stars were found. At the same time much of the observational material was gathered for the preparation of our six-volume catalogue of about fifty thousand of the

brightest galaxies in the northern half of the celestial sphere
and of ten thousand clusters of galaxies seen in the same
area. For the construction of the 18-inch Schmidt telescope, its housing, a full-size objective prism, a small re-
muneration for my assistant, and the operational costs for
the whole project during ten years, only about fifty thousand dollars were expended. This probably represents the
highest efficiency, as measured in results achieved per dollar
invested, of any telescope presently in use, and perhaps of
any ever built, with the exception of Galilei's little refractor.

Even after making allowances for Zwicky's notorious egotism,
I have to agree with his claims for the 18-inch Schmidt. His exploration of the world of the supernovas was of immense importance
to the future of astronomy. He found enough supernovas that he
could classify them into various types and observe regularities in
their behavior. His sky survey set the style for many later surveys
done with bigger instruments and bigger investments of manpower and money. He was the first astronomer to search deliberately for the most violent events in the universe, and he was the
first to understand that if you want to search efficiently for tran-
sient events you must cover the whole sky repeatedly. Insofar as
the modern style in astronomy is to concentrate attention on
short-lived and violent processes, Zwicky was the first modern
astronomer. And the 18-inch Schmidt gave him the chance to
show what he could do.

In another passage taken from his 1966 autobiography, Zwicky
discusses more recent developments:

In the future entirely new types of telescopes will become available. Among these novel devices, which are already being used in a preliminary way, the photoelectronic
telescope of Professor A. Lallemand in Paris is so far the
most outstanding and successful. Astronomers therefore
expect that photoelectronic devices of small apertures and
light weight will eventually outperform the giant 200-inch
Hale reflector on Palomar mountain. In any case these new
instruments will be indispensable if we intend seriously to

explore the universe with the aid of rocket-borne instrumentation.

Here Zwicky correctly predicts the line of development that led to the launch and successful operation of the IUE twelve years later. The key invention that made IUE possible was the Secondary Electron Conduction, or SEC, Vidicon television camera. The SEC Vidicon took the basic idea of Lallemand's photoelectronic telescope and made it practical by translating it from vacuum-tube to solid-state hardware. After the IUE was launched, the technology of light detection advanced a big step further with the development of the charge-coupled device or CCD. Modern telescopes, both on the ground and in space, use CCD television cameras as their primary means of observation. Zwicky would not have been guilty of exaggeration if he had said that a small telescope with a CCD would outperform the 200-inch Hale telescope as it existed at Palomar in 1966. A small telescope with a CCD is for many purposes better than a big telescope with an old-fashioned photographic plate.

But Zwicky did not take into account the fact that the 200-inch telescope would soon have its CCD detectors too. The CCD does not care whether the telescope to which it is attached is big or small. The CCD works equally well for both. Today the 200-inch is used routinely with CCD detectors of various sizes and shapes. As a consequence, the 200-inch telescope today is ten times as productive as it was in 1966 when Zwicky wrote his book. In the old days when the telescope was dependent on photographic plates, an exposure of many hours was needed to record a single spectrum of a faint object. Often a whole night would be spent in taking one or two deep exposures. Today with the CCD, a deep exposure takes twenty or thirty minutes, and ten or twenty exposures are made in a night. The forty-year-old 200-inch telescope has been rejuvenated by the new detectors and is now pouring out astronomical discoveries at a greater rate than ever before.

2. ZWICKY AND BAADE

Zwicky was wrong to claim that small telescopes with electronic detectors would put the 200-inch Hale out of business. Zwicky was blinded by his dislike of Walter Baade, the astronomer who did most of the observing with the 200-inch during the first ten years of its operation. When Zwicky wrote that small electronic telescopes would outperform the 200-inch, what he had in mind was that Zwicky would outperform Baade. Both of them were great astronomers. Now that they are both dead and we can look at them with historical detachment, we can see that neither of them outperformed the other. Zwicky was a cantankerous genius, quick in thinking of useful schemes and energetic in carrying them out. Besides his pioneering supernova search and his great catalogue of clusters of galaxies, he also founded and organized the Committee for Aid to War-Stricken Scientific Libraries, which during the years after World War 2 collected and distributed a million dollars' worth of books and journals to rebuild libraries in France, Germany, Japan, Korea, Taiwan, the Philippines, and Lebanon. Baade, in contrast, was an artist, a virtuoso performer who played the 100-inch telescope on Mount Wilson and the 200-inch on Palomar like violins. His great contribution to astronomy was the identification of the two populations of stars in the universe, the young Population I to which the sun and all its neighbors in our local region of our galaxy belong, and the old Population II which is seen in globular clusters and in the central regions of other galaxies. The decisive step in the discovery of Population II was to resolve into stars the great red blob at the center of the Andromeda galaxy M31. Baade was able to see these stars only by pushing the 100-inch telescope to the limit of its capabilities under conditions of excellent seeing. For this purpose any smaller telescope would have been useless.

Once in their lives, when Zwicky and Baade were both young and before they had become enemies, before either Zwicky's 18-inch telescope or Baade's 200-inch existed, they wrote together a theoretical paper of extraordinary originality. Their paper appeared in 1934 with the title "Cosmic Rays from Supernovae." This was just two years after James Chadwick had discovered the neutron. At the end of their paper Baade and Zwicky put the following paragraph:

> With all reserve we advance the view that a supernova represents the transition of an ordinary star into a neutron

star, consisting mainly of neutrons. Such a star may possess a very small radius and an extremely high density. As neutrons can be packed much more closely than ordinary nuclei and electrons, the gravitational packing energy in a cold neutron star may become very large, and under certain conditions may far exceed the ordinary nuclear packing fractions. . . .

These remarks of Baade and Zwicky were ignored for a long time. They were ignored by astronomers for thirty-three years, until neutron stars were discovered by radio astronomers. Now we know that almost everything Baade and Zwicky were saying in 1934 was true. It was a great loss to science that they did not continue their collaboration. Each of them alone was a great astronomer, but together they would have been greater. If they had remained friends, neutron stars might have been discovered twenty-five years sooner, in 1942 instead of in 1967. It happened that in 1942 Baade used the 100-inch telescope to take the classic pictures of the Crab Nebula, the most spectacular visible remnant of a supernova. Baade's pictures show the Crab Nebula looking like a tumbleweed with a shell of fine filaments on the outside and an amorphous glow on the inside. Baade knew that the Crab Nebula was the debris from the supernova explosion of the year 1054. He also knew that there is a peculiar star at the center of the nebula, which he suspected of being the stellar remnant of the explosion. According to the Baade-Zwicky paper of 1934, the stellar remnant ought to be a neutron star. Baade asked his friend Rudolf Minkowski to take a spectrum of the star. Minkowski, also using the 100-inch telescope, took a spectrum and found it completely featureless, with no lines at all, unlike any other star in the sky. Minkowski calculated the temperature of the star and found it to be half a million degrees, ten times as hot as any other star. The spectrum made it certain that this was in fact the supernova remnant, a star with weird and unique properties. But Baade and Minkowski did not go further. They did not look at the star again. They did not in their 1942 publications mention the possibility that it might be a neutron star. They seem to have silently excluded this possibility from their minds. They seem to have felt no strong curiosity, no burning desire to find out whether this weird object was a neutron star or not.

How can their disinterest be explained? How did it happen that Baade and Minkowski in 1942 could ignore the question which Baade and Zwicky had so clearly stated in 1934? The simplest hypothesis to explain Baade's lack of interest in neutron stars in 1942 is that the more speculative part of the 1934 Baade-Zwicky paper was written by Zwicky alone. If that were so, it is easy to imagine that by 1942 Baade had come to consider a neutron star to be merely one of Zwicky's crazy ideas from which Baade was glad to disassociate himself. From a human point of view such a reaction is understandable. But from a scientific point of view it was a great opportunity missed.

Zwicky was in 1942 busy designing rockets for the United States Army. He had little time at that moment for astronomy. He was barely on speaking terms with Baade. Still, it is interesting to imagine what might have happened if Zwicky had been collaborating with Baade and Minkowski when they explored the Crab Nebula in 1942. Zwicky would certainly have seized on Minkowski's spectrum as prima facie evidence for the existence of a neutron star. Zwicky would not have forgotten what he had written in 1934. Zwicky with his inventiveness and his love of gadgetry might even have thought of building an instrument to look for rapid variations in the light from the remnant star. Light variations on a time scale of milliseconds would be conclusive proof that the star was a neutron star. Nothing less compact than a neutron star could vary on a time scale shorter than a second. The star in the Crab Nebula does in fact, as we now know, flash on and off thirty times a second. To observe the flashes is not difficult once you know they are there. A few years ago we had a graduate student observing the flashes and measuring their changing period with a 1-meter telescope on the Princeton campus. Whatever a Princeton graduate student could do with a 1-meter telescope under the polluted sky of New Jersey, Zwicky could have done just as well with his 18-inch telescope under the clear sky of Palomar. All that Zwicky needed to do was to put a recording photodetector with a fast response at the focus of his telescope instead of a photographic plate. This was the way the flashes were finally discovered in 1969 by Cocke, Disney, and Taylor. Zwicky could have done it twenty-five years earlier.

Zwicky was uniquely qualified to be the discoverer of neutron stars. He was one of the few astronomers in those days who took neutron stars seriously. He was one of the few who saw the potential of electronic photodetection. And he was one of the few who had unlimited observing time on a good small telescope. If he had put his mind to the problem, he could have seen the star in the Crab Nebula flashing in 1942, and the whole subsequent history of astronomy would have been changed. He missed his chance because he was not talking to Baade and Minkowski.

I told this story of the missed discovery of the neutron star at some length because it shows that "being the right size" is not enough. The moral of the story is that you miss making important discoveries if you work with big telescopes alone or with small telescopes alone. You need a big telescope to get good spectra of faint objects. You need a small telescope to search the sky for objects you did not know existed. You need a big telescope to detect objects out to the extreme limits of faintness. You need a small telescope to keep watching a variable object to see how it changes from night to night or from month to month. But it is not enough to have both big and small telescopes. You need also to have big-telescope astronomers and small-telescope astronomers talking to each other. Zwicky was a classic case of a small-telescope astronomer doing great work with limited means. Baade was a classic big-telescope astronomer, like his predecessor Edwin Hubble at the 100-inch telescope, searching the far distances of the universe. I do not attempt to apportion the blame between Zwicky and Baade for the fact that they stopped being friends. Both were to blame for missing the chance to put their combined talents to work to solve the mystery that lies at the heart of the Crab Nebula.

3. PULSARS

When the thirty-times-a-second flashing of the star in the Crab Nebula was finally seen in 1969, the job was done with a small telescope. Three young astronomers put a recording photomultiplier at the focus of a 1-meter telescope at the Steward Observatory (Kitt Peak) in Arizona. They saw the flashes immediately, as soon as they pointed the telescope at the right place in the sky. They used a small telescope because it was handy and not in great demand. If they had chosen to make their observation with a big telescope, they would have had to wait for weeks or months until a free night became available. On the 1-meter telescope they were given four nights and had enough time to study the flashing star in detail.

One might say that the discovery of the flashing star by Cocke, Disney, and Taylor was a victory for the small telescope. But such a conclusion would be misleading. The 1-meter telescope did not do the job all by itself. The reason why Cocke, Disney, and Taylor decided to look for optical flashes in 1969 was because radio astronomers had seen radio flashes coming from the direction of the Crab Nebula a few months earlier. Staelin and Reifenstein, two radio astronomers at the National Radio Astronomy Observatory at Green Bank, West Virginia, used a 90-meter radio telescope to detect the flashes. It was the big and the small telescope working together that established the unique character of the Crab Nebula source.

By the time the Crab Nebula star was proved to be a neutron star by the discovery of its radio and optical pulsations, other neutron stars had already been identified on the basis of radio observations alone. The first neutron stars were found in 1967. They were called pulsars because they emitted radio pulses with a time scale of the order of a second or shorter. They were seen with a radio telescope in England designed for a different purpose. The telescope was big but cheap and technically primitive, consisting of an array of 2,048 dipole antennas strung up like clotheslines over five acres of land near Cambridge. A large part of the array was built by one graduate student, Jocelyn Bell, who was also responsible for looking at the strip charts on which the output of the telescope was recorded. She actually discovered the pulsars although her supervisor, Antony Hewish, collected the Nobel Prize. The discovery owed nothing to Baade and Zwicky. By 1967 the paper of Baade and Zwicky, predicting neutron stars as supernova remnants, appears to have been totally forgotten. Not one of the early pulsar papers refers to it.

The discovery of pulsars may justly be scored as a victory for big telescopes. But it was not a victory for big money and big organization. Antony Hewish's observatory was a shoestring operation, technically old-fashioned even in 1967, costing far less than the more modern instruments that were being built at the same time in other places around the world. Hewish earned his Nobel Prize by building a telescope that went flatly against the fashionable trends. The big money, then as now, was going into radio telescopes that could observe short wavelengths, because shorter wavelengths gave higher angular resolution. Hewish went the other way, to a wavelength of three meters. The big modern instruments, then as now, processed their data with long integration times in order to separate weak signals from noise. Hewish went the other way, to short integration times and rapid readout of data. Hewish needed long waves and rapid readout because he was interested in observing the scintillation of distant radio sources. Scintillation is the twinkling produced by irregular motions in the plasma, the rarefied interstellar gas of positive and negative electric charges, along the line of sight from the source to the earth. The time structure of the scintillations gives information about the spatial structure of the plasma. Hewish needed long waves because the plasma diffracts long waves more strongly than short waves. He needed rapid readout because scintillations are rapid. His telescope was a magnificently economical tool for studying scintillations. If everything had gone according to Hewish's plan, Jocelyn Bell would have spent a year or two measuring scintillations and Hewish would have assembled the results into a determination of the properties of the interplanetary and interstellar plasmas.

Fortunately, things did not go according to plan. Jocelyn Bell looked at the strip charts and found her famous "bit of scruff," a place on the chart where the pen wiggled unaccountably. As the days went by, she found more bits of scruff. When the scruff was plotted on an expanded scale, it showed occasional signs of regular pulsation. When the direction of the scruff was measured over several weeks, the signal was seen to be coming from a source fixed on the sky and not from a source on the Earth. And so the first pulsar had been discovered. Hewish had, as things turned out, built a telescope ideally suited to the study of pulsars. Pulsars, like scintillations, are best seen at long wavelengths and with short integration times. Even after the first pulsars had been discovered and their positions and periods were known, it was difficult for other radio telescopes to see them. If Hewish had not stubbornly

insisted on building a telescope that swam against the tide of
fashion, the discovery of pulsars might have been delayed for
many years.

   The moral of the pulsar story is not "small is beautiful." Hewish's telescope was not small. The moral of the story is "different
is beautiful." Hewish's telescope was different from others in
many ways, not only in its long wavelength and its primitive data-
recording system, but also in its purpose and mode of operation.
It was a special-purpose instrument, not designed like most big
telescopes to accommodate a variety of users. It was designed to
be used full-time by Hewish's little group of associates and students. Hewish could do what he liked with it. As soon as Jocelyn
Bell found the scruff, Hewish could decide to put his telescope
and his team to work full-time on clearing up the mystery. For all
these reasons Hewish's telescope was particularly well placed to
make a major unexpected discovery. If you are hoping to find
something unexpected, to be different is an advantage. It is an
even greater advantage if you can be, like Hewish, lucky. It was
Hewish's luck that pulsars exist. He was also lucky to have had
Jocelyn Bell for a student. But that was not only a matter of luck.
Hewish showed uncommonly good judgment in choosing her to
work on the project and in giving her responsibilities equal to her
talents. In one of the major radio-astronomical observatories run
on more orthodox lines, no matter how gifted a graduate student
might be, she would not be given enough time or enough responsibility to discover something radically new.

   Another moral of the pulsar story is, be prepared for surprises.
Always remember that the universe is, as J. B. S. Haldane said,
"not only queerer than we suppose but queerer than we *can* suppose." Do not for a moment assume, when you are discussing the
building of new telescopes or new accelerators, that you are smart
enough to imagine in advance the things that the new instruments
will discover.

4. BIRMINGHAM AND BRISTOL

The stories now switch from telescopes to accelerators, from astronomy to particle physics. There are fundamental differences

between astronomy and particle physics. One of the main differences is that accelerators have short working lives, whereas telescopes last forever. An accelerator usually does its most important work within five years of being switched on. At the age of ten it is ready to be scrapped or converted into an injector for a larger machine. Telescopes are still young at forty. The forty-year-old 200-inch at Palomar is still as productive as it has ever been. The seventy-year-old 100-inch at Mount Wilson was recently retired, not because the telescope itself was obsolete but because the growth of the city of Los Angeles had made the sky too bright for serious astronomy. Almost all the major telescopes that have ever been built are still in use.

Why is there this difference in longevity between accelerators and telescopes? One reason is the difference in subject matter. An accelerator can only fire a limited set of projectiles at a limited set of targets. If it is a modern accelerator using colliding beams, it does not even have a choice of targets. An accelerator can do only a limited number of different experiments. When these experiments have been done, the accelerator is ready for retirement. The sky, on the other hand, contains a practically unlimited variety of objects for telescopes to look at. The 200-inch could continue taking spectra for a thousand years before it would run out of stars. Another reason for the difference between accelerators and telescopes is that accelerators are expensive to use while telescopes are cheap. Roughly speaking, to use an accelerator with maximum efficiency requires spending one-fifth of the capital cost of the machine each year. To use an optical telescope efficiently, even with modern electronic detectors and computer analysis of data, you need to spend only about one-twentieth of the capital cost per year. It is cost-effective to keep old telescopes alive and to kill old accelerators. The Darwinian struggle for existence among particle physicists is fiercer than it is among astronomers.

I go back again to the past to find examples of wisdom and folly in the building of accelerators. One of the vivid memories of my youth is the accelerator at the University of Birmingham in England. We called the accelerator the White Oliphant because it was built by Mark Oliphant and it was no good for doing physics. It was a 1-billion-volt proton synchrotron and was under construction when I went to Birmingham in the summer of 1949. In those days a billion volts was high-energy. If the machine had been finished on schedule, it would have been for a while the highest-energy machine in the world. Oliphant had a dream that by building this machine he could make Birmingham a world leader in particle physics.

Meanwhile, world leadership in particle physics had come unexpectedly to the University of Bristol, a rival institution only a hundred miles from Birmingham. Cecil Powell at Bristol, exploiting brilliantly the technique of tracking particles in photographic emulsion, had started a revolution in particle physics by discovering several new varieties of fundamental particle. He identified the particles, known as mesons, that are carriers of the strong forces that hold nuclei together. Powell needed no accelerator. He found his mesons in the interactions of cosmic rays with atoms in his emulsions. His preeminence in the art of finding new particles arose from his ability to inspire a small army of skilled and dedicated scanners, who did the tedious work of examining emulsions micron by micron under their microscopes. I visited Bristol at that time and was amazed at the high morale and enthusiasm of Powell's scanners. To keep this enthusiasm alive, month after month, was Powell's unique gift. At that game no other physicist in the world could beat him. At that moment in the history of particle physics, success depended on human qualities rather than on machines.

At Birmingham, morale among the experimental physicists was considerably lower. The building of the synchrotron was delayed. The quality of the magnets was not up to specifications. Worst of all, no serious preparations were made for using the machine to do science. The machine was in a hole in the ground, with insufficient space around it for setting up experiments. It looked as if Oliphant were only interested in building the machine but not seriously interested in using it. The machine was ultimately finished after I left Birmingham, but it never did any important experiments.

The Birmingham synchrotron was a textbook example of how not to do particle physics. The decision to build it was motivated more by political considerations than by science. The driving force behind it was a desire to beat the Americans in the race to have the highest-energy machine. The politicians who supplied the money for it were persuaded that England needed only to have the highest-energy machine in order to be a world leader in science. They were not told that the machine would be useless without adequate funds and space for experiments. The British government, the Birmingham University administrators, and Oliphant himself regarded the machine as an end in itself rather than as a tool for doing science. The result of their efforts was a scientific disaster for England, for Birmingham, and for Oliphant. The fiasco was particularly tragic for Rudolf Peierls, my friend and teacher, who had built up an excellent school of theoretical physics in Birmingham and hoped in vain to see experimental particle physics flourish there too.

The White Oliphant was not the only example of an accelerator that did lasting damage to the scientific community in which it was built. Oliphant, having learned nothing from his failure in Birmingham, went to Australia and built a second White Oliphant in Canberra. The Canberra accelerator was a high-current machine which had the same effect on particle physics in Australia as the Birmingham machine had had in England. A high-visibility accelerator project, driven by political prestige rather than by scientific need, usually sets back the progress of particle physics in a country by about ten years. The prestige project absorbs the funds that would otherwise be available for more modest and scientifically useful machines. It also leads to the frustration and disillusionment of a generation of young experimenters. This I saw happen in Birmingham in 1950. It happened later at least twice in the Soviet Union, with the 12-billion-volt machine at Dubna in the 1950s, and with the 70-billion-volt machine at Serpukhov in the 1970s. Soviet experimental physics has still not recovered from these disasters. In each case we see the same pathological symptoms, a machine built with great fanfare, without adequate facilities for experiments, and without an active experimenter in charge.

In Bristol in the 1940s we saw the opposite syndrome, an experimental genius in charge, an ample supply of the essential experimental tools, high-quality microscopes and well-trained scanners, with no accelerator and no political fanfare. The essential difference between Bristol and Birmingham was that Powell was doing science while Oliphant was building a machine. The triumph of Bristol as a world leader in particle physics was inevitably short-lived. Very soon, accelerators became so efficient in producing particles that cosmic rays could no longer compete. When this happened, Bristol withdrew from the particle physics game and continued to run a first-class cosmic ray laboratory. The first priority in Powell's laboratory was always to explore nature, not to build apparatus. Meanwhile, Birmingham and Canberra were left with their White Oliphants, Dubna and Serpukhov with their white elephants.

5. THE PERILS OF BEING ORIGINAL

After Cecil Powell at Bristol, the next person I met who was doing particle physics in a highly original fashion was Donald Glaser at Ann Arbor. In 1950, Don Glaser was a graduate student in the Physics Department at the University of Michigan. At that time there were two practical methods for observing the tracks of particles, the old cloud chamber of Charles Wilson and the new photographic emulsion technique of Cecil Powell. The cloud chamber and the emulsion both had severe limitations. The cloud chamber was a temperamental device. The tracks it registered were hard to measure accurately, and the interesting particle interactions rarely occurred in the gas of the chamber because the gas had too low a density. The photographic emulsion had to be scanned laboriously under the microscope and was useless for experiments involving large amounts of data. Because of these deficiencies of the cloud chamber and the emulsions, most particle physics experimenters at that time did not try to observe tracks at all. Instead, they relied on simple particle counters to tell where the particles were going. Counters were good enough for many purposes, but for studying complicated particle decay processes a track detector would have been much better.

When I came to Ann Arbor in the summer of 1950, Don Glaser was dreaming of a detector that would detect particle tracks with bubbles in a superheated liquid. He was only a graduate student, and hardly anybody took him seriously. He had no outside funding. One person who took him seriously was George Uhlenbeck, a theoretical physicist with no expertise in particle physics.

Uhlenbeck scrounged money from the University of Michigan to keep Don Glaser alive. With tiny amounts of money, Glaser built tiny bubble chambers holding a few teaspoonsful of liquid. It took him five years to work the bugs out of the plumbing and the optical systems, so that tracks could be seen and measured. After five years he had a small bubble chamber that worked. Only then did particle physicists become interested in what Glaser was doing. Luis Alvarez invited him to Berkeley and provided him with the resources to build bubble chambers of useful size. Within a few years bubble chambers had given Berkeley world leadership in particle physics. Within another few years, bubble chambers had become standard equipment in particle physics laboratories all over the world.

Meanwhile, I had come to know another young man who was doing particle physics in a fashion as original as Don Glaser's. In those happy days, if you published a paper in the *Physical Review,* they gave you a free copy of the journal. This was worth a lot, since we did not yet have Xerox machines. I had two papers on spin-waves published in the issue of June 1, 1956, and so I got two free copies of that issue to take home and read. That was a vintage issue. It had, among other good things, a letter to the editor from a young instructor at Princeton University, Gerard O'Neill. The letter had the title, "Storage-Ring Synchrotron: Device for High-Energy Physics Research." In two pages it laid down the path which experimental particle physics has followed for the subsequent thirty-four years.

If you read O'Neill's letter now, you can see that almost everything in it was right. But it took a long time before most of us understood how right it was. O'Neill said that future accelerators should have two colliding beams rather than one beam with a fixed target. To produce colliding beams of sufficient intensity, they would need storage rings accumulating particles for a long time. The expert experimenters did not take O'Neill seriously, just as they had not taken Glaser seriously six years earlier. Storage rings were a neat idea but obviously unpractical. O'Neill had to work and fight for many years before the storage ring came to life. He had to build a storage ring himself at Stanford to convince people that it was feasible. With the benefit of hindsight we can find one serious mistake in O'Neill's letter. O'Neill was too conservative. He grossly underestimated the possible improvement of high-vacuum techniques. He claimed that a storage ring could hold a beam with a lifetime of a few seconds. If he had said hours instead of seconds, nobody would have believed him. In fact, it did not take many years before storage rings with lifetimes of several hours became routine. And now, thirty years later, almost all major particle physics accelerators include storage rings as an essential component.

I have sometimes had disagreements with O'Neill. I have sometimes been wrong. I have in my files a letter to O'Neill that I wrote in 1970. I said, "There is a question whether all of us may not have grey hair before any storage rings in the energy-range you are talking about get built." Now several storage rings in this energy range have been built and are doing world-class science, and neither O'Neill nor I yet has grey hair.

Particle physics in the United States has remained happily free from the White Oliphant syndrome. Or at least it was so until recently. Accelerators were built in many places, not as public monuments but as instruments for doing physics. The people in charge, Lawrence and Alvarez at Berkeley, Fermi at Chicago, Wilson at Cornell, Panofsky and Richter at Stanford, Wilson and Lederman at Fermilab, were interested in doing experiments. Most of the accelerators they built were scientifically productive. The same happy state of affairs prevailed at many of the laboratories of Western Europe. One of the places which was not so fortunate was Princeton. We had a large accelerator in Princeton, operated jointly by Princeton University and the University of Pennsylvania. The Princeton-Penn accelerator was an engineering success but a scientific failure. It was not a disastrous failure like the machine at Birmingham. It did some useful experiments. But nobody could think of anything for it to do which would be exciting enough to justify the cost of running it. It finally died on April 9, 1972.

I do not blame Milton White, the builder and director of the Princeton-Penn accelerator, for the fact that his machine did not live up to his expectations. He was unlucky. Science is always a gamble. Milton White was a gambler who lost. He happened to build his machine to accelerate particles at an energy where nature had no big surprises. He was as good a scientist as many others who were luckier. Fortunately, the machine he built was not extravagantly large. It was small enough that the funding agencies could make the decision to close it down on scientific grounds, without becoming involved in questions of national politics and national prestige. The demise of the accelerator was a local setback for Princeton and Penn, but not a setback for particle physics as a whole. Even at Princeton and Penn, the physics communities continued to flourish. The moral of the Princeton-Penn story is that it does no great harm to gamble, provided you do not gamble more than you can afford to lose. Gambling only becomes dangerous and destructive when the stakes are so high that you can't afford losing. This is another criterion for deciding the right size for a scientific project. The right size means a size at which you can afford to take a gamble. If you are too big to gamble, you are too big to do creative science.

This is the basic reason why the Superconducting Supercollider, or SSC, oversteps the limits of reasonable size for a scientific project. The SSC is supposed to cost about twenty times as much as the Princeton-Penn accelerator, after allowing for inflation. This difference in size implies a difference in political environment. The SSC is too big to take a gamble. I see a distressing similarity between the political forces now impinging on the SSC and the political forces that drove the accelerator projects at Birmingham, Dubna, and Serpukhov. In each case the political authorities decided to build the accelerator because it would be the highest-energy accelerator in the world and would be good for national prestige, and the result was a scientific disaster. I fear that similar circumstances may produce a similar disaster in the case of the SSC. Fortunately, nature is unpredictable. It still could happen that the SSC, like Hewish's radio telescope or Powell's photographic emulsion, will reward us with discoveries in a totally unexpected direction.

CHAPTER 5

Sixty Years of Space Science, 1958–2018

.....

1 9 8 8

I. THE ROAD NOT TAKEN

I am looking at the history of the space science enterprise over a period of sixty years, half in the past and half in the future, centered on the year 1988. This period is a good one to look at, long enough to include a good sample of successes and failures. It goes far enough into the future to allow some radical changes in our present arrangements for doing space science.

The sixty years begin in 1958, the year after the launch of the first Sputnik. I actually go back a little further, to the year 1952, when Wernher von Braun published in the German magazine *Weltraumfahrt* (Space Travel) a long article with the title "Das Mars Projekt." This was published in English the following year as a hardcover book with the title *The Mars Project*. Von Braun's Mars Project was only a dream. It was a road not taken. At the time the book was published, only the hard-core space cadets and science fiction enthusiasts took it seriously. But it was a dream with great consequences. The components of the dream were pieces of hardware. The details of the hardware were worked out lovingly and professionally. Traces of von Braun's dream can be seen in many of the space vehicles that we are using today. The dream set the stage for almost everything that came later.

The Mars Project was a manned exploration of Mars, using the

Freeman Dyson

technology of World War 2 and conducted in the style of a military campaign. Seventy men were supposed to arrive in orbit around Mars, with fifty of them descending to the surface. Ladies need not apply. The descent to the surface is made in three landing boats, one landing on skis on one of the polar snowfields, the other two landing on wheels near the equator. The boat with skis lands first, carrying vehicles and equipment for its crew to travel from pole to equator and prepare a smooth runway for the two boats with wheels to land on. After all three boats have landed, the fifty men stay on the surface for a terrestrial year conducting scientific investigations. The two wheeled boats, minus their wings, then carry all fifty men up into Mars orbit where they join their twenty waiting comrades for the trip back to Earth. To give a feeling for the scale of these operations, each landing boat is a glider with a wing span of 150 meters and a wing area of three-quarters of an acre. These dimensions were based on an assumed value, now known to be much too high, for the density of the Martian atmosphere.

Von Braun's landing boats were the top layer of a three-tiered pyramid. The middle layer was a fleet of ten interplanetary space ships, assembled in orbit around the Earth and designed to travel in convoy from Earth orbit to Mars orbit and back again. The bottom layer was a fleet of forty-six ferry vessels or space shuttles, designed to carry passengers and freight up and down between Earth and Earth orbit. These imagined ferry vessels of von Braun were the ancestors of the space shuttle that flew thirty years later.

The main difference between von Braun's shuttle and the modern version was the frequency of flights and the quickness of turn-around. To launch his expedition von Braun had his shuttles flying four missions every day for eight months, a total of 950 flights to Earth orbit and back. Each shuttle vehicle would make the round trip, including loading and unloading, once every twelve days. These numbers did not seem absurd in 1952. At that time the success of the Berlin airlift of 1948 was fresh in everybody's mind. What von Braun was proposing for his ferry vessels was comparable with the Berlin airlift. His ferry vessels were supposed to be cheap, rugged, and easy to service, like the DC-3 airplanes that flew day after day in and out of Berlin. His flight rate seems absurd only when we compare it with the experience

48

of the modern shuttle, a far more complicated and delicate vehicle, which has never been able to operate with a turnaround time shorter than three months. If von Braun's simple and rugged shuttle had been built, would it have done the job he designed it to do? We will never know. History passed it by, leaving behind only dreams.

The overall scale of von Braun's project was, as he said, "no greater than a minor military expedition extending over a limited theater of war." It was comparable in size and cost, as it was in style, to the operations with which von Braun had been involved in World War 2. Here are some numbers summarizing the dimensions of the enterprise:

Total launch weight at takeoff from Earth: 6 million tons
Total payload at Earth orbit: 37,000 tons
Total payload at Mars orbit: 4,200 tons
Total payload on Mars surface: 150 tons
Total bandwidth for communication by radio from Mars
  to Earth: 1 kilohertz

The last item demonstrates most dramatically the difference between World War 2 technology and the space technology of today. A bandwidth of one kilohertz is too narrow for telephony, let alone television. Communication between von Braun's troops and Earth would have been by telegraphy only, messages spelled out in Morse code. The bulk of the scientific data would have been brought home, as it was in the nineteenth century, on the ship with the explorers.

What would have been the scientific harvest of von Braun's argosy if it had sailed as he intended? That would have depended mainly on the scientific quality of the crew. Concerning the scientific activities of the expedition, von Braun is silent. He was more interested in getting to Mars and getting back safely than in the intervening year of trudging the Martian soil. All that he says about scientific objectives is contained in a single paragraph:

Let us assume for a moment that a small group of men were actually to land on Mars or on some other planet. How could they probe its inner mysteries? To do so they

49

would require means of transportation and some form of movable pressurized housing if they were to explore any considerable portion of the planetary surface. While a man encased in an impressively clumsy pressure-suit, walking importantly around the base of a space vessel, makes a fine and interesting figure in a lunar or Martian moving picture, it is unlikely that he will gather much useful data about the heavenly body on which he stands.

Von Braun wisely left the discussion of scientific objectives to the scientists. His job as an engineer was only to provide them with the necessary mobility and life support for their explorations. If his dreams had come true, the scientific harvest might have been immense or it might have been negligible. In my opinion, there was a real chance of bringing back an immense harvest. It might have happened, as it happened with the voyage of HMS *Beagle* in 1831–36 and again with the voyage of HMS *Challenger* in 1872–76, that a single ship exploring a large territory could lay the foundations for a major scientific revolution. The *Beagle* brought back a large part of the evidence for Darwin's theory of evolution. The *Challenger* brought back the first comprehensive view of the ecology of the world's oceans. The *Beagle* was fortunate to have Charles Darwin on board. The *Challenger* was fortunate to have the oceanographer John Murray. I find nothing absurd in the picture of a young geochemist or microbiologist, following in the footsteps of Darwin, exploring Mars as a member of von Braun's crew, and discovering enough new facts to overthrow all our accepted notions of planetary and prebiotic evolution.

On the other hand, a year is too short a time, even for a genius like Darwin, to absorb the riches of a new world. The *Beagle* voyage lasted five years, the *Challenger* voyage four. Neither ship would have changed the history of science if its voyage had been cut short after a year. A year is barely enough time to get the scientific equipment unpacked and running reliably. It takes longer than a year to see which are the important questions to answer. So the more probable outcome of the von Braun expedition would have been a hasty reconnaissance without any deep scientific probing. Especially if the reconnaissance had been conducted as von Braun envisaged it, in the style of a military operation, the chance of achieving a scientific output proportionate to the investment would have been minimal.

Should we feel sorry or glad that von Braun's road was the road not taken? Speaking for myself, I must confess that I am sorry. The Mars project was a magnificent venture. It would have opened the Solar System to mankind. After the ships came home from their first exploration of Mars, the entire infrastructure would still have been in place for further expeditions to Mars or to other places. Only one landing boat and parts of two others would have been left behind on Mars. Only three of the ten interplanetary space ships would have been left in Mars orbit. The remaining seven interplanetary space ships in Earth orbit and the fleet of forty-six ferry vessels on the ground were designed to be reusable, and could have embarked on new voyages as soon as new crews and new landing boats could be assembled. Even if, as is likely, the first expedition to Mars made no major contribution to science, later expeditions using the same infrastructure would have had a good chance of doing so. Later expeditions could have left scientists on the planet for five years rather than one, long enough for Darwin to find his finches.

2. APOLLO AS IT MIGHT HAVE BEEN

But these are idle dreams. Von Braun's infrastructure was never built. Instead, we were left with the Apollo project and the space shuttle. Both Apollo and the shuttle embodied fragments of von Braun's dream. Each Apollo mission to the moon was a miniature Mars Project, with the time scale compressed by a factor of a hundred from three years to a week, the time for exploring compressed from a year to three days. The space shuttle is in essence von Braun's ferry vessel, converted from a single-purpose to a multipurpose vehicle, and detached from the interplanetary mission for which von Braun intended it.

I do not need to recapitulate here the histories of Apollo and the shuttle. Apollo was a brilliant success, the shuttle a dismal failure. I am concerned with the general lessons that success and failure might teach us. What is to be learned from this success and this failure?

The success of Apollo was mainly due to the fact that the project was conceived and honestly presented to the public as an international sporting event and not as a contribution to science. The order of priorities in Apollo was accurately reflected by the first item to be unloaded after each landing on the Moon's surface, the television camera. The landing, the coming and going of the astronauts, the exploring of the Moon's surface, the gathering of Moon rocks and the earthward departure, all were expertly choreographed with the cameras placed in the right positions to make a dramatic show on television. This was to me the great surprise of the Apollo missions. There was nothing surprising in the fact that astronauts could walk on the Moon and bring home Moon rocks. There were no big scientific surprises in the chemistry of the Moon rocks or in the results of magnetic and seismic observations that the astronauts carried out. The big surprise was the quality of the public entertainment that the missions provided. I had never expected that we would see in real time astronauts hopping around in lunar gravity and driving their Rover down the Lincoln-Lee scarp to claim a lunar speed record of eleven miles per hour. Intensive television coverage was the driving force of Apollo. Von Braun had not imagined the possibilities of television when he decided that one kilohertz would be an adequate communication bandwidth for his Mars Project.

The brilliant success of Apollo as a sporting event came at a high cost for science. In many ways Apollo was a missed opportunity for science. It is interesting to speculate upon the shape that Apollo would have taken if science rather than television had been the primary objective. One possible shape for Apollo would have been an expedition following the pattern of the Mars Project more closely. The Apollo hardware could have been used with far greater cost-effectiveness if a smaller number of astronauts had been able to live and work on the Moon for a longer time. The main thing that the astronauts lacked on the Moon was time. Everything they did had to be done in a hurry, with one eye on the clock. That is not a good way to do science. To give them time von Braun provided his Mars Project astronauts with "some form of movable pressurized housing," that is to say, tractors and house trailers. A mobile laboratory building was envisaged in the early plans for Apollo but never reached the Moon.

Let us take a rough look at the numbers, to see how the Apollo payloads were used and how they might have been used. There were six lunar landings. Each of the six missions put roughly 50 tons into orbit about the Moon. Each mission was self-contained and allowed 2 astronauts to spend up to 3 days on the Moon, a total of 36 man-days for exploration and science. Of the 50 tons in lunar orbit, 35 tons were used to return to Earth, 15 tons to land on the Moon and return to orbit. Of the 15 tons that descended from lunar orbit, about 5 were needed for the return to orbit and about 2 were used for life support and transportation and exploration on the Moon. So the actual Apollo missions used about 12 tons of payload on the Moon for about 36 man-days of activity. This was an extremely inefficient use of resources. It makes no sense scientifically to bring a roving vehicle to the Moon and then use it only for 3 days.

The corresponding numbers for the Mars Project were 150 tons of payload on Mars to support 50 men for 400 days. So the Mars Project was supposed to achieve 130 man-days per ton while Apollo achieved 3 man-days per ton. Perhaps 130 man-days per ton would mean uncomfortably tight rations, but people could certainly live comfortably for 40 man-days per ton, which is 13 times the endurance of Apollo. Beyond this, we could have achieved another factor of five improvement in the cost-effectiveness of Apollo by using half the missions for passengers and half for freight. This was the way von Braun planned his logistics for the trip to Mars. Three Apollo missions could have been passenger missions, bringing two astronauts each to the Moon and back, while the other three could have been unmanned freight missions. Each freight mission, starting with 50 tons in lunar orbit, could have made a soft landing on the Moon with 18 tons of payload. In this way the useful payload on the Moon could have been increased from 12 to 60 tons, while the number of astronauts was reduced from 12 to 6.

Finally, if we had 6 astronauts landed on the Moon with 60 tons of payload, and if we assume they could live for 40 man-days per ton, then they could all stay on the Moon together for 400 days, just as long as von Braun's team was supposed to stay on Mars. This would have given them a chance to do some real exploring. Provided with a mobile habitat and traveling only about 15 miles per day, they could have circumnavigated the Moon, passing over both poles and traversing the back side. They might have been lucky enough to find a supply of native ice frozen in the perpetually shaded bottoms of the polar craters. Given a local supply of water, the explorers could have lengthened their stay beyond 400 days and could have prepared the ground for a permanent lunar settlement. All this might have been done within the budget and time span of Apollo. It was a great opportunity missed. Instead, we had some good shows on television.

The moral which I draw from this analysis is that the Apollo project was the right size for a major planetary exploration. The Mars Project with its 50 explorers on the ground was extravagantly large. It would have been more cost-effective to have fewer people and to let them stay on Mars longer. My hypothetical version of Apollo, with 6 people on the ground for a year, could have done a good job of exploring the Moon. Much less than this would be inadequate to the task, much more would have been impossibly expensive. Apollo was not too small or too big for its mission. Its scientific deficiencies had little to do with size. Its deficiencies arose from the fact that science was not its primary purpose. The opportunity to do cost-effective science on the Moon was missed. But not forever. The opportunity is still open, whenever humanity may decide the time is ripe for a big new effort of lunar exploring. And next time, if we do it right, we will have good science and good television too.

3. THE SHUTTLE

The failure of the shuttle is more difficult to explain than the success of Apollo. The shuttle failed in many different ways. It was supposed to be cheap, it was supposed to be reliable, it was supposed to be easy to service and reuse, it was supposed to be a frequent flyer, it was supposed to be safe. It turned out to be none of these things. The shuttle turned out to be a turkey. The word "turkey," in air force slang, means a bird which is barely able to fly.

Long experience in the development and use of airplanes has taught us to beware of turkeys. The appearance of a turkey is unpredictable. Turkeys appear in unlikely places. High technical credentials and industrial competence cannot give us a guarantee against turkeys. My own first acquaintance with a turkey was in the British Bomber Command of World War 2. We had a bomber called the Halifax, manufactured by a consortium of companies under the leadership of Sir Frederick Handley Page. Sir Frederick persuaded our government to buy Halifaxes in great quantity as the main delivery system for our strategic bombing of Germany. Meanwhile, a smaller company called Avro designed another bomber called the Lancaster, and our government bought some Lancasters too. The Lancaster was a makeshift affair, made by sticking two extra engines onto an old two-engined bomber that nobody wanted. But when we flew Halifaxes and Lancasters side by side in Bomber Command, we discovered unexpectedly that the Lancaster was more than three times as cost-effective as the Halifax. First, the Halifax cost 50 percent more than the Lancaster. Second, the Lancaster could carry a 50 percent larger load of bombs. And third, the Halifax had a 50 percent greater chance of being shot down. Multiplying together three factors of one and a half gives roughly a factor of three and a half in cost-effectiveness in favor of the Lancaster. In other words, the Halifax was a turkey. After recognizing this fact, and turning a deaf ear to Sir Frederick Handley Page's vigorous lobbying campaign in London, our Bomber Command switched its squadrons to Lancasters as rapidly as possible. The strange thing about this story is that nobody ever understood why the Halifax was a turkey. It just was so. The Halifax was built by competent people, it had no obvious flaws, and still it was a turkey. If the Lancaster had not happened to come along, we would not even have known that the Halifax was a turkey. That is the way it is with airplanes. Some are turkeys and some are not, and it is impossible to predict in advance which is which.

In view of this history, it is not surprising that the shuttle turned out to be an even worse turkey than the Halifax. The more complicated a flying machine is, the greater the chance that it will be a turkey. All the steps in the evolution from von Braun's simple ferry vessel to the modern shuttle were making the bird increasingly complicated, and therefore increasingly in danger of becoming a turkey. The fact that the shuttle was a turkey became clear to many of us in the space science community long before the *Challenger* disaster made it clear to the public. But the political authorities and the leaders of NASA made the mistake of neglecting to prepare a backup system in case the shuttle failed. They had no Lancaster ready when the Halifax shuttle started to grow turkey feathers.

The history of the shuttle is a typical example of a generic problem that occurs frequently in the development of science and technology, the problem of premature choice. Premature choice means betting all your money on one horse before you have found out whether she is lame. Politicians and administrators responsible for large projects are often obsessed with avoiding waste. To avoid waste they find it reasonable to choose one design as soon as possible and shut down the support of alternatives. So it was with the shuttle. We have seen the same pattern of premature choice in many other large enterprises, in nuclear power stations, in controlled thermonuclear fusion programs, in the American automobile industry, as well as in space propulsion and space science. The evolution of science and technology is a Darwinian process of the survival of the fittest. In science and technology, as in biological evolution, waste is the secret of efficiency. Without waste you cannot find out which horse is the fittest. This is a hard lesson for politicians and administrators to learn.

When I first came as a student from England to Cornell University in 1947, I was immediately impressed by two things, the quality of the science at Cornell and the wastefulness of the supply system. In England we were rationing bread and carefully reusing envelopes to save paper. At Cornell they were circulating interoffice mail in big fresh envelopes and throwing bread away. It occurred to me then that there might be a connection between the wastefulness and the flourishing of science at Cornell. If you want to do well in science, you had better not be too much concerned with saving envelopes.

The problem of premature choice is primarily a problem of size. Waste is politically embarrassing only when it occurs in large chunks. Politicians usually do not insist on making premature choices when their largesse is scattered over a multitude of small items. It is when projects grow big that the wastefulness of the Darwinian process becomes embarrassing and the pressure to anticipate Nature's judgment becomes irresistible. If we have three large projects competing for funds, and one looks better than the others, why waste money on the others? It is hard for a politician to see why. But in science and technology what looks better today will often turn out tomorrow to be a turkey. This is especially true if the decision between the alternatives is made by a committee. Committees usually decide in favor of the biggest project, simply because the biggest project has more votes on the committee. But Nature does not decide by majority vote. Frequently, Nature prefers the unfashionable and less popular alternative. This is why premature choice is dangerous, and why big science is in greater danger than small science of finding itself stuck with a horse that Nature declares unfit.

Please excuse me for mixing metaphors, for describing the shuttle first as a turkey and then as a lame horse. Both metaphors are good. Each captures a particular weakness of the shuttle. The shuttle is a turkey because it can only just fly into orbit, and a very low orbit at that, with no margin of performance to allow it to put payloads into higher orbits which would be more useful for science. The shuttle is a lame horse because, every time you fix one problem, you find another problem appearing somewhere else.

Fortunately, it is not true that the United States has no alternative to the shuttle. There are alternatives, if we can persuade our government to free itself from its obsession with the shuttle and give the alternatives some serious support. Instead of listing the alternatives, I will discuss only one, the International Ultraviolet Explorer, or IUE, mission which I mentioned in chapter 3. The IUE is a typical example of the new technology of space exploration that has grown up in the thirty years since von Braun conceived his Mars Project. The new technology, growing in Darwinian fashion from small beginnings, has already made the technology of the Mars Project and the shuttle obsolete.

4. INTERNATIONAL ULTRAVIOLET EXPLORER

The International Ultraviolet Explorer is a small telescope sitting in a geosynchronous orbit above equatorial South America, about

one-tenth of the way from the Earth to the Moon. It recently cel-
ebrated its twelfth birthday in space. It was launched in January
1978 from Cape Canaveral by a Delta rocket, one of the old reliable expendable rockets. The IUE is a joint enterprise, built and
operated by three agencies, the European Space Agency (ESA),
the British Science and Engineering Research Council (SERC),
and the United States NASA. The spacecraft and the optical mirrors were supplied by NASA, the television detection system by
SERC, and the solar power supply by ESA. The observer who
uses the telescope may sit either at the Goddard Space Flight Center in Maryland or at Villafranca in Spain.

The purpose of the IUE is to explore the universe in ultraviolet
light which is invisible to ground-based telescopes. The universe
is immensely rich in objects which are bright in this waveband.
Anything substantially hotter than the Sun will appear bright to
IUE. There is no danger that IUE will run out of interesting objects to look at. It looks at hot young stars, variable stars of many
varieties, white dwarfs, novae and supernovae, the interstellar gas,
globular clusters, active galactic nuclei, quasars, and other kinds
of peculiar objects that do not yet have names. Geosynchronous
orbit is an ideal place to have a telescope. From up there, the Earth
obscures less than 1 percent of the sky. The telescope keeps busy
for twenty-four hours every day, independent of weather and
moonshine and city lights. All day and all night it is pouring data
down to Earth at the rate of twenty kilobits per second, twenty
times as much as von Braun planned to send home from Mars.

The wonderful thing about the IUE is that it does so much
good science with so little hardware. The whole thing weighs
only nine hundred pounds, about a fiftieth of a shuttle payload
and about one–eighty-thousandth of the payload in Earth orbit of
the Mars Project. And the harvest of science produced by the IUE
is greater than the harvest of any shuttle or Apollo mission. To
give one recent example of what the IUE can do, it has provided
the most complete and accurate supernova light curve ever obtained. When a supernova was discovered in the Large Magellanic
Cloud on February 23, 1987, the IUE was immediately put to
work on it. Over the succeeding years, the IUE has continued to
measure its output with a continuity and precision that no
ground-based telescope can rival. And this is for the IUE only a

minor distraction from the regular program of observations. Most of the observations are of fainter objects which take longer to observe. A typical observation takes about an hour and produces a detailed spectrum of an object. There are more than eight thousand hours in a year and the IUE has already studied more than fifty thousand objects. Some objects are more interesting than others. Astronomers normally concentrate their attention on the most interesting objects, especially on those that are mysterious or variable and need to be observed repeatedly.

Since the IUE is a unique instrument with unique capabilities, it does not need to be large. The telescope mirror is 18 inches in diameter, a size that is nowadays within reach of the wealthier amateur astronomers on the ground. This little amateur-size telescope has been pouring out professional-quality science at a rate that not one of the big telescopes on the ground can match. In the first eight years of its life, the IUE had already produced more than a thousand papers in professional astronomical journals. A thousand guest observers have come to Goddard and Villafranca to use it. Why is the IUE so popular? There are two main reasons. This little telescope happens to be both user-friendly and universe-friendly. It is user-friendly because the guest observer sitting at the console at Goddard or Villafranca can watch the data coming down on the television monitor in real time. I have twice sat in on observing sessions at Goddard. It is delightful to see how informal the whole operation is—the observer, in this case a young graduate student, herself deciding which stars to look at and interpreting the spectra as they come in. You save a lot of valuable time if you can see at once that a star is uninteresting and cut the observation short. Or, if you see that a star is doing something unexpected, you can stop and take a more careful look at it and maybe discover something important. Looking at the sky with the IUE telescope is almost as good as being there.

The IUE is universe-friendly because it happens to be well matched to the processes that are going on out there. Almost every object that looks interesting when we see it with visible light from the ground turns out to be even more interesting when we look at it in the ultraviolet band covered by the IUE. The purpose of astronomy is not just to see things but to understand them. It happens very often that things seen in telescopes on the

ground are understood much better after they have been observed
with the IUE.

The results of the first nine years of observing with the IUE
were summarized in a fat book, *Exploring the Universe with the
IUE Satellite,* with forty chapters describing forty different kinds
of objects. Not bad for the scientific harvest of a small telescope.
And the IUE is still in business. It was designed to operate for
three years and it has now been operating for twelve. The weak
point of the system is the attitude-control gyros. Everything else
is still working well, but four out of six gyros have failed. The
gyros have to keep spinning and they cannot be expected to last
forever. Fortunately, the designers put in six gyros for an attitude-
control system that only needs three. The first gyro failed after
one year, the second and third after four years. After four years,
things looked bad. We were down to three gyros, and one more
failure would put the attitude-control system out of action. At this
point the engineers started to fight back. They worked out a new
and ingenious program by which the satellite could be oriented
with only two gyros. The new system was held in reserve for
three years while three gyros were still running. Then, seven years
from launch, the fourth gyro failed and the new system was carefully nursed into operation. At present, after twelve years, the
bird is flying smoothly on two gyros. And the engineers have another even more ingenious system in reserve so that when the fifth
gyro fails, IUE can probably continue to function with one gyro.
There is even talk of a zero-gyro system, using optical sensors and
momentum wheels only. That will be tough, but not impossible.
I will not be surprised if these engineers succeed in keeping the
IUE operational for another decade. The ultraviolet universe has
still to be explored, and the Hubble Space Telescope does not
make the IUE obsolete.

We will still need the IUE, even when the Hubble Telescope has
overcome its technical troubles and is operating at full capacity.
Hubble is a big telescope designed to look at very faint objects
with very high angular resolution. It has angular resolution about
fifty times sharper than the IUE and can see things about ten
thousand times fainter than the IUE. This means that Hubble will
discover a vast number of things that the IUE could not reach.
But the greater outreach of Hubble comes at a high price. I do not
mean the price in dollars. I mean the price in observing time. If

you observe with Hubble at the limit of its capabilities, you need to wait a long time to collect the light. Since most of the interesting objects in the sky are faint, Hubble will never have enough time to observe as many of them as we would like. Hubble will be, as far into the future as we can see, terribly overbooked, with astronomers from all over the world standing in line for years to obtain a few hours of observing time. The shortage of observing time is made worse by the low orbit. Unlike the IUE, Hubble can only see half of the sky at a time, and the time it can point at a particular object is interrupted as it swings around the earth. The precious observing time of Hubble will always be oversubscribed, and no time will be allotted to any astronomer to look at things which could be looked at just as well with the IUE. That is the reason why Hubble will not make the IUE obsolete. The two instruments complement each other without significant overlapping. Hubble is needed for deep exploration and high-resolution imaging; the IUE is needed for rapid and wide coverage of brighter objects.

It is a curious paradox that the Hubble Telescope has attracted such intense attention from the public while the IUE is almost unknown. This is partly due to the fact that Hubble is big while the IUE is small. Partly it is due to the fact that Hubble is caught in the shuttle morass while the IUE is not. Still, it is a paradox that the public, and even the scientifically educated public, is poorly informed about one of the most successful and cost-effective of all our scientific ventures in space. Perhaps we should draw a moral from this paradox. Perhaps it is no accident that the most successful projects are the least conspicuous. Perhaps scientific merit and big publicity are incompatible. If this is so, then we should be careful not to talk too loud about the IUE. Let us be thankful that the shuttle and its misfortunes have distracted the attention of the public, while the international community of astronomers associated with the IUE has been quietly getting on with the job of exploring the universe.

5. THE NEXT THIRTY YEARS

I now make another jump in time, a jump of thirty years to the year 2018. I will not try to sketch a program of space missions for the next thirty years. Our primary need is to have more missions like the IUE, international collaborations of modest size, modest cost, and long duration. Whether the IUE itself lives or dies, we shall have many such missions, flown by the Europeans and the Japanese and the Russians if NASA is unwilling to do the job. These are the missions that efficiently exploit the technology of the 1970s and 1980s, microcomputers and software and imaging electronic detectors. We already have a new infrared imaging detector which will allow us to explore the universe in the infrared as efficiently as the IUE has explored in the ultraviolet. A satellite like the IUE, working in the infrared, will yield a harvest of science at least as rich as the IUE. This is a job for the next decade. If we are wise, we shall have several such satellites flying before the year 2000. I talk now about things that we may do later, not with the technology of 1988 but with the technology of 2018.

I have sketched in a rough fashion how space-technology jumped in the past thirty years, from 1958 to 1988. The von Braun Mars Project represented the technology of 1958. The IUE represented the technology of 1988. The Mars Project was the best you could have done with space exploration in 1958, while the IUE was the best you could do in 1988. The point of this comparison is that the jump in cost-effectiveness from the Mars Project to the IUE is not just a factor of 10 or 100 but more like a factor of 10,000 or 100,000. The jump is so great that you cannot measure it by a single number. Compared with the Mars Project, the IUE has:

1. 20 times as many people actively observing.
2. 20 times the data rate for returning information.
3. 10 times the mission duration.
4. 100 times less cost.
5. 80,000 times less mass in orbit.

It is a matter of taste how many of these numbers you multiply together to obtain an index of cost-effectiveness. No matter how you do it, the IUE wins at least by a factor of ten thousand. This huge jump did not come from technical improvements in rocket propulsion. It came from a radical change in style. The style of the Mars Project was based on World War 2 military operations and the Berlin airlift. The style of the IUE was based on thirty years of experience with television cameras, microcomputers, and remote-control software.

When we look ahead to 2018, we should expect big steps forward in science to come once again from changes in style rather than from marginal improvements in technology. I am saying that another jump by a factor of ten thousand in cost-effectiveness is possible. The next big jump will not come from anything included in the present plans of NASA. The present NASA program, with its emphasis on a massive space station in low Earth orbit, is not even pointing in the right direction. To improve cost-effectiveness by a factor of ten thousand, we need spacecraft that are radically cheaper, smaller, and quicker than anything we can build with 1988 technology. Spacecraft should weigh pounds rather than tons, they should cost tens of thousands rather than tens of millions of dollars, and they should fly missions at a rate of several per day rather than several per year.

I am not pretending that I can predict the future. I am not saying that a jump by a factor of ten thousand in cost-effectiveness is bound to happen. I am saying only that it might happen and that we ought to try to make it happen. There are two ways in which the jump could happen. The two ways are called nanotechnology and genetic engineering. Nanotechnology means the building of machines and structures on a microscopic scale by manipulation of individual atoms and molecules. Genetic engineering means the use of nature's nanotechnology of genes and enzymes to grow living creatures of our own design. Both mechanical nanotechnology and genetic engineering are vigorously growing industries, and are likely to be transforming our Earth-bound economy during the next thirty years. At present, nanotechnology is mainly confined to the production of electronic devices and semiconductor chips, while genetic engineering is mainly confined to the production of drugs and vaccines. By the year 2018 both technologies will be available for a greater variety of purposes. Either of them or both could be adapted to the production of radically smaller, cheaper, and more capable spacecraft.

The chief prophet of nanotechnology is Eric Drexler, who wrote a book, *Engines of Creation,* explaining his ideas, and founded an institution, the Foresight Institute, to explore their consequences. I agree with him that nanotechnology might take us to the promised land of cheap and widely proliferated space-craft, but I expect genetic engineering to get there first. Those of you who are still alive in 2018 will see who won the race. Probably both nanotechnology and genetic engineering will have an impor-tant role to play in space science. The two technologies are likely to grow together and ultimately merge, so that it will be difficult to tell which is which. In the end, nanotechnology will give us scientific instruments having the alertness and agility of living creatures, while genetic engineering will give us living creatures having the sensitivity and precision of scientific instruments. The spacecraft of 2018 may well be a hybrid, making use of nanotech-nology for its sensors and communications, genetic engineering for its legs, wings, and brain.

Here is a rough sketch of one possible shape that the 2018 spacecraft might take. I call this model the Astrochicken because it is about as big as a chicken and about as smart. It is a product of genetic engineering. It does not look like a chicken. It looks more like a butterfly. It has wide and thin solar sails instead of wings, and a high-resolution spectroscopic imaging system instead of eyes. With its solar sails it flies around the inner solar system as far as the main belt of asteroids. At any one time there will be hun-dreds of such birds flying, programmed to make specialized ob-servations of Earth, Moon, Sun, planets, and asteroids as well as of the heavens beyond. Other cousins of the Astrochicken will have legs for landing and hopping around on asteroids, or solar-powered ion-jet engines for exploring the outer solar system as far as Pluto.

The high-performance space telescope of 2018 will not have a monolithic mirror like the Hubble Telescope. It will be a light and flexible optical array composed of a hundred astrochickens flying together in space and linked by a network of optical interferome-ters. Such an optical array might give us angular resolution a hun-dred times better than Hubble with a smaller total weight. And meanwhile there will be a variety of more modest Astrochicken observatories, continuing and extending the mission of the IUE, and costing a few thousand dollars apiece.

Why should anybody believe such fantasies? The Astrochicken is a fantasy, not a prediction. We know that Astrochickens are a theoretical possibility. The same laws of nature which allow us to produce chickens also allow us to produce Astrochickens. A chicken is no less a miracle than an Astrochicken.

6. TO MARS NEXT TIME

That is my sixty-year program for space science, beginning with the Mars Project of Wernher von Braun, payload 4,700 tons, and ending with the Astrochicken, payload a couple of pounds. To do well in science we must vigorously exploit the new technologies that make our instruments smaller, cheaper, and smarter. The Astrochicken stands as a symbol of the radical improvements that twenty-first-century technology will make possible.

I said nothing about the big missions that space enthusiasts inside and outside NASA are now promoting. I said nothing about future manned missions to Mars. According to the plans of the enthusiasts, manned missions to Mars and other interesting places should be under way by the year 2018, before my sixty-year program ends. Do these plans make sense? Are manned missions to Mars foolish? Should we give up on manned missions and leave space science to the chickens?

Von Braun's Mars Project was a wonderful idea when he proposed it in the 1950s. A manned mission to Mars in 2018 is still a wonderful idea. But the Astrochickens should go there first. A manned mission with the technology of the 1950s made sense in the 1950s, and a manned mission with the technology of 2018 will make sense in 2018. What will not make sense is a manned mission in 2018 using the technology of 1988.

Whether big manned missions make sense or not is a question of ecology. Big missions make sense if they are embedded in an ecology of numerous smaller missions, sharing the work of exploration in a cost-effective manner. The Apollo missions to the Moon were fruitful because they were supported by a variety of smaller unmanned missions. A manned mission to Mars, helped and preceded by a variety of unmanned missions, could open the planet in a decisive fashion to human exploration. A manned mission to Mars without the accompanying ecology of small missions would be an empty political gesture, as costly and as

65

counterproductive for science as the telescope at Zelenchukskaya. The order of priorities in any scientific exploration must be, first, the small missions, and then the big. Unless the small missions come first, the big ones will be largely wasted.

When we try to imagine the environment in which a group of human explorers on Mars could creatively function, the word "ecology" has a double meaning. The first meaning is metaphorical, the second literal. The metaphorical ecology means the environment of scientific missions, large and small, which give depth to the explorers' vision and enable them to understand what they see. The literal ecology means the environment of living creatures and machines, the plants and animals and vehicles and habitats, which will enable the explorers to settle down on Mars and live there in some degree of ease and comfort. Before humans can go and explore Mars in a cost-effective style, large numbers of un-manned missions must prepare the ground scientifically, and large numbers of biologically engineered creatures must prepare the ground physically for human settlement. The Astrochicken and its cousins will serve us in both capacities.

The driving force behind the idea of manned missions to Mars, both in America and in the Soviet Union, is territorial expansion rather than science. And that is as it should be. We shall go to Mars, not just to study its physics and chemistry but to bring a dead planet to life. In bringing a dead planet to life, even more than in the pursuit of scientific knowledge, the name of the game is ecology.

CHAPTER 6

The Importance of
Being Unpredictable

.....

1990

This is a good time to talk about the unpredictability of human affairs. The winter of 1989 was the season of revolutions. Who predicted them? Who even believed a year earlier that they were possible? Certainly not I, even though I have family connections in East Germany and consider myself well informed. So far as we can tell, these revolutions were not even foreseen by the people who carried them out. The leaders were swept along by events which they neither planned nor controlled. The best guide to the understanding of these events is Tolstoy's *War and Peace*. Tolstoy describes the great campaign of 1812 as similarly unplanned and uncontrolled. The nominal leaders on the two sides, Napoleon and Kutuzov, were never really in control. Since Kutuzov was aware of this and Napoleon was not, Kutuzov made fewer mistakes. But in the end, according to Tolstoy, the outcome was determined by the individual actions of hundreds of thousands of ordinary soldiers, whose decisions, to fight bravely or to run away, nobody could have predicted. "Napoleon," says Tolstoy, "in his activity all this time was like a child, sitting in a carriage, pulling the straps within it, and fancying he is moving it along." The same could be said of the dethroned tyrants of 1989, Honecker and Zhivkov and Ceauşescu and all the rest of them.

It is not only in Eastern Europe that the most important human affairs are unpredictable. Who predicted forty years ago that Japan would beat the United States at our own game of industrial productivity? Who predicted the rapid growth of poverty and homelessness in American cities? Who predicted the onslaught of the AIDS epidemic? Nobody was in charge of these events, and nobody knew how to prevent them. They happened, like the chaotic retreat from Moscow in 1812, because the people who imagined themselves to be in charge were deluding themselves. The leaders of our industrial establishment thought they could handle the productivity problem, the leaders of our political establishment thought they could handle the poverty problem, the leaders of our medical establishment thought they could handle the problem of infectious disease. American leaders were as impotent as the leaders of Eastern Europe when history took an unexpected turn. Tolstoy's image of the child pulling the straps in his carriage applies equally to them all.

The names of the individuals now alive who will most decisively influence the future course of history are probably unknown to us. How many people at the beginning of the twentieth century had heard the names of Lenin and Einstein? How many educated Romans during the peaceful reign of the emperor Tiberius heard the name of Jesus of Nazareth? The next major shift in the course of history will probably be as unexpected as any that happened in the past. The worst folly is to believe, as Karl Marx believed, that history marches to a predictable tune.

Since I am a scientist, I am a specialist in unpredictability. Science is even more unpredictable than history. Every important discovery in science is by definition unpredictable. If it were predictable, it would not be an important discovery. The purpose of science is to create opportunities for unpredictable things to happen. When nature does something unexpected, we learn something about how nature works. It used to be said, before the recent era of revolutionary discoveries, that science was organized common sense. In the modern era it would be more accurate to define science as organized unpredictability.

To illustrate the unpredictability of science, here is a little story about Francis Crick, the great biologist who discovered, with James Watson, the double helix. They discovered the double helix in 1953, and thereby created the new science of molecular genet-

FROM EROS TO GAIA

ics. Eight years before that I met Francis Crick for the first time. He was in Fanum House, a dismal office building in London where the Royal Navy kept a staff of scientists. Crick had been working for the navy for a long time and was depressed and discouraged. He said he had missed his chance of ever amounting to anything as a scientist. World War 2 had hit him at the worst time, putting a stop to his career as a physicist and keeping him away from science for six years. The six best years of his life, squandered on naval intelligence, lost and gone forever. Crick was good at naval intelligence, and did important work. But military intelligence bears the same relation to intelligence as military music bears to music. After six years in this kind of intelligence, it was far too late for Crick to start all over again as a student and learn all the stuff he had forgotten. No wonder he was depressed. I came away from Fanum House thinking, "How sad. Such a bright chap. If it hadn't been for the war, he would probably have been quite a good scientist."

A year later I met Crick again. The war was over and he was much more cheerful. He said he was thinking of giving up physics and making a completely fresh start as a biologist. He said the most exciting science for the next twenty years would be in biology and not in physics. I was then twenty-two years old and very sure of myself. I said, "No, you're wrong. In the long run biology will be more exciting, but not yet. The next twenty years will still belong to physics. If you switch to biology now, you will be too old to do the exciting stuff when biology finally takes off." Fortunately, he didn't listen to me. He went to Cambridge and began thinking about DNA. It took him only seven years to prove me wrong. The moral of this story is clear. Even a smart twenty-two-year-old is not a reliable guide to the future of science.

Here is another story about another great scientist who worked for the Royal Navy. Patrick Blackett had been a particle physicist before World War 2 and won a Nobel Prize for taking pictures of particles interacting in cloud chambers. After the war he gave a lecture in London. I came to listen, expecting to hear exciting things about new particles. I was disgusted to find that he had lost interest in particles and only talked about some dull stuff that he had done for the navy, measuring the magnetization of mud and rocks on the bottom of the sea. For some inscrutable reason he

69

seemed to think the patterns of magnetization on the sea bottom were scientifically exciting. I decided that too many years of working for the navy had addled the man's brains. How sad. Another good man lost to science because of the war. It took Blackett a little longer than it took Crick to prove me wrong. Seventeen years after his lecture, a systematic program of measurements of magnetization of ocean sediments on both sides of the mid-Atlantic ridge provided the crucial evidence that established the reality of continental drift and gave birth to the new science of plate tectonics.

That is the way science is. The big jumps ahead are taken by people who disregard the conventional wisdom and do something unexpected. The big jumps are unpredictable. And the same unpredictability reigns also in economics and international politics.

The great task before us now, as citizens of the world, is to learn to organize our societies in such a way that unpredictable things have a chance to happen. A number of revolutions in our thinking are long overdue. We need a collapse of nationalism and a rising commitment to international institutions. We need a collapse of greed and a commitment to decent treatment of the poor. We need a collapse of military rivalry and a commitment to a worldwide effort to preserve our planet as a fit home for mankind and other living creatures. The conventional wisdom says that none of these revolutions will happen. But we have seen in the last year a number of revolutions that the conventional wisdom had declared impossible. The overdue revolutions are unpredictable but not impossible. It is our task, both in science and in society at large, to prove the conventional wisdom wrong and to make our unpredictable dreams come true.

CHAPTER 7

Strategic Bombing in World War 2 and Today
Has Anything Changed?

.....

1990

I. A VISIT TO FAIRCHILD AIR FORCE BASE

I am not a historian. I have not done the research that would be needed to trace the history of strategic bomber forces from World War 2 to the present. Instead of history, I give you anecdotes. Instead of analysis, I give you opinions. My anecdotes and opinions make no claim to be objective. I claim only that they are authentic, based on firsthand experience. I talk about things that I saw with my own eyes. At the end I try to distill a meaning from what I have seen.

Let me begin with things that are still fresh in memory. On July 18, 1989, I spent a day at Fairchild Air Force Base, one of the Strategic Air Command bases at which B-52 bombers are maintained on alert. The phrase "on alert" means that a certain fraction of the bombers stand fully fueled and loaded with bombs, their crews close enough to jump into the planes and take off within a small number of minutes. Each plane carries some of its hydrogen bombs in the bomb bay and the rest in Air-Launched Cruise Missiles (ALCM) mounted externally on pylons attached to the wings.

I came to the base because I was studying technical problems concerning verification of arms-control treaties. One of the central issues in the START treaty negotiations is whether to limit the numbers of nuclear cruise missiles. Rules for counting cruise missiles must first be agreed, and then procedures must be worked out for verifying the numbers and for distinguishing nuclear from nonnuclear missiles. In order to talk sense about these matters, it is useful to see and touch a cruise missile in its real-world environment. The officers of the 92nd Bombardment Wing courteously allowed me to spend the day with one of the alert crews and to climb around inside their B-52. I was able to gain an impression, not only of the hardware but of the human beings who hold the fate of the world in their hands.

The first thing that strikes you when you arrive at Fairchild is the peace and beauty of the surroundings. The base is near Spokane, at the eastern end of Washington State. All around stretches the landscape of golden hills, like California but cooler and less crowded. At night you hear the distant hooting of trains carrying the wheat harvest to market. The base is a neat little old-fashioned American town, with church and school and playground and children running free. At the guesthouse they give you a comfortable room for ten dollars a night. They also give you a bumper sticker with the coat of arms of the 92nd Bombardment Wing, a two-edged sword with sunshine on one side of it and a lightning flash on the other. Under the coat of arms there is a Latin motto, "Duplum Incolumitatis," which I take to mean "Double Security." The atmosphere of the place is the atmosphere of a small college town in the 1950s. Here, it seems, time has been standing still. The civic pride and the simple virtues of the 1950s still flourish. The only evidence of changing times is the fact that several of the senior officers running the 92nd Bombardment Wing are female.

When I encountered the alert crew with whom I was to spend the day, I was relieved to find that they did not resemble the crew of the B-52 "Leper Colony" in the movie *Doctor Strangelove*. They are not imbued with fierce desire to engage in nuclear combat, toe-to-toe with the Russkies. They are seven young men who enlisted in the air force because it offered them a free college education in exchange for six years of service. They take their job seriously but without fanaticism. They do not expect to receive an order to drop a bomb in anger. They expect to finish their six years of practice flying and then find jobs in the civilian world. They talked about their future careers and about their families. In spirit, they are already civilians. In half a day I could not expect to penetrate far into their inner thoughts, but my contact with them gave me no reason to doubt their technical competence and moral sanity. They take at face value the official motto of the Strategic Air Command, "Peace Is Our Profession." Sitting at lunch with these young men in the cafeteria within the alert area, I had the feeling that peace is in good hands. Steady, courteous, reliable, these young men embody the virtues one expects to find in a Greyhound bus driver.

And yet, the B-52 is no Greyhound bus. When I was clambering around the airplane, the images which came to my mind were not of peace but of war. I remembered clambering around a similar airplane, a Lancaster belonging to the Pathfinder Force of the Royal Air Force Bomber Command, forty-five years earlier, in January 1944. The Lancaster was standing, fueled and heavily loaded with bombs, ready to take off for the next night attack on Berlin. That was at Wyton Air Force Base in England. In those days I was not concerned with arms-control treaties but with keeping bombers from getting shot down. Wyton was the home of 83 Squadron. The Lancasters of 83 Squadron had lower losses than average, not because our electronic countermeasures protected them but because they always flew at the front of the bomber stream. The German night fighters usually arrived late and picked off a larger fraction of the bombers at the back of the stream.

How immeasurably the world has changed between 1944 and 1989! And in spite of all the changes in technology and in society, the fall of empires and the rise of nations, the basic design of strategic bombers has hardly changed at all. The Lancaster and the B-52 are amazingly alike. The crew still consists of seven men with roughly the same jobs that they had in 1944. The accommodations for the crew are still almost as uncomfortable as they were in 1944. And the long slender bombs in the bomb bay look very much like the Tallboy high-penetration bombs that sank the German battleship *Tirpitz* in Tromsö Fjord in 1944. Superficially, the B-52 is a modified Lancaster with jet engines instead of propellers.

I was happy to see that one of the mechanical problems that used to plague the Lancaster crews in the old days is still alive and well. After we had examined the bombs in the bomb bay of the B-52, the commander pressed the switch to close the bomb bay doors. Nothing happened. He tried several other switches. Still nothing happened. The problem was solved by the entire crew standing in line beneath the bomb bay and forcing the doors shut with a heave of seven broad shoulders.

The picture of these seven young men, with their friendly smiles and good-humored banter slamming the bomb bay shut, came into jarring conflict with another picture in my mind. The second picture is the inner workings of the hydrogen warheads inside those elegant silverfish in the bomb bay. It was the first time in my life that I had come within a few feet of a hydrogen bomb. For many years I have been theoretically aware that these bombs exist. To see and touch them with my own hands gave their existence a different meaning. They are no longer theoretical. They are there.

I sat in the commander's seat in the cockpit and had my hand on the red switch which the commander turns to allow the bomb aimer to release the bombs. This switch is also no longer theoretical. It is there. We know that there is a permissive action link, or PAL, an electronic control which prevents the red switch from functioning unless the correct coded signal is received from the Strategic Air Command or from an even higher authority. I do not know, and I do not wish to know, how the command-and-control system operates between the National Command Authority and the bomber in the air. All I know is that the command-and-control system is complicated and that it involves human beings. It demands an orderly military hierarchy in order to function safely.

2. STRATEGIC STABILITY AND POLITICAL TURMOIL

While I was at Fairchild, I was struck by the thought that similar bombers are sitting loaded with similar bombs with similar young men on alert and similar command-and-control systems at various air force bases scattered around the Soviet Union. We have no reason to doubt that their command-and-control systems are technically as robust as ours. But we now have reason to doubt that their society is robust.

The calm day-to-day existence of Fairchild Air Force Base makes sense in a stable world governed by stable institutions. When you look at Fairchild with its simple well-ordered life, it is easy to see why it continues to exist. It exists because large bureaucratic organizations resist change. It exists because it perpetuates the organization of strategic bomber forces that were created during World War 2. It exists because people find security in clinging to established routines. So long as the Soviet Union was likewise governed by bureaucratic inertia and was clinging to established routines, you could believe in a stable equilibrium, with the red switches on both sides controlled by rational command authorities. But now the world has changed. Bureaucratic inertia can no longer be relied on. The real threat to our existence comes not from the Soviet command authority but from Soviet command confusion.

During the day at Fairchild I also witnessed the ritual of a generated alert. "Generated alert" is air force jargon for bringing out the bombs and putting them on board the B-52 bombers that are not already on alert. The generated alert is an impressive performance, with hydrogen bombs moving around on trolleys, and stern-faced men with machine guns ready to take care of unauthorized visitors. I was duly impressed. The internal security of the base is in good hands. There was no way I could have hijacked one of the trolleys and taken it out of the base. Only one thing went wrong during the generated alert. The process is organized as a competitive sport, with the various teams of ground crew competing with each other to get the bombs loaded as quickly as possible. Our team was expected to win, but they had the misfortune to have a substitute truck driver replacing one of their team who had the flu. To place the cruise missiles on the wing of the B-52, the driver had to drive the trolley under the wing backward, with no margin for error either in position or angle. The substitute driver struggled to hit the right spot while the rest of the team impatiently watched the seconds ticking by. In the end, the missiles were successfully attached, but our team had lost the game by several minutes.

After watching this performance of the generated alert, I felt that I understood for the first time the meaning and purpose of Fairchild Air Force Base. Not only the ceremony of the alert, but the entire base with all its bombs and planes and dedicated young men, is a ritualized reenactment of the strategic bombing campaigns of World War II. Hydrogen bombs are no longer useful for fighting wars, but they are excellent for adding solemnity to a ritual. The whole Strategic Air Command is engaged in perpetuating such rituals. Just as wolves fighting for dominance in a pack have learned to fight ritualistically so that they do not get torn apart, showing their teeth but being careful not to use them, so we fight ritualistically with our hydrogen bombs. The rituals give us a comforting illusion of security. And so long as the rituals are faithfully observed, nobody gets hurt.

3. BACK TO WORLD WAR 2

In the old days I used to know Wing-Commander Tait, the man who sank the *Tirpitz* in Tromsö Fjord in November 1944. He was commander of 617 Squadron, a special squadron of Lancasters which took no part in the routine mass bombings but carried out small operations requiring high precision. This squadron became famous because of its suicidal low-level attack on the Ruhr dams in May 1943. In that attack they lost eight out of nineteen Lancasters. From a military point of view the attack was more costly to England than to Germany. Like many other such follies, it was a public-relations triumph and was made into a successful movie. But Wing-Commander Tait was determined to waste no more lives for the moviemakers. He looked around for other more sensible things to do with his squadron. Since he was exempt from the grind of regular bombing operations, he had time to come to Bomber Command Headquarters and chat with his old friend Reuben Smeed, who happened to be my boss. Smeed was the expert on German defenses. Tait understood that the official Bomber Command policy of ignoring the defenses was not a sensible way to fight a war. He was one of the few bomber pilots who had time to think critically about what he was doing.

I was usually invited to come in and listen when Tait and Smeed were discussing the progress of the war. They talked freely about the failures of the strategic bombing offensive. The basic reason for our failures was that the German defenses were too strong. If the bombers attacked from low altitude they took unacceptable losses. If they attacked from high altitude they could not bomb accurately enough to hit anything smaller than a city. And even at high altitude the losses were still heavy. Tait decided that the most useful thing his squadron could do was to develop a technique for accurate bombing from high altitude. He had his squadron equipped with Tallboy bombs. The Tallboy was the only bomb streamlined and slender enough to follow a predictable trajectory from twenty thousand feet to the ground. The squadron practiced with special stabilized bombsights until they could hit practice targets with an error of less than a hundred feet. This was about five times as accurate as a normal bomber bombing on a practice range with a normal bombsight and normal bombs. It was about fifty times as accurate as a normal bomber bombing a defended target in Germany.

In 1944, Wing-Commander Tait had his squadron of bombers ready and trained with their beautiful Tallboy bombs. His problem then was to find suitable targets that were not too heavily defended. The concrete submarine pens on the west coast of France made ideal targets. The Germans had built these pens to give their U-boats secure bases for operations in the Atlantic. While the Battle of the Atlantic was raging in 1942 and 1943, the pens were repeatedly attacked with ordinary high-explosive bombs. Ordinary bombs could do no significant damage to the massive reinforced concrete roofs of the pens. The U-boat crews inside could listen calmly to the patter of bombs exploding over their heads, and then go about their business. Finally, in 1944, 617 squadron went to work on the pens with Tallboy bombs. The Tallboy bombs did what they were supposed to do, smashing through the concrete and making the pens useless. Unfortunately, this triumph of technology occurred when the Allied armies were already landed in France and the Battle of the Atlantic was already won.

During the last autumn of the war, Tait was able to find a few targets inside Germany which his Tallboy bombs could demolish. In September 1944 he breached the aqueduct of the Dortmund-

Ems Canal and left thirty-three barges stuck in the mud. In October he breached the Kembs Dam on the Rhine River in an operation described in the official history as "brilliant." The military value of this operation was even smaller than the value of the famous Ruhr dams attack a year and a half earlier, but this time no bombers were lost. Tait was happy. He had finally created a small force of bombers that could bomb accurately without getting wiped out.

In November came Tait's greatest exploit, the sinking of the *Tirpitz*. The battleship *Tirpitz*, sister ship of the *Bismarck*, had been in earlier years a major threat to the Arctic convoys carrying supplies around the North Cape to Murmansk. The mere existence of the *Tirpitz* in a Norwegian base was a constant anxiety to the British navy. By November 1944 the *Tirpitz* was not in fact a threat to anybody. She was still afloat, lying in Tromsö Fjord in the extreme north of Norway, but she had been so badly damaged in earlier attacks by submarines and aircraft that the Germans had decided not to attempt to bring her back to a German port for repair. Her top speed in her damaged condition was seven knots. These facts about her seaworthiness were not known to the British navy or to Wing-Commander Tait.

The German defenses at Tromsö Fjord were negligible. The Germans had not even deployed their customary smokescreen when Tait arrived with his Tallboy bomb. Tait had the satisfaction of bombing an ideal target under ideal conditions with perfect visibility. He dropped the first bomb and scored a direct hit. A few minutes later there was another direct hit, followed by an internal explosion that split the ship open from keel to deck. Tait was already on his way home when the *Tirpitz* turned over and sank. Fortunately, more than half the crew survived. Tait did not lose a single man. In this way it happened, in November 1944, that the classic victory of air power over sea power was won.

What I saw at Fairchild Air Force Base in 1989 was a ritualized version of the things Tait had been doing with his squadron of Lancasters forty-five years earlier. But the ritualization of strategic warfare did not begin with the 92nd Bombardment Wing. It began in 1944. When Tait's Lancasters were taken away from regular bombing operations, equipped with technically superior bombs and bombsights, and allowed to choose their own targets in areas peripheral to the main theater of war, ritualization was already far advanced. The process of ritualization was gradual. Not all of Tait's operations were showpieces. But his fundamental purpose was to conduct bombing operations with technical precision and without getting hurt. This purpose led him inevitably in the direction of showpieces. And the final result, the sinking of the *Tirpitz,* was the greatest showpiece of all.

I do not remember whether Tait, in his conversations with Reuben Smeed at Bomber Command Headquarters, ever enunciated explicitly the philosophy of ritualization as the basis of his bombing tactics. Probably not. He was, after all, a flying officer, not a strategic philosopher. Our conversations were mainly concerned with the details of the German defenses and how best to avoid them. But ritualization was the logical response to the situation as Tait saw it. Tait knew as well as we did that the successful operations of Bomber Command, achieved at enormous cost in aircraft and lives, had come too late in the war to have any decisive effect on the outcome. He found himself in command of an elite squadron with glorious traditions and superb crews. He wanted to contribute as best he could to the prosecution of the war, but his first priority was to avoid throwing away the lives of his men in acts of useless heroism. What was he to do? He had to weigh his responsibility to his crews against his responsibility to his commander in chief, Bert Harris. He chose the best practical compromise between these responsibilities. He chose to keep his squadron busy with operations which were technically brilliant, emotionally satisfying to the British public, and not too dangerous to his crews. Bert Harris, usually a hard man to please, loved these cheap and spectacular victories. The cheapest and most spectacular of all was the sinking of the *Tirpitz*. So it happened that Tait achieved the ritualization of strategic bombing operations, even before the war was over. And the operational exercise at Fairchild was only the same process of ritualization carried to its logical conclusion.

I have been talking about the British experience of strategic bombing in World War 2 because that was where I was. The American experience was different. The American strategic bombing of Japan in the spring of 1945 was successful. General Curtis LeMay's operations over Japan were as technically brilliant as Tait's operations over Germany. LeMay's operations, unlike Tait's, were strategically decisive. LeMay did not confine his attention to easy targets. LeMay was fighting a real war, not a ritualized war.

The reason why LeMay succeeded while Bert Harris failed was that the Japanese did not have effective defenses. LeMay was able to ignore such defenses as there were over Japan. The fact that the Japanese defenses were negligible is well known. Another fact is not so well known. The Japanese might have had an effective defense when LeMay attacked. It was, like the Battle of Waterloo, a close-run thing. The Japanese had a twin-engined night fighter, called by them the Gekko and by the Americans the Irving. The sole surviving Irving is sitting in the National Air and Space Museum in Washington. It was described recently in one of the excellent museum publications, *Moonlight Interceptor* by Robert Mikesh and Osamu Tagaya. The Irving was as good as any German night fighter. The Irving was also equipped with upward-firing guns, as lethal against a B-29 as the German "Schräge Musik" which shot down so many thousand Lancasters. All that the Irvings lacked was numbers. A few hundred night fighters were enough to cripple the British bomber offensive against Germany and make accurate bombing impossible. A few hundred Irvings could have had the same effect over Japan. If the Japanese had given priority to air defense, a few hundred Irving night fighters might have been operational when LeMay attacked, and the B-29s over Tokyo might have shared the fate of the Lancasters over Berlin. As it was, the Japanese produced only 486 Irvings altogether, and only a small fraction of them were used as night fighters. A handful of Irvings succeeded in shooting down a few dozen B-29s. They became a forgotten footnote in the history of the war.

The success of General LeMay's campaign in 1945 made little difference to the long-term future of the Strategic Air Command. For many years SAC operated as if real war-fighting campaigns in the style of 1945 were still possible. During the later phases of the war in Vietnam, B-52 bombers were in action, dropping large quantities of nonnuclear bombs on a variety of targets. The results were disappointing. From time to time, B-52s were shot down by surface-to-air missiles. Since B-52s were no longer being produced, SAC could not afford to lose many of them. It soon became clear that the bombing was ineffective in Vietnam as it had been in Germany. The reason for the failure was the same in

Vietnam as in Germany. The defenses were too strong. Against competent defenses, nonnuclear strategic bombing is a losing proposition.

After the attempt to achieve victory through air power in Vietnam had failed, SAC continued to pursue its primary mission, the strategic bombing of the Soviet Union with nuclear weapons. But inevitably, as fission bombs and hydrogen bombs and intercontinental missiles were deployed in larger numbers in the Soviet Union, the practical feasibility of nuclear war fighting became more and more dubious. The situation of the B-52s today is similar to the situation of Tait's Lancasters in World War 2. The B-52s today, like Tait's Lancasters in 1944, can be highly effective against undefended targets, but they cannot solve our security problems. The hydrogen bomb in its elegant streamlined shell, like its predecessor the Tallboy, is powerless to protect us from the dangers of living in a chaotic world.

4. A VISIT TO THE USS *PRINCETON*

I now leave the air force and turn to the navy. The navy with its Trident submarines has become a major player in the strategic-bombing game. The main driving force of the strategic arms race has not been American-Soviet rivalry but rather the rivalry between the navy and the air force in the United States. Interservice rivalries exist in the Soviet Union and in other countries too. Wherever you have navies and air forces, you have these intense rivalries. The service with the newest strategic weapons gets the biggest share of the budget. The weapons become symbols of political status for the service that owns them, whether or not they are militarily useful. The conversion of strategic weapons into status symbols is a part of the process of ritualization that I saw at Fairchild. It is an old and familiar story.

Now, in the United States, the old game of interservice rivalry has developed a new twist. The United States has two navies, a submarine navy and a surface navy. The submarine navy has long enjoyed the political clout that comes with possession of massive strategic forces. The surface navy has been shut out of the strategic-weapons game. Into this situation came recently a new factor, the Tomahawk cruise missile. The Tomahawk belongs to both navies. It can be launched either from submarine torpedo tubes or from launchers on the decks of cruisers. It satisfies the demands of interservice rivalry on two levels simultaneously. It is the navy's answer to the air force's air-launched cruise missile, and it is the surface navy's answer to the submarine navy's Trident.

In the course of my study of cruise missile treaty verification problems, I visited the missile-carrying cruiser USS *Princeton* at the Long Beach naval base. I also visited a General Dynamics factory where Tomahawks are manufactured. The *Princeton* is a beautiful ship, clean and spacious and full of high-tech gadgetry. In the officers' wardroom stands a handsome silver bowl presented by the graduating class of Princeton University on the occasion of her commissioning. Down below is the combat command center, where the captain sits surrounded by a crowd of people with computer screens. The *Princeton* is sister ship to the *Vincennes,* which recently shot down an Iranian airliner over the Persian Gulf. Sitting in that crowded command center, I could easily imagine how such a tragic accident could happen. No human being could possibly assimilate the information coming in on all those computer monitors in real time. If the captain of the *Vincennes* had been up on the bridge, he would have had a better feeling for what was going on in the real world around him.

Everywhere I went, on ships and in factories, I was impressed by the professional pride and dedication of the people in charge. The navy knows how to inspire such devotion. And the centerpiece of their pride is the Tomahawk missile. The Tomahawk is indeed a masterpiece of design. It is, as Robert Oppenheimer said of the hydrogen bomb, technically sweet. Slender enough to be launched from a standard torpedo tube, it flies on wings as small as a whistling swan's. It can carry either a nuclear warhead or conventional high explosive. The nuclear version has a range of over a thousand miles and accuracy better than a ballistic missile. It can destroy any target on earth that is within five hundred miles of an ocean. The U.S. government claims for the purposes of treaty negotiation that the Tomahawk is not a strategic weapon. The people who build it and own it, General Dynamics and the surface navy, know better. They know what it can do.

Fewer than half of the existing Tomahawks are nuclear. The nonnuclear Tomahawks come in various versions. One version of nonnuclear Tomahawk is a ship-to-ship missile. Nonnuclear antiship cruise missiles are nothing new. The Soviet navy has deployed them in quantity for many years. The nonnuclear antiship Tomahawk is unambiguously a tactical weapon, having nothing to do with strategic warfare. The nuclear Tomahawk, on the other hand, is fundamentally ambiguous. It is possible to imagine it being used to destroy ships in a tactical nuclear war at sea. But tactical nuclear war is not a plausible method of exercising sea power. The more plausible mission for nuclear Tomahawks is to destroy targets on land at long range. That is to say, the plausible mission for nuclear Tomahawks is strategic.

With the nuclear Tomahawk, we fell into the trap of deploying a powerful new weapons system before we had decided what we wanted to do with it. The United States has no clearly defined need for such a weapon. In the long run, the existence of nuclear cruise missiles constitutes a permanent threat to our security. Cruise missiles are widely proliferated among the navies of many countries. Any country that has access to nuclear warheads can easily slip a nuclear package into a cruise missile. And of all the countries in the world, the United States has the most tempting array of cruise missile targets open to surprise attack from offshore.

While I was inspecting Tomahawks at various stages of their manufacture and deployment, I could see the pride and joy which these weapons inspire in those who handle them. That is the tragedy of the Tomahawk. It is a genuine work of art. It is an expression of human genius. Thousands of talented and dedicated people are devoting their lives to it. My friend and colleague Sidney Drell said, after visiting one of our cruise missile assembly plants, "these people build cruise missiles the way Stradivarius built violins." Why must our skilled craftsmen and engineers find their fulfillment in building such lethal toys? Why can't they build violins?

5. CONCLUSIONS

It is time to summarize conclusions from the experiences that I described. My conclusions come in two parts. First, ideas about treaty verification, the issue that I was officially supposed to be studying. Second, a little sermon about the larger issues, whether we need to deploy strategic weapons at all and how we might go about getting rid of them.

Nuclear cruise missiles bring into sharp focus the question that underlies all discussions of treaty verification. How much verification is enough? The major strategic weapons, B-52s, intercontinental ballistic missiles, and Trident submarines, are comparatively easy to identify and to count by means of satellite photography. The B-52s at Fairchild carry, as required by treaty, little fins on the fuselage which distinguish them from nonnuclear B-52s. The fins are called EODs, externally observable differences. Big Brother in the Sky can keep track of the B-52s and the EODs from day to day. With Tomahawks the situation is different. They are small and normally hidden from view. The nuclear and nonnuclear versions look alike. Any verification scheme which could accurately keep track of them would be intrusive.

The Tomahawk raises serious problems for arms controllers who believe in the necessity of accurate verification. American political leaders frequently say that no treaty should be signed unless it is verifiable. The necessity of accurate verification has become for many people an unquestioned dogma. This dogma may be harmful to our health.

The desirability of an arms-control treaty should be judged by weighing the risks and benefits of three possible situations which I call A, B, C. A is the situation which exists if we have no treaty. B is the situation where we have a treaty faithfully observed by both sides. C is the situation where we have a treaty observed by us but violated by the other side. Obviously, we should prefer B to C if that were the choice open to us. The purpose of verification is to make B likely and C unlikely. But the real choice before us is between A and an unknown combination of B and C. The choice between B and C is not ours. In making our choice we have to weigh $(B-A)$, the gain in security resulting from a faithfully observed treaty, against $(A-C)$, the loss in security resulting from a violated treaty. Both the gain and the loss must be measured relative to the existing situation A.

In the case of a treaty abolishing nuclear sea-launched cruise missiles, the gain in security $(B-A)$ is large since our coasts are highly vulnerable to such missiles, while the loss in security

(A − C) is small since we are almost as vulnerable without a treaty as we would be with a violated treaty. Our gain is great if the other side is honest and our loss is small if the other side cheats. In this case a treaty is advantageous, even if the verification is imperfect. The importance of verification is more political than military. We need verification because a treaty violation would be damaging to international relations in general, not because a violation would seriously increase our existing vulnerability to cruise missile attack. For a treaty limiting deployments of Tomahawks and other cruise missiles, intrusive verification with technically accurate counting of missiles and warheads is not required. In this case "enough verification" means a verification system capable of detecting gross or flagrant violations.

The comparison of situations A, B, and C can be applied to any proposed arms-control treaty, not only to treaties concerned with cruise missiles. In general, we find that possible treaties can be divided into two classes, which I call good and bad. Good treaties are those for which (B − A) is larger than (A − C), that is to say, the potential gain in security if the opponent is honest is large compared with the potential loss if the opponent is dishonest. The abolition of nuclear cruise missiles is an example of a good treaty. Bad treaties are those for which (A − C) is larger than (B − A), the risk is larger than the potential gain. Now what does this classification imply for verification? If a treaty is good by this criterion, it needs only moderate verification. With a verification system that only detects gross violations with reasonable certainty, the treaty is still on balance advantageous. On the other hand, if a treaty is bad by this criterion, it needs precise verification to make it advantageous, and even with precise verification the potential advantage is not great. In general, treaties that require precise verification are not worth the trouble they cause. So the conclusion of the argument is simple. Negotiate only good treaties and stay away from bad ones. Then you will never be in the situation where your security depends on accurate verification. Verification will play its proper role, adding stability and confidence to an emerging international order. And if history turns sour, if confidence fails and treaties are violated, your losses will be limited.

That is all I have to say about treaty verification. I end with some more general remarks about strategic weaponry. Why do we have this enormous apparatus of destruction, the B-52s and the Tomahawks and all the rest, together with the equally enormous apparatus on the Soviet side? That is the main question I am forced to ask myself after my visits to Fairchild and to the good ship *Princeton*. Why do we have all this stuff? When you see a big room full of hydrogen bombs, you cannot help asking the question "Why?" These things are inordinately dangerous, they are absorbing the talents and skills of a huge number of competent people, and they do not have much redeeming social value. Why do they exist? The best answer I can find to this question is, bureaucratic inertia. All this stuff is there because the organizations to produce it and maintain it are there. And the organizations, industrial and military and scientific, are there because they were built up to fight World War 2 and never built down. Big bureaucratic organizations do not spontaneously vanish. Both in the United States and in the Soviet Union, the military bureaucracies are still perpetuating in ritualized form the functions that they performed in World War 2. If you do not believe this, you should spend a day at Fairchild Air Force Base.

I came back from my visit convinced that the time is now ripe for drastic measures to get rid of strategic forces on a massive scale. The whole apparatus is an absurd anachronism. And the only way to get rid of it is to get rid of it. Negotiate cuts in forces down to zero or as near to zero as we can get. Close the bases, chop the budgets, dismantle the bureaucracies and the bombs. I do not delude myself into believing that any of this will be easy. But it is possible, and it is in the long run necessary to our survival. Why not do it now?

I see three factors which happily reinforce each other, to make the prospects for getting rid of nuclear weaponry now more promising than they were a few years ago. The first factor is the political revolution in the Soviet Union and Eastern Europe. The second factor is the crumbling of the nuclear weapons production apparatus in the United States. For forty years nuclear weapons have been politically popular in the United States because they were supposed to be cheap, efficient, and safe. Now the means of production of nuclear materials have run into difficulties which prove them to be expensive, inefficient, and unsafe. The military-industrial complex supporting the production of nuclear weapons is revealed to be technologically obsolescent. The third factor supporting the abolition of nuclear weaponry is the emergence of environmental dangers as a major concern of the political leadership in all industrialized countries.

These three factors acting together have opened a new era of history. The new era has begun and will continue, whether or not Mr. Gorbachev remains in charge in the Soviet Union. The new era brings hope that arms-control agreements and political settlements may be achieved with greater speed and greater scope than seemed possible in the past. We now have a chance to move beyond the piecemeal reduction of military deployments, to move directly to the dismantling of strategic forces and the building of a peaceful international order. We have a chance to forget the nuclear arms race and to apply our technological resources on a massive scale to the relief of human suffering. We have a chance to consolidate peaceful relations by practical cooperation in solving the great ecological problems of Planet Earth.

Here is the final moral of my story. Strategic weapons belong to the past. We have clung to them too long. They have no future.

[*Postscript, December 1991*] The older chapters are generally less out-of-date than the newer. This chapter, one of the most recently written, is the most outdated of all. It describes a world that has vanished in the international upheavals of 1991. The title should now be "Strategic Bombing in World War 2 and Yesterday." The world of strategic bomber forces changed more in the one year 1991 than in the previous forty-five. Everything I saw in my tour of the West in 1989 was swept aside by President Bush's decision in September 1991 to demobilize nuclear forces unilaterally. The B-52 bombers are no longer standing on alert. The hydrogen bombs are no longer trundling around Fairchild Air Force Base on trolleys. The nuclear Tomahawks are no longer on the ships. And a reciprocal act of demobilization was announced a week later in the Soviet Union. For these unprecedented and wise decisions we must be profoundly grateful. I decided to keep this chapter in the book as a memorial to a bygone age, to remind us how far we have come in a short time and how far we have still to go.

PART II

Things
∘∘∘∘

Do not destroy what you cannot create.

LEO SZILARD,

"TEN COMMANDMENTS"

CHAPTER 8

Field Theory

.....

1 9 5 3

I. A DESCRIPTIVE THEORY

"It is perhaps surprising that no new meson was reported during the symposium, though almost a month had passed since a previous meeting of nuclear physicists in Copenhagen." This learned joke in the British journal *Nature,* commenting on an international physics conference last summer, sums up the present chaotic situation in theoretical physics. We have become accustomed during the last few years to the discovery of new particles. About twenty different kinds are now known. Everybody expects that many more will be discovered as experimental techniques are improved. Yet nobody has succeeded in classifying the known particles, or in predicting the properties of unknown ones. Nobody understands why such and such particles exist, why they have the various masses that are observed, or why some of them interact strongly and some do not.

How do theoretical physicists spend their time, if they are not able to attack the basic problem of the nature of elementary particles? Of what use can the existing theories be, if they do not throw light on this problem? These awkward questions are asked frequently when experimental and theoretical physicists come together. I shall try to answer them, and to explain why theoretical physicists believe that their theories are useful even though there is so much they do not understand.

First, let me make one point clear. There is a generally accepted theory of elementary particles, known as quantum field theory. While theoretical physicists often disagree about the details of the theory, and especially about the way it should be applied to practical problems, the great majority agrees that the theory in its main features is correct. The minority who reject the theory, although led by the great names of Albert Einstein and Paul Dirac, do not yet have any workable alternative to put in its place. In this chapter I adopt the point of view of the majority. When I talk about the concept of field, I mean the concept as it is used in present-day quantum field theory. The majority believes that this concept is so useful and illuminating that it will survive the changes and revolutions that the theory will inevitably undergo in the future. Henceforward, I omit the phrase "in the opinion of the majority," or "in my opinion," which should stand at the beginning of every sentence.

Next, a remark about the purpose of the theory. This concerns the failure of the theory to give us an understanding of why the observed particles exist and no others. The point is that the theory is descriptive and not explanatory. It describes how elementary particles behave; it does not attempt to explain why they behave so. To draw an analogy from a familiar branch of science, the function of chemistry as it existed before 1900 was to describe precisely the properties of the chemical elements and their interactions. Chemistry described how the elements behave; it did not try to explain why a particular set of elements, each with its particular properties, exists. To answer why, completely new sciences were needed: atomic and nuclear physics. Looking backward, it is now clear that nineteenth-century chemists were right to concentrate on the how and to ignore the why. They did not have the tools to begin to discuss intelligently the reasons for the individualities of the elements. They had to spend a hundred years building up a good descriptive theory before they could go further. And the result of their labors—the classical science of chemistry—was not destroyed or superseded by the later insight that atomic physics gave.

The quantum field theory treats elementary particles just as nineteenth-century chemistry treated the elements. The theory starts from the existence of a specified list of elementary particles, with specified masses, spins, charges, and interactions with one another. All these data are put into the theory at the beginning. The purpose of the theory is to deduce from this information what will happen if particle A is fired at particle B with a given velocity. We are not yet sure whether the theory will be able to fulfill even this modest purpose. Many technical difficulties have still to be overcome. One of the difficulties is that we do not yet have a complete list of particles. Nevertheless, the successes of the theory in describing experimental results have been striking. It seems likely that the theory in something like its present form will describe accurately a wide range of possible experiments. This is the most that we would wish to claim for it.

Our justification for concentrating attention on the existing theory, with its many arbitrary assumptions, is the belief that a working descriptive theory of elementary particles must be established before we can expect to reach a more complete understanding at a deeper level. The numerous attempts to by-pass the historical process, and to understand the particles on the basis of general principles without waiting for a descriptive theory, have been as unsuccessful as they were ambitious. The more ambitious they are, the more unsuccessful. These attempts seem to be on a level with the famous nineteenth-century attempts to explain atoms as "vortices in the ether."

2. CLASSICAL FIELDS

Physicists talk about two kinds of fields: classical fields and quantum fields. Actually, we believe that all fields in nature are quantum fields. A classical field is just a large-scale manifestation of a quantum field. But since classical fields were discovered first and are easier to understand, it is useful to say what we mean by a classical field first, and to talk about quantum fields later.

A classical field is a kind of tension or stress that can exist in empty space in the absence of matter. It reveals itself by producing forces, which act on material objects that happen to lie in the space the field occupies. The standard examples of classical fields are the electric and magnetic fields, which push and pull electrically charged objects and magnetized objects respectively. Michael Faraday discovered that these two fields also exert effects on each other. He found that a changing magnetic field produces electric forces (an effect now known as induction), and his finding made possible the development of practical electric generators. Later the exact laws of behavior of electric and magnetic fields were formulated mathematically by James Clerk Maxwell. He found that in any space where a changing magnetic field exists, an electric field must exist also, and vice versa. In order to describe completely the state of the fields in a given region of space, it is necessary to specify the strength and the direction of both the electric and magnetic fields at every point of the region.

Maxwell was the first to realize that electric and magnetic fields can exist not only near charges and magnets but also in free space disconnected from material objects. From his equations he deduced that in empty space such fields would travel with the velocity of light. Hence, he made the epoch-making guess that light consists of traveling electromagnetic fields. We now know that his guess was correct, and we are able to generate traveling electromagnetic fields ourselves and use them for various purposes. These artificial traveling fields we call radio.

Another example of a classical field is the gravitational field. This has the special property that it acts on all material objects in a given region of space. It is difficult to experiment with, because the gravitational field produced by any object of convenient laboratory size is absurdly weak. For this reason we have never been able to detect any effects of freely traveling gravitational waves, which presumably exist in the neighborhood of a rapidly vibrating mass. It is also impossible to measure the possible interactions of gravitational and electromagnetic fields. This is the main reason why we know so much less about gravitation than about the other fields.

What, then, is the picture we have in mind when we try to visualize a classical field? Characteristically, modern physicists do not try to visualize the objects they discuss. In the nineteenth century it was different. Then it seemed that the universe was built of solid mechanical objects, and that to understand an electric field it was necessary to visualize the field as a mechanical stress in a material substance. It was possible, indeed, to visualize electric and magnetic fields in this way. To do so, people imagined a material substance called the ether, which was supposed to fill the whole of space and carry the electric and magnetic stresses. But as the theory was developed, the properties of the ether became more and more implausible. Einstein in 1905 finally abandoned the ether and proposed a new and simple version of the Maxwell theory in which the ether was never mentioned. Since 1905 we gradually gave up the idea that everything in the universe should be visualized mechanically. We now know that mechanical objects are composed of atoms held together by electric fields, and therefore it makes no sense to try to explain electric fields in terms of mechanical objects.

It is still convenient sometimes to make a mental picture of an electric field. For example, we may think of it as a flowing liquid which fills a given space and which at each point has a certain velocity and direction of flow. The velocity of the liquid is a model for the strength of the field. But nobody nowadays imagines that the liquid really exists or that it explains the behavior of the field. The flowing liquid is just a model, a convenient way to express our knowledge about the field in concrete terms. It is a good model only so long as we remember not to take it seriously. We must not expect that the equations of motion of the electric field will be the same as those of any self-respecting liquid. To a modern physicist the electric field is a fundamental concept which cannot be reduced to anything simpler. It is a unique something with a set of known properties, and that is all there is to it. This being understood, the reader may safely think of a flowing liquid as a fairly accurate representation of what we mean by a classical electric field. The electric and magnetic fields must then be pictured as two different liquids, both filling the whole of space, moving separately and interpenetrating each other freely. At each point there are two velocities, representing the strengths of the electric and magnetic components of the total electromagnetic field.

It is characteristic of a classical field that its strength at a given point varies smoothly as the point moves around in space. Therefore, the liquid model must be imagined as an ideal liquid, not composed of atoms but filling all space uniformly and having a well-defined velocity at every point.

The idea that killed the ether was the principle of relativity, introduced by Einstein in 1905. This principle states that the properties of empty space are always the same, regardless of the velocity with which an experimenter is moving through it. Even if there is a material ether filling space, the experimenter is unable to measure its velocity. For practical purposes the ether is unobservable. If it does exist, it is of no interest to us. Our picture of the world becomes simpler if we abandon the ether and speak only about electric and magnetic fields in empty space. Einstein made a complete theory of the classical electromagnetic field and its interactions with matter, using the principle of relativity as his starting point. In 1916 he extended the idea of relativity to construct his theory of the classical gravitational field. These theories stand today substantially as Einstein left them.

The classical field theories of Einstein, electromagnetic and gravitational, together give us a satisfactory explanation of all large-scale physical phenomena. They explain everything in the physical world that can be explained without bringing into view the fact that the world is built of particles. There is every reason to believe that the classical field theories are correct so long as we are talking about objects much bigger and heavier than an atom. But they fail completely to describe the behavior of individual atoms and particles. To understand the small-scale side of physics, physicists had to invent quantum mechanics and the idea of a quantum field.

3. QUANTUM FIELDS

Unfortunately, the quantum field is even more difficult to visualize than the classical field. The basic axiom of quantum mechanics is the uncertainty principle. This says that the more closely we look at any object, the more the object is disturbed by our looking at it, and the less we can know about the subsequent state of the object. Another, less precise, way of expressing the same principle is to say that objects of atomic size fluctuate continually; they cannot maintain a precisely defined position for a finite length of time. Their quantum fluctuations are never precisely predictable, and the laws of quantum mechanics tell us only the statistical behavior of the fluctuations when averaged over time. The universal existence of these fluctuations, and the general correctness of the laws of quantum mechanics, have been verified by a wealth of experiments during the last thirty years.

How do quantum fluctuations affect classical fields? The answer is, not at all. The fluctuations are not observable with ordinary large-scale equipment. Looked at with large-scale apparatus, the quantum field behaves exactly like a classical field. Only when we measure the effects of an electromagnetic field on a single atom do the quantum fluctuations of the field become noticeable. The physicists Willis Lamb and Robert Retherford at Columbia University have observed the effects of electromagnetic fields on single hydrogen atoms. They were able to measure the effects of the fields with great accuracy. The effect of the quantum fluctuations, itself a small part of the total effect of the fields, was measured to an accuracy better than one part in a thousand. Within this margin of possible error, the effect agreed with the conclusions of quantum field theory. The Lamb-Retherford experiment is the strongest evidence we have for believing that our picture of the quantum field is correct in detail.

At the risk of making some professional quantum theoreticians turn pale, I shall describe a mechanical model that may give some idea of the nature of a quantum field. Imagine the flowing liquid which served as a model for a classical electric field. But suppose that the flow, instead of being smooth, is turbulent, like the wake of an ocean liner. Superimposed on the steady average motion there is a tremendous confusion of eddies, of all sizes, overlapping and mingling with one another. In any small region of the liquid the velocity continually fluctuates, in a more or less random way. The smaller the region, the wilder and more rapid the fluctuations. In a real liquid these fluctuations are limited by two factors: the viscosity or stickiness of the liquid, which damps out turbulent motions, and the atomic structure of the liquid, which sets a minimum size for eddies, since it is meaningless to talk about eddies containing only a few atoms. In our model of the quantum field, however, we assume that neither of these factors operates. There is no dissipation of energy by viscosity, nor any minimum size of eddies. The velocity in a given region can continue to fluctuate without diminution forever, and the fluctuations grow more intense without limit as the size of the region is reduced.

The model does not describe correctly the detailed quantum-mechanical properties of a quantum field; no classical model can do that. But it gives a reasonably valid picture of the general appearance of the thing. In particular, the model makes clear that it is meaningless to speak about the velocity of the liquid at any one point. The fluctuations in the neighborhood of the point become infinitely large as the neighborhood becomes smaller. The velocity at the point itself has no meaning. The only quantities that have meaning are velocities averaged over regions of space and over intervals of time. This property of the model is a true representation of a property of a quantum field. The strength of a quantum field at a point can never be measured. Quantum field theory is a theory of the behavior of field strengths averaged over finite regions of space and time.

4. THE PARTICLES EMERGE

Now comes the climax of the story. We have put into the theory of the quantum field two big ideas: the idea of quantum mechanics and the idea of relativity. These two ideas force us to construct a mathematical theory which in its main lines is fixed. The only freedom left to us is in matters of detail. When we deduce the consequences of this mathematical theory, we find that a miracle has occurred. Automatically, there emerges a third big idea, that the world is built of elementary particles. This idea is a consequence of the fact that, in a quantum field, energy can exist only in discrete units which we call quanta. When we work out the theory of these quanta, we find that they have precisely the properties of the elementary particles that we observe in the world around us.

It is not possible to explain in nontechnical language how particles arise mathematically out of the fluctuations of a field. It cannot be understood by thinking about a turbulent liquid or any other classical model. All I can say here is that it happens. And it is the basic reason for believing that the concept of a quantum field is a valid concept and will survive any changes that may later be made in the details of the theory.

The picture of the world that we have finally reached is the following. Some ten or twenty different quantum fields exist. Each fills the whole of space and has its own particular properties. There is nothing else except these fields; the whole of the material universe is built of them. Between various pairs of fields there are various kinds of interaction. Each field manifests itself as a type of elementary particle. The particles of a given type are identical and indistinguishable. The number of particles of a given type is not fixed, for particles are constantly being created or annihilated or transmuted into one another. The properties of the interactions determine the rules for creation and transmutation of particles.

In this picture of the world, the electromagnetic field appears on an equal footing with the other fields. The particle corresponding to it is the light quantum, or photon. The photon appears to be different from other elementary particles only because its laws of interaction make it especially easy to create and annihilate. So the photon appears to be less permanent than the electron. But this is only a difference of degree. All particles, including the electron, can be rapidly annihilated under suitable conditions.

The elementary particle corresponding to the gravitational field has been named the graviton. There can be little doubt that in a formal mathematical sense the graviton exists. However, nobody has ever observed an individual graviton. Because of the extreme weakness of the gravitational interaction, only large masses produce observable gravitational effects. In the case of large masses, the number of gravitons involved in the interaction is large, and the field behaves like a classical field. Consequently, it may never be possible to observe an individual graviton. Whether the graviton has a real existence is one of the important open questions in physics.

The electromagnetic and gravitational fields have one essential property in common. They are long-range fields, making their effects felt over great distances. This is connected with the fact that the photon and the graviton have no rest mass and always travel at a fixed velocity, the velocity of light. Almost all other fields in nature have a short range, less than the size of an atom, and their effects cannot be felt beyond this distance. The short-range fields cannot be detected in a classical way by measuring their effects on large objects. They never behave like classical fields in any experimental situation. This is why the field corresponding to the electron was never recognized as a field until quantum field theory was invented. Even now, the electron field seems more foreign to us than the electromagnetic field. Fundamentally, the two are very similar. The main difference between them is the short range of the electron field, which has the consequence that the electron possesses a rest mass and can travel slowly or remain bound in an atom. Most of the other known particles—protons, neutrons, the many varieties of mesons—also have a rest mass and are associated with short-range fields.

The most spectacular success of quantum field theory is its treatment of charged fields. According to the theory, a quantum field may or may not carry an electric charge. For example, the electron field carries a charge, while the electromagnetic field does not. The theory predicts that any charged field must be represented by two types of particle, precisely alike in all respects except that one has a positive and the other a negative charge. The theory also predicts that under suitable conditions a pair of such particles, one positive and one negative, can be created or annihilated together in a single event. All these predictions of the theory have been confirmed in the case of the electron field. There exists a particle, the positron, which is exactly like an electron except that it has the opposite charge. There are also at least two varieties of meson that exist in positive and negative forms. The theory predicts that there should be an antiproton, a particle negatively charged but otherwise identical with a proton. The antiproton has not yet been detected. It presents an outstanding challenge to experimental physicists to discover it, or to theoretical physicists to explain why it should not exist.

Even to a hardened theoretical physicist, it remains perpetually astonishing that our solid world of trees and stones can be built of quantum fields and nothing else. The quantum field seems far too fluid and insubstantial to be the basic stuff of the universe. Yet we have learned gradually to accept the fact that the laws of quantum mechanics impose their own peculiar rigidity upon the fields they govern, a rigidity which is alien to our intuitive conceptions but which nonetheless effectively holds the earth in place. We have learned to apply, both to ourselves and to our subject, the words of Robert Bridges:

> *Our stability is but balance, and our wisdom lies*
> *In masterful administration of the unforeseen.*

CHAPTER 9

Innovation in Physics

.....

1 9 5 8

I. UNDERSTANDING MAXWELL

One of the most entertaining scientific autobiographies is *From Immigrant to Inventor,* by Michael Pupin. The name Pupin may be seen over the door of the physics laboratory of Columbia University. For the younger physicists of today, the name belongs to the building and the man is forgotten. This is a pity, for he was a colorful as well as a great man. He arrived in America from the backwoods of Hungary at the age of sixteen, and after various adventures became a Columbia professor when he was thirty-four. He was born with a restless curiosity and a fixed determination to master the science of his time.

His book is interesting in two ways. It gives a vivid picture of American society in the 1870s, seen from the point of view of the penniless immigrant. It also describes, with well-observed detail, the physics and the physicists of that time. Physics then was dominated by one transcendent innovation, James Clerk Maxwell's theory of the electromagnetic field. Pupin set out to understand the Maxwell theory like a knight in quest of the Holy Grail. First he went to Columbia, but found nobody there who could explain Maxwell. Then he went to Cambridge, where Maxwell had worked; but Maxwell was dead, and Pupin's tutors were mainly interested in cramming him for the mathematical tripos examination. Finally, he went to Berlin, and there he found Hermann von Helmholtz. Helmholtz had understood the Maxwell theory, and he taught Pupin what he knew. Pupin was amazed to find out, as he says, "how few were the physicists who had caught the meaning of the theory, even twenty years after it was stated by Maxwell in 1865."

The features of the theory which seem most significant to us now are not those which seemed most important to Maxwell. From our modern point of view, the basic idea of the theory is that nature has a double-layered structure. In the lower layer there are electric and magnetic fields, which satisfy simple wave equations and travel freely through space in the form of light or radio waves. In the upper layer there are material objects, energies, and forces. Only the upper layer is directly accessible to our observation. A lower-layer object such as an electric field can only be observed by looking at the energies and forces which it produces in the upper layer. And these energies and forces are always proportional to the square of the field strength. The field strength itself is a mathematical abstraction. The fact that a field strength is not directly measurable can be seen simply by looking at the unit in which it is conventionally supposed to be measured. The unit is the square root of an erg per cubic centimeter. An erg is an ordinary unit of energy and can be measured with ordinary instruments such as thermometers and calorimeters. But nobody has ever imagined an instrument that will measure directly the square root of an erg, or the square root of a cubic centimeter. The field strengths, the basic quantities with which the Maxwell theory deals, are in their nature abstract and not simply related to things that we can see and touch.

The reason why new concepts in any branch of science are hard to grasp is always the same; contemporary scientists try to picture the new concept in terms of ideas which existed before. The discoverer himself suffers especially from this difficulty. He arrived at the new concept by struggling with the old ideas, and the old ideas remain the language of his thinking for a long time afterward. In the preface to his *Treatise on Electricity and Magnetism*, Maxwell writes: "I shall endeavour to place in as clear a light as I can the relations between the mathematical form of this theory and that of the fundamental science of Dynamics, in order that we may be in some degree prepared to determine the kind of dynamical phenomena among which we are to look for illustrations or explanations of the electromagnetic phenomena." This was written seven years after the original publication of Maxwell's theory. It still did not occur to him that he had created a new science having an equal claim with Newtonian dynamics to the adjective "fundamental."

The basic difficulty of the Maxwell theory in those days was that no one could conceive of an electric field except in terms of a mechanical model; Maxwell himself was an ingenious inventor of such models. The previously existing physical ideas were material particles, fluids, and elastic solids, all obeying the laws of Newton's dynamics. The physicists of that time had no other way to think of an electric field. They were forced to start from some complicated picture of mechanical objects in motion, and in these terms the Maxwell equations appeared neither simple nor natural. Only very slowly did it become possible to forget the mechanical models and to picture an electric field as something basic and indivisible, a physical object which exists in its own right and does not need to be explained in terms of something else. It took about thirty years for physicists to make this change in their way of thinking. Once the change was made, the simplicity and beauty of the Maxwell equations were no longer hidden, and it was hard to understand what all the fuss had been about.

2. UNDERSTANDING QUANTUM MECHANICS

We stand today in relation to quantum mechanics just as Pupin stood in relation to the Maxwell theory. Quantum mechanics has a reputation for being strange, difficult, and incomprehensible to ordinary mortals. Yet I believe it is not more difficult to understand quantum mechanics now than it was to understand Maxwell in 1885. Again, from our modern point of view, the fundamental idea of quantum mechanics is merely the extension to matter of the two-layered view of nature already inherent in Maxwell's treatment of electricity and magnetism. Quantum mechanics ultimately makes no distinction between matter and electricity. The two-layered view of nature thus becomes consistent and universal. In the lower layer are put electric and magnetic fields, together with mathematical abstractions of a similar kind called wave functions which describe the behavior of matter. In the upper layer are now only energies, forces, and probabilities. The wave functions are also not directly accessible to measurement, and it is only the squares of wave functions that are seen in observations at the upper level. There are many differences in detail between quantum mechanics and Maxwell's theory, between the behavior of matter and of electromagnetism, but in the broad view the two pictures are the same. The reason why quantum mechanics seems to us now more difficult to grasp is that our intuitions of the solid nature of matter are more deep-rooted than our intuitions about electricity.

There is hope that quantum mechanics will gradually lose its baffling quality. The Maxwell theory is not easy to explain to nonspecialists, but the difficulties now are in the details and not in the basic conceptions. Today we may find it hard to remember the various terms in Maxwell's equations with the correct plus and minus signs, but the general physical picture of an electric and magnetic field in empty space is not conceptually difficult. We do not suffer the agonizing bafflement that the scientists of the 1880s felt in trying to imagine an electric field. It is even difficult for us to understand precisely what the difficulty was; that is why Pupin's book is valuable. So the essential ideas of quantum mechanics (though not the details) may likewise be taught to future generations of schoolchildren and may in time become familiar to the general public.

I have observed in teaching quantum mechanics, and also in learning it, that students go through an experience similar to the one that Pupin describes. The student begins by learning the tricks of the trade. He learns how to make calculations in quantum mechanics and get the right answers, how to calculate the scattering of neutrons by protons and so forth. To learn the mathematics of the subject and to learn how to use it takes about six months. This is the first stage in learning quantum mechanics, and it is comparatively painless. The second stage comes when the student begins to worry because he does not understand what he has been doing. He worries because he has no clear physical picture in his head. He gets confused in trying to arrive at a physical explanation for each of the mathematical tricks he has been taught. He works very hard and gets discouraged because he does not seem to be able to think clearly. This second stage often lasts six months or longer. It is strenuous and unpleasant. Then, unexpectedly, the third stage begins. The student suddenly says to himself, "I understand quantum mechanics," or rather he says, "I understand now that there isn't anything to be understood." The difficulties which seemed so formidable have mysteriously vanished. What has happened is that he has learned to think directly and unconsciously in quantum-mechanical language. He is no longer trying to explain everything in terms of prequantum conceptions.

The duration and severity of the second stage are decreasing as the years go by. Each new generation of students learns quantum mechanics more easily than their teachers learned it. The students are growing more detached from prequantum pictures. There is less resistance to be broken down before they feel at home with quantum ideas. Ultimately, the second stage will disappear entirely. Quantum mechanics will be accepted by students from the beginning as a simple and natural way of thinking, because we shall all have grown used to it. By that time, if science progresses as we hope, we shall be ready for the next big jump into the unknown.

The Maxwell theory and quantum mechanics are examples of physical innovation at the deepest level. Such innovations occur when experimental facts are incomprehensible within the bounds of earlier conceptions. A new style of reasoning and imagining has to be groped for, slowly and painfully, in the dark. For the last ten years it has been clear to most physicists that a basic conceptual innovation will be needed in order to come to grips with the properties of elementary particles. A great part of our present effort in experimental physics is devoted to the study of these particles. The justification for studying them so intensively is the belief that here, more than elsewhere in physics, we have a situation ripe for radical innovation. Let us now look at the historical perspectives and inquire how and when a radical innovation is likely to occur.

A few months ago two of the great historic figures of European physics, Werner Heisenberg and Wolfgang Pauli, believed that they had made an essential step forward in the direction of a theory of elementary particles. Pauli happened to be passing through New York, and was prevailed upon to give a lecture explaining the new ideas to an audience that included Niels Bohr, who had been mentor to both Heisenberg and Pauli in their days of glory thirty years earlier when they made their great discoveries. Pauli spoke for an hour, and then there was a general discussion during which he was criticized sharply by the younger generation. Finally, Bohr was called on to make a speech summing up the argument. "We are all agreed," he said, "that your theory is crazy. The question which divides us is whether it is crazy enough to have a chance of being correct. My own feeling is that it is not crazy enough."

The objection that they are not crazy enough applies to all the attempts which have so far been launched at a radically new theory of elementary particles. It applies especially to crackpots. Most of the crackpot papers that are submitted to the *Physical Review* are rejected, not because it is impossible to understand them, but because it is possible. Those that are impossible to understand are usually published. When the great innovation appears, it will almost certainly be in a muddled, incomplete, and confusing form. To the discoverer himself it will be only half-understood. To everybody else it will be a mystery. For any speculation that does not at first glance look crazy, there is no hope.

The pace of fundamental advance in physics is set by human stupidity. The pace is, and has always been, very slow. The rapid expansion of experimental work in the last ten years has had the consequence that experimental knowledge is now far ahead of theory. This is a healthy situation. But fundamental understanding will not be hurried. It could easily happen that all conceivable experiments that can be done with accelerators by bashing elementary particles together will be done, and the results will be accurately recorded, and still we will have no understanding of what is happening. Then we will have to sit and wait for ideas, or for radically new kinds of experiments. Somehow, sometime, we believe the logjam will be broken. But we can push at only one log at a time, and few of them move when we push them.

3. PAST INNOVATIONS

There have been many innovations in physics, some of supreme importance, which did not involve any radically new ways of

thinking. One of these was the discovery of the atomic nucleus by
Ernest Rutherford. Another was the recent proposal by C. N.
Yang and T. D. Lee that left-right symmetry might be violated in
subatomic processes. The history of both these innovations shows
again the incapacity of even the best of us to see far beyond the
end of our noses.

Rutherford discovered the nucleus in 1911. He deduced, from
the fact that alpha particles passing through a thin metal foil are
sometimes deflected at large angles, that the entire mass and positive charge of an atom must be concentrated within a sphere of
radius a thousand times smaller than the radius of the atom. This
work was published in May 1911. One might have expected that
it would create some stir in the world of physics. But in a recent
lecture Edward Andrade, a friend and collaborator of Rutherford,
said of this event, "At the time, I was working in Lenard's laboratory in Heidelberg, a very active center of research on electronic
physics. I have no recollection of any attention aroused by Rutherford's atom." In 1913, Rutherford published a book, *Radioactive
Substances and their Radiations,* in which the structure of the atom,
consisting of a nucleus with surrounding electrons, is for the first
time clearly spelled out. The book was reviewed in *Nature* by
Lord Rayleigh, surely as broad-minded and versatile a physicist as
one could find. The review does not mention the subject of
atomic structure.

It is perhaps not surprising that the clear evidence for an atomic
nucleus should have been so long ignored by Rutherford's contemporaries. They had been accustomed to regard speculations
about the insides of atoms as belonging to metaphysics rather than
to physics. They naturally closed their minds to any information
concerning a field that had for centuries been the domain of char-
latans and philosophers. It is more surprising that Rutherford
himself took several years to wake up to the importance of his
own work. When he first announced his discovery in a letter to
Otto Hahn in April 1911, he said, "I have been working recently
on scattering of alpha and beta particles and have devised a new
atom to explain the results, and also a special theory of scattering." It seems he was then more intrigued by his ability to calculate the deflection of a particle, acted on by a force varying as the
inverse square of the distance from a fixed center, than by the
mystery of what this massive fixed center might really be. In his

1913 book the nucleus still occupies a very minor place. Otherwise it could hardly have been overlooked by Lord Rayleigh. One could almost say it was Niels Bohr who first called Rutherford's attention to the importance of what he had done.

The work of Yang and Lee has revealed similar blindness in the physicists of a younger generation. This I know from personal experience. Yang and Lee wrote their paper entitled "Question of Parity Conservation in Weak Interactions" in June 1956. A copy of it was sent to me, and I read it. I read it twice. I said, "This is very interesting," or words to that effect. But I didn't have the imagination to say, "By golly, if this is true it opens up a whole new branch of physics." Other physicists at that time, with very few exceptions, were equally unimaginative.

In their paper Yang and Lee proposed several specific experiments by which the question of parity conservation could be tested. One might suppose that every experimentalist who heard of these proposals was itching to go to work on them. Here was the long-awaited chance to do a crucial experiment that would unambiguously reveal a new law of nature. But the experimentalists, except for Chien Shiung Wu and a few others, calmly went on doing what they had been doing before. Chien Shiung Wu, with her collaborators at the National Bureau of Standards, had the courage to spend six months in preparing the decisive experiment. Her positive results were announced in January 1957. By that time there were three other groups who were preparing similar experiments, in Chicago, in Leiden, and in Moscow. Four groups of people, among all the experimental physicists in the world, were ready to lay aside their regular work and gamble on a new idea.

I remember that in October 1956 I met Yang and said, "It will be exciting if this Wu experiment shows up something." "Yes," he said, "it will be exciting," and he went on to talk about his calculations in the theory of imperfect gases. I believe even Yang at that time had no clear idea of how exciting it would be. In this respect he was no better and no worse than Rutherford.

It may be said as a general rule, to which there are some notable exceptions, that every great innovation in physics is merely the decisive moment in a gradual growth of understanding that extends over about sixty years. Thirty years commonly pass between the recognition of a puzzling phenomenon and the birth of the new idea that will explain it. Another thirty years pass between the birth of the idea and the working out of its major consequences. The first thirty years are a time of struggle and searching for a solution, the second thirty a time of readjustment and assimilation of strange conceptions. From Michael Faraday's discovery of electromagnetic induction to Maxwell's theory was thirty years. From Maxwell's theory to Heinrich Hertz's demonstration of electromagnetic waves, or to Pupin's transmission lines, was another thirty. It took thirty years to go from Rutherford's nucleus to a rough understanding of nuclear structure and nuclear reactions. It took thirty years from Heisenberg's quantum mechanics to John Bardeen's new theory of superconductivity, although most physicists have long believed what Bardeen has now brilliantly demonstrated, that superconductivity is merely a spectacular large-scale manifestation of quantum-mechanical principles.

In the case of the work of Lee and Yang, we can see the past but not the future. Thirty years ago Enrico Fermi gave the first general description of the weak interactions responsible for the decay of radioactive nuclei by the emission of electrons, and formulated the problem of describing these interactions precisely. This problem remained unsolved for thirty years, although an enormous number of experiments, becoming more ingenious and exact as the years went by, was devoted to its elucidation. Then came the breaking of the logjam by the suggestion of Lee and Yang that a violation of left-right symmetry might be an essential feature of weak interactions. Within a year of the first experimental confirmation of the Lee–Yang idea, new experiments came in a flood—experiments measuring and exploiting the left-right asymmetries. These experiments have finally solved the problem posed by Fermi. We now know, at least for the case of nuclear radioactivity, what the weak interactions are. But it is clear to everybody that we are only halfway through the story. The existence of left-right asymmetry in weak, but not in strong, interactions is not in any basic sense understood. It is now for the first time possible to begin thinking realistically about the fundamental properties of weak interactions. We can confidently predict that thinking on this subject will go on and on and never stop, until the full meaning of the discovery of Lee and Yang is brought to light. If historical precedents are followed, the task will keep us busy for the next thirty years or more.

4. WHAT NEXT?

I have given a brief and fragmentary survey of some of the main innovations in physical theory during the last hundred years. I do not mean to overstress the similarities and regularities that these examples show. There are no historical laws in science, so far as I can see. I have emphasized the slower and wider process of enlargement of human understanding that precedes and follows every significant innovation. The work that must be done by scientists great and small, to absorb and assimilate an innovation after it has occurred, is as long, as hard and as important as the work that pushed and groped along the way to the innovation's birth. The best description of the whole process is to be found in the words that Sir Arthur Eddington wrote in 1934: "When we see these new developments in perspective they appear as the natural unfolding of a flower."

Finally, what of the future? Can we predict or in any way influence the course of future innovations? The answer is clearly no, except in the vaguest and most conjectural sense. Nevertheless, I shall hazard a few guesses about the shape of things to come.

There are two points of view commonly held about the present situation in elementary-particle physics. One view, which may be called the optimistic view, holds that we are in a situation comparable to that of 1925, when classical and atomic physics were in glaring conflict. At that time the heroic intellectual struggles of Bohr, Kramers, de Broglie, Schrödinger, Dirac, and Heisenberg brought order out of chaos by giving birth to quantum mechanics. The optimistic view is that a similarly epoch-making innovation, which will put an end to the present confusions of particle physics, is just around the corner. The opposing view is often called pessimistic, but I prefer to call it skeptical, since I hold it myself and I do not admit my joy in the works of nature to be any less than that of the optimists. The skeptical view believes in a longer time scale. It assigns a more modest place to the problems and capabilities of the present generation of physicists, and it has more faith in the inexhaustible richness of nature.

The skeptical view places our generation in somewhat the same position as the eighteenth-century successors of Newton. After Newton had completed the framework of dynamics, his successors had two great tasks. One task was to work out and fully understand the mathematical consequences of Newton's ideas. This task was the lifework of the great applied mathematicians of the eighteenth and nineteenth centuries: Euler, Lagrange, Laplace, Jacobi, and Hamilton. It was not finished for 150 years after Newton's *Principia*. The second task was to study and reduce to order those physical phenomena that Newton left outside the scope of his dynamics, especially light, electricity, and magnetism. This task occupied the efforts of the leading physicists for some 200 years after Newton, and was accomplished only with the work of Faraday and Maxwell.

Quantum mechanics could not have been discovered by anybody, no matter how great his genius, until after Hamilton and Maxwell had completed their work. If somebody had said, thirty years after Newton, "We need a radical innovation in dynamics in order to explain the behavior of light and electricity," and had sat down and tried to invent quantum mechanics, he would have been wasting his time. Without Hamilton's deep mathematical analysis of Newtonian dynamics to suggest the form of the new theory, and without Maxwell's detailed theory of electrical forces to suggest its physical content, nobody could have had any inkling of the kind of innovation that would prove necessary.

My view, the skeptical one, holds that we may be as far away from an understanding of elementary particles as Newton's successors were from quantum mechanics. Like them, we have two tremendous tasks ahead of us. One is to study and explore the mathematics of the existing theories. The existing quantum field theories may or may not be correct, but they certainly conceal mathematical depths that will take the genius of an Euler or a Hamilton to plumb. It may well be that the approach to a new theory cannot begin until the mathematical nature of the old theories is clearly understood. Our second task is to press on with the exploration of the wide range of physical phenomena that the existing theories do not explain. This means pressing on with experiments in the fashionable area of particle physics, but it also means much more. Outstanding among the areas of physics which have been left out of recent theories of elementary particles are gravitation and cosmology. Einstein's theory of gravitation is an outstanding innovation which has still after forty years not begun to be absorbed into the mainstream of physics. Cosmology is to most physicists, like the insides of atoms to the contemporaries of Rutherford, not a respectable subject to think about. It is probable that a satisfactory theory of elementary particles will demand as an essential ingredient a description of the boundary conditions that the universe had to satisfy at its beginning. If this is so, then we can expect no final clarification of particle physics until the great open questions of cosmology have been answered by observation.

My guess then is that important innovations will occur in physics as they have in the past, at intervals of twenty-five or fifty years, approximately the length of time it takes for one innovation to be digested before the next can be gestated. I guess that an innovation of the magnitude of Newtonian dynamics or quantum mechanics is not likely within a hundred years from now. And I guess that the next important innovation will arise, within twenty-five years, out of gravitational or astronomical observations made possible by elaborate equipment assembled in interplanetary space.

Tomonaga, Schwinger, and Feynman Awarded Nobel Prize for Physics

.....

1 9 6 5

The 1965 Nobel Prize for physics has been awarded to three theorists, Sin–Itiro Tomonaga of Tokyo, Julian Schwinger of Harvard, and Richard Feynman of the California Institute of Technology. The prize was given for their creation of the modern theory of quantum electrodynamics. This is the theory which brought order and harmony into the vast middle ground of physics, excluding gravitation on the one side and nuclear forces on the other, but including the laws of atomic structure, radiation, creation and annihilation of particles, solid-state physics, plasma physics, maser and laser technology, optical and microwave spectroscopy, electronics, and chemistry. Quantum electrodynamics unifies all these diverse phenomena into a small number of principles of great generality and elegance, weaving together special relativity with quantum mechanics in a seamless fabric. It is in a certain sense the most perfect and the most highly developed part of physics.

Since its completion in 1948 the theory has been tested by means of a succession of experiments of steadily increasing accuracy. For example, the magnetic moment of the electron was recently measured by Richard Crane at the University of Michigan with an error of less than one part in ten million. This was a beautiful and formidably difficult experiment, but unfortunately the result attracted little attention; it only proved that quantum electrodynamics was right to two more places of decimals.

Just this year there have been experimental indications of a possible deviation from the theory in the behavior of electron-positron pairs produced at energies of billions of volts. If confirmed, this deviation will by no means invalidate the theory, but will only show for the first time where the boundary lies between quantum electrodynamics and the world of high-energy particles. It is still one of the major mysteries of physics how quantum electrodynamics, a theory which deliberately excludes from consideration all particles except the well-known electron, positron, and photon, can give so amazingly accurate a representation of reality over so wide a range of conditions.

The three creators of the theory did their work independently but not simultaneously. Tomonaga kept alive in Japan during World War 2 a school of theoretical physics which was in some ways ahead of the rest of the world. In these conditions of total isolation he published his fundamental paper in Japanese in 1943. Schwinger and Feynman were meanwhile fully occupied with the development of radar and nuclear energy respectively. When they returned to academic life after the war, their interest was aroused by a series of new experiments on the fine details of the hydrogen atom. The experiments had become possible as a result of the wartime development of microwave techniques, and were about a thousand times more accurate than the best prewar measurements. The new experiments made glaringly obvious the lack of a satisfactory theory of radiative processes, and so Schwinger and Feynman were led along different paths to invent such a theory. Each of them completed his work during the winter of 1947–48, just at the time the first English-language translations of the papers of Tomonaga and his students began to arrive from Japan. It was interesting to find that, although the new experiments had played a decisive role in the thinking of Schwinger and Feynman, Tomonaga had been able to reach an essentially identical insight on the basis of theoretical considerations alone.

The fact that the theory had three discoverers rather than one proved fruitful for its further development. Each of the three brought a different viewpoint and a different style, and so the theory gained in breadth and richness. Tomonaga was most concerned with basic physical principles; his papers were simple, clear, and free from elaboration of detail. Schwinger was most concerned with the construction of a complete and massive mathematical formulation; his papers were monuments of formal ingenuity. An unkind critic once said: "Other people publish to show you how to do it, but Julian Schwinger publishes to show you that only he can do it." Schwinger was in fact the first to hack his way through the mathematical jungle and arrive at a definite numerical value for the magnetic moment of the electron.

Feynman's approach was the most original of the three; he was willing to take nothing for granted, and so he was forced to reconstruct almost the whole of quantum mechanics and electrodynamics from his own point of view. He was concerned with deriving simple rules for the direct calculation of physically observable quantities. His invention of "Feynman graphs" and "Feynman integrals" made it easy to apply the theory to concrete problems. In the end, Feynman's rules of calculation have become standard tools of theoretical analysis, not only in quantum electrodynamics but in high-energy physics as a whole. And Feynman's insistence on discussing directly observable quantities led to the growth of the "S-matrix point of view," which now dominates current thinking about the fundamental particles and their interactions.

The theory which came to triumph in 1948 is not an easy one to describe in nontechnical language. It must be placed in the context of some earlier history. The pioneers of quantum mechanics—Dirac, Heisenberg, Pauli, and Fermi—had worked out the physical basis for quantum electrodynamics during the late 1920s. The basis consisted in a direct application of the methods of quantum mechanics to the Maxwell equations describing the electromagnetic field. The resulting theory seemed to give a qualitatively correct account of radiation processes, but it failed to give exact predictions; when pushed beyond the first approximation, it always gave infinite or meaningless answers. In the face of this situation, the physicists of the 1930s mostly looked for radical changes in the theory. It was generally believed that the "divergence difficulties" were symptoms of fundamental errors, and were only to be escaped by altering the theory drastically. So from

1935 to 1945 there was a succession of fruitless attempts to cure the divergence disease of quantum electrodynamics by methods of radical surgery.

Tomonaga, Schwinger, and Feynman rescued the theory without making any radical innovations. Their victory was a victory of conservatism. They kept the physical basis of the theory precisely as it had been laid down by Dirac, and only changed the mathematical superstructure. By polishing and refining with great skill the mathematical formalism, they were able to show that the theory does in fact give meaningful predictions for all observable quantities. The predictions are in all cases finite, unambiguous, and in agreement with experiment. The divergent and meaningless quantities are indeed present in the theory, but they appear in such a way that they automatically eliminate themselves from any quantity which is in principle observable. The exact correspondence between quantities which are unambiguously calculable and quantities which are observable becomes, in the end, the theory's most singular virtue.

The theory, as Tomonaga, Schwinger, and Feynman left it, has stood the test of time for seventeen years. It describes only a part of physical reality, and it makes no claim to finality. But its success within its area of applicability has been so complete that it seems sure to survive, at least as a special limiting case, within any more comprehensive theory that may come later to supersede it.

CHAPTER II

Energy in the Universe

.....

1 9 7 1

I. THE MEANING OF ENERGY

Man has no Body distinct from his Soul;
for that called Body is a portion of Soul
discerned by the five Senses,
the chief inlets of Soul in this age.

Energy is the only life and is from the Body;
and Reason is the bound or outward circumference of Energy.

Energy is Eternal Delight.

> William Blake,
> *The Marriage of Heaven and Hell*
> (1793)

One need not be a poet or a mystic to find Blake's definition of energy more satisfying than the definitions given in textbooks of physics. Even within the framework of physical science, energy has a transcendent quality. On many occasions, when revolutions in thought have demolished old sciences and created new ones, the concept of energy has proved to be more valid and durable than the definitions in which it was embodied. In Newtonian mechanics, energy was defined as a property of moving masses. In the nineteenth century energy became a unifying principle in the construction of three new sciences, thermodynamics, quantitative chemistry, and electromagnetism. In the twentieth century energy again appeared in fresh disguise, playing basic and unexpected roles in the twin intellectual revolutions that led to relativity theory and quantum theory. In the special theory of relativity, Albert Einstein's equation $E = mc^2$, identifying energy with mass, threw a new light on our view of the astronomical universe, a light whose brilliance no amount of journalistic exaggeration has been able to obscure. And in quantum mechanics, Max Planck's equation $E = h\nu$, restricting the energy carried by any oscillation to a constant multiple of its frequency, transformed in an even more fundamental way our view of the subatomic universe. It is unlikely that the metamorphoses of the concept of energy, and its fertility in giving birth to new sciences, are yet at an end. We do not know how the scientists of the next century will define energy, or in what strange jargon they will discuss it. No matter what language the physicists use, they will not come into contradiction with Blake. Energy will remain in some sense the lord and giver of life, a reality transcending our mathematical descriptions. Its nature lies at the heart of the mystery of our existence as animate beings in an inanimate universe.

The purpose of this chapter is to give an account of the movement of energy in the astronomical world, insofar as we understand it. I shall discuss the genesis of the various kinds of energy that are observed on the Earth and in the sky, and the processes by which energy is channeled in the evolution of stars and galaxies. This overall view of the sources and flow of energy in the cosmos is intended to put in perspective the problems of the use of energy by mankind on the Earth. In looking to our local energy resources, it is well to consider how we fit into the larger scheme of things. Ultimately, what we can do here on the Earth will be limited by the same laws that govern the economy of astronomical energy sources. The converse of this statement may also be true. It would not be surprising if it should turn out that the origin and destiny of the energy in the universe cannot be completely understood in isolation from the phenomena of life and consciousness. As we look out into space, we see no sign that life has intervened to control events anywhere except precariously on our own planet. Everywhere else, the universe appears to be mindlessly burning up its reserves of energy, inexorably drifting toward the state of final quiescence described imaginatively by Olaf Stapledon: "Presently nothing was left in the whole cosmos but darkness and the dark whiffs of dust that once were galaxies." It is conceivable, however, that life may have a larger role to play than we have yet imagined. Life may succeed against all the odds in molding the universe to its own purposes. And the design of the inanimate universe may not be as detached from the potentialities of life and intelligence as scientists of the twentieth century have tended to suppose.

The cosmos contains energy in various forms—for example, gravitation, heat, light, and nuclear energy. Chemical energy, the form that plays the major role in present-day human activities, counts for very little in the universe as a whole. In the universe the predominant form of energy is gravitational. Every mass spread out in space possesses gravitational energy, which can be released or converted into light and heat by letting the mass fall together. For any sufficiently large mass, this form of energy outweighs all others.

The laws of thermodynamics decree that each quantity of energy has a characteristic quality called entropy associated with it. The entropy measures the degree of disorder associated with the energy. Energy must always flow in such a direction that the entropy increases. Thus, we can arrange the different forms of energy in an "order of merit," the highest form being the one with the least disorder or entropy. Energy of a higher form can be degraded into a lower form, but a lower form can never be wholly converted back into a higher form. The direction of energy flow in the universe is determined by one basic fact, that gravitational energy is not only predominant in quantity but also highest in quality. Gravitation carries no entropy and stands first in the order of merit. It is for this reason that a hydroelectric power station, converting the gravitational energy of water to electricity, can have an efficiency close to 100 percent, which no chemical or nuclear power station can approach. In the universe as a whole, the main theme of energy flow is the gravitational contraction of massive objects, the gravitational energy released in contraction being converted into energy of motion, light, and heat. The flow of water from a reservoir to a turbine situated a little closer to the center of the Earth is in essence a controlled gravitational contraction of the Earth, on a more modest scale than astronomers are accustomed to consider. The universe evolves by the gravitational contraction of objects of all sizes, from clusters of galaxies to planets.

When one views the universe in broad outline in this way, a set of paradoxical questions at once arises. If thermodynamics favors the degradation of gravitational energy to other forms, how does it happen that the gravitational energy of the universe is still predominant after 10 billion years of cosmic evolution? If large masses are unstable against gravitational collapse, why did they not all collapse long ago and convert their gravitational energy into heat and light in a quick display of cosmic fireworks? If the universe is on a one-way slide toward a state of final death in which energy is maximally degraded, how does it manage, like King Charles, to take such an unconscionably long time a-dying? These questions are not easy to answer. The further one goes in answering them, the more paradoxical the apparent stability of the cosmos becomes. It turns out that the universe as we know it survives, not by any inherent stability, but by a succession of seemingly accidental "hang-ups." By a hang-up I mean an obstacle, usually arising from some quantitative feature of the design of the universe, that arrests the normal processes of degradation of energy. Psychological hang-ups are generally supposed to be bad for us, but cosmological hang-ups are absolutely necessary for our existence.

2. A CATALOGUE OF HANG-UPS

The first and most basic hang-up built into the architecture of the universe is the size hang-up. A naive person looking at the cosmos has the impression that the whole thing is extravagantly, even irrelevantly, large. This extravagant size is our primary protection against a variety of catastrophes. Most important for our survival is protection against the catastrophe of gravitational collapse. If matter of any kind is distributed in space, the matter cannot collapse gravitationally in a time shorter than the "free-fall time," which is the time it would take to fall together in the absence of any other hang-ups. According to Newton's law of gravitation, the free-fall time depends only on the average density of the matter. For example, the Earth has average density five times the density of water, and a free-fall time of fifteen minutes. This means that if the Earth's rocks could by some miracle lose all their strength while retaining their weight, and if the Earth were not rotating, the Earth would collapse to its center in fifteen minutes. Newton's law says that there is a simple relation between density and free-fall time. The free-fall time varies inversely with the square root of the density. This relation implies that, when we have an extravagantly big volume of space, which means an extravagantly small density, the free-fall time becomes so long that gravitational collapse is postponed to a remote future.

For the universe as a whole, the average density of mass is about one atom per cubic meter, and the corresponding free-fall time is about 100 billion years. This is longer than the probable age of the universe (10 billion years), but only by a factor of ten. If the matter in the universe were not spread out with such an exceedingly low density, the free-fall time of the universe would already have ended, and our remote ancestors would long ago have been engulfed and incinerated in a universal cosmic collapse.

The matter inside our own galaxy has an average density about a million times higher than that of the universe as a whole. The free-fall time for the galaxy is therefore about 100 million years, a thousand times shorter than the free-fall time of the universe. Within the time span of life on the Earth, the galaxy is not preserved from gravitational collapse by size alone. Our survival requires other hang-ups besides the hang-up of size.

Another form of degradation of gravitational energy, less drastic than gravitational collapse, would be the disruption of the Solar System by close encounters or collisions with other stars. Such a degradation of the orbital motions of the Earth and planets would be just as fatal to our existence as a complete collapse. We have escaped this catastrophe only because the distances between stars in our galaxy are also extravagantly large. Again, a calculation shows that our galaxy is barely large enough to make the damaging encounters unlikely. Even within our galaxy, the size hang-up is necessary to our preservation, although it is not by itself sufficient.

The second on the list of hang-ups is the spin hang-up. An extended object cannot collapse gravitationally if it is spinning rapidly. Instead of collapsing, the outer parts of the object settle into stationary orbits revolving around the inner parts. Our galaxy as a whole is preserved by this hang-up, and the Earth is preserved by it from collapsing into the Sun. Without the spin hang-up, no planetary system could have been formed at the time the Sun condensed out of the interstellar gas. The spin hang-up has produced ordered structures with an impressive appearance of permanence, not only galaxies and planetary systems but also double stars and Saturn's rings. None of these structures is truly permanent. Given sufficient time, all will be degraded by slow processes of internal energy dissipation or by random encounters with other objects in the universe. The Solar System seems at first sight to be a perfect perpetual-motion machine, but in reality its longevity is dependent on the combined action of the spin hang-up and the size hang-up.

The third hang-up is the thermonuclear hang-up. This hang-up arises from the fact that hydrogen "burns" to form helium when it is heated and compressed. The thermonuclear burning is actually a fusion reaction between the nuclei of hydrogen atoms. It releases energy which opposes any further compression. As a result, any object such as a star that contains a large proportion of hydrogen is unable to collapse gravitationally beyond a certain point until the hydrogen is all burned up. For example, the Sun has been stuck on the thermonuclear hang-up for 4.5 billion years, and will take another 5 billion years to burn up its hydrogen before its gravitational contraction can be resumed. Ultimately, the supply of nuclear energy in the universe is only a small fraction of the supply of gravitational energy. But the nuclear energy acts as a delicately adjusted regulator, postponing the violent phases of gravitational collapse and allowing stars to shine peacefully for billions of years.

There is good evidence that the universe began its existence with all the matter in the form of hydrogen, with perhaps some admixture of helium but few traces of heavier elements. The evidence comes from the spectra of stars moving in our galaxy with very high velocities relative to the Sun. The high velocities mean that these stars do not take part in the general rotation of the galaxy. They are moving in orbits oblique to the plane of the galaxy, so that their velocity and the Sun's combine to give a relative velocity of the order of hundreds of kilometers per second. Such a velocity distinguishes these stars from the common stars, which orbit with the Sun in the central plane of the galaxy and show relative velocities of the order of tens of kilometers per second. The high-velocity stars form a "halo," or spherical cloud, bisected by the flat rotating galactic disk which contains the bulk of the ordinary stars.

The obvious explanation of this state of affairs is that the high-velocity stars are the oldest. They condensed out of the primeval galaxy while it was still in a state of free fall, before it encountered the spin hang-up. After the spin hang-up the galaxy settled down into a disk, and the ordinary stars were formed in orbits within the disk where they have remained ever since. This picture of the history of the galaxy is dramatically confirmed by the spectroscopic evidence. The spectra of the extreme high-velocity stars show extremely weak absorption lines for all the elements except hydrogen. These stars contain less than a tenth, sometimes less than a hundredth, as much of the common elements carbon, oxygen, and iron as we find in the Sun. Such major deficiencies of the common elements are almost never found in low-velocity stars. Since hydrogen burns to make carbon and iron, but carbon and iron cannot burn to make hydrogen, the objects with the least contamination of hydrogen by heavier elements must be the oldest. We can still see a few high-velocity stars in our neighborhood dating back to a time so early that the contamination by heavier elements was close to zero.

The discovery that the universe was originally composed of rather pure hydrogen implies that the thermonuclear hang-up is a universal phenomenon. Every mass large enough to be capable of gravitational collapse must pass through a prolonged hydrogen-burning phase. The only objects exempt from this rule are masses of planetary size or smaller, in which gravitational contraction is halted by the mechanical strength of the material before the ignition point of thermonuclear reactions is reached. The preponderance of hydrogen in the universe ensures that our night sky is filled with well-behaved stars like our Sun, placidly pouring out their energy for the benefit of any attendant life forms, and giving to the celestial sphere its historic attribute of serene immobility. It is only by virtue of the thermonuclear hang-up that the heavens have appeared to be immobile. We now know that, in corners of the universe other than our own, violent events are the rule rather than the exception. The prevalence of catastrophic outbursts of energy was revealed to us through the rapid progress of radio astronomy over the past thirty years. These outbursts are still poorly understood. It seems likely that they occur in regions of the universe where the thermonuclear hang-up has been brought to an end by the exhaustion of hydrogen.

It may seem paradoxical that the thermonuclear hang-up has such benign and pacifying effects on extraterrestrial affairs, while our terrestrial thermonuclear devices are neither peaceful nor particularly benign. Why does the sun burn its hydrogen gently for billions of years instead of blowing up like a bomb? To answer this question it is necessary to invoke yet another hang-up. The crucial difference between the Sun and a bomb is that the Sun contains ordinary hydrogen with only a trace of the heavy hydrogen isotopes, whereas the bomb is made mainly of heavy hydrogen. Heavy hydrogen can burn explosively by strong nuclear interactions, but ordinary hydrogen can react with itself only by the weak interaction process. In the weak process two ordinary hydrogen nuclei (protons) fuse to form a heavy hydrogen nucleus (deuteron). The proton-proton reaction proceeds about a billion billion times more slowly than a strong nuclear reaction at the same density and temperature. It is this weak interaction hang-up that makes ordinary hydrogen useless to us as a terrestrial source of energy. However, the hang-up is essential to our existence in at least three ways. First, without this hang-up we would not have a sufficiently long-lived and stable sun. Second, without it the ocean would be an excellent thermonuclear explosive and would constitute a perennial temptation to builders of "doomsday machines." Third and most important, without the weak interaction hang-up it is unlikely that any appreciable quantity of hydrogen would have survived the initial hot, dense phase of the evolution of the universe. Almost all the matter in the universe would have been burned to helium before the first galaxies started to condense, water would be a rare substance, and all solid planets would be as dry as the Moon.

FROM EROS TO GAIA

If one looks in greater detail at the theoretical reasons for the existence of the weak interaction hang-up, our survival seems even more providential. The hang-up depends decisively on the nonexistence of an isotope of helium of mass two, with a nucleus consisting of two protons and no neutrons. If helium-two existed, the proton-proton reaction would yield a helium-two nucleus, and the helium-two nucleus would afterward decay into a deuteron. The first reaction being strong, the hydrogen would burn fast to produce helium-two, and the subsequent weak decay of the helium-two would not limit the rate of burning. It happens that there does exist a well-observed state of the helium-two nucleus, but the state is unbound so that the two protons do not stick together. The nuclear force between two protons is strong and attractive, but it just barely fails to produce a bound state. If the force had been a few percent stronger, there would have been no weak interaction hang-up.

I have discussed four hang-ups: size, spin, thermonuclear, and weak interaction. The catalogue is by no means complete. There is an important class of transport or opacity hang-ups, which arise because the transport of energy by conduction or radiation from the hot interior of the Earth or the Sun to the cooler surface takes millions of years. It is the transport hang-up that keeps the Earth fluid and geologically active, giving us continental drift, earthquakes, volcanoes, and mountain uplift. All these processes derive their energy from the original gravitational condensation of the Earth 4 billion years ago, supplemented by a modest input of energy from subsequent radioactivity of the earth's rocks.

Last on my list is a special surface tension hang-up that has enabled the fissionable nuclei of uranium and thorium to survive in the Earth's crust until we are ready to use them. These nuclei are unstable against spontaneous fission. They contain so much positive charge and so much electrostatic energy that they are ready to fly apart at the slightest provocation. Before they can fly apart, however, their surface must be stretched into a nonspherical shape, and this stretching is opposed by an extremely powerful force of surface tension. A nucleus is kept spherical in the same way that a droplet of rain is kept spherical by the surface tension of water, except that the nucleus has a tension about a billion billion times as strong as that of the raindrop. In spite of this surface tension, a nucleus of uranium does occasionally fission spontaneously, and the rate of the fissioning can be measured. Nonetheless, the hang-up is so effective that less than one in a million of the Earth's uranium nuclei has disappeared in this way since the Earth was formed.

3. A VIOLENT BUT FRIENDLY UNIVERSE

No hang-up can last forever. There are times and places in the universe at which the flow of energy breaks through all hang-ups. Then rapid and violent transformations occur, of whose nature we are still ignorant. Historically, it was physicists and not astronomers who recorded the first evidence that the universe is not everywhere as quiescent as traditional astronomy had pictured it. The physicist Victor Hess discovered sixty years ago that even our quiet corner of the galaxy is filled with a cloud of the extremely energetic particles now called cosmic rays. We still do not know in detail where these particles come from, but we know that they represent an important channel in the overall energy flow of the universe. They carry, on the average, about as much energy as starlight.

The cosmic rays must certainly originate in catastrophic processes. Various attempts to explain them as by-products of familiar astronomical objects have proved quantitatively inadequate. In the past thirty years half a dozen strange new types of object have been discovered, each of which is violent and enigmatic enough to be a plausible parent of cosmic rays. These include the supernovas (exploding stars), the radio galaxies (giant clouds of energetic electrons emerging from galaxies), the Seyfert galaxies (galaxies with intensely bright and turbulent nuclei), the X-ray sources, the quasars, and the pulsars. All these objects are inconspicuous in our view of the sky, only because they are extremely distant from us. We are protected once again by the size hang-up. The vastness of the interstellar spaces has diluted the cosmic rays enough to save us from being fried or sterilized by them. If sheer distance had not effectively isolated the quiet regions of the universe from the noisy regions, no long-continued biological evolution would have been possible.

The longest-observed and least mysterious of the violent objects are the supernovas. These appear to be ordinary stars, more massive than the Sun, that have burned up their hydrogen and passed into a phase of gravitational collapse. In various ways the rapid release of gravitational energy can cause the star to explode. There may in some cases be a true thermonuclear detonation, with the core of the star, composed mainly of carbon and oxygen, burning instantaneously to iron. In other cases the collapse may cause the star to spin so rapidly that hydrodynamic instability disrupts it. A third possibility is that a spinning magnetic field becomes so intensified by gravitational collapse that it can drive off the surface of the star at high velocity. Probably several different kinds of supernova exist, with different mechanisms of energy transfer. In all cases the basic process must be a gravitational collapse of the core of the star. By one means or another some fraction of the gravitational energy released by the collapse is transferred outward and causes the outer layers of the star to explode. The outward-moving energy appears partly as visible light, partly as the energy of motion of the debris, and partly as the energy of cosmic rays. In addition, a small fraction of the energy may be converted into nuclear energy of unstable atoms of thorium and uranium, and small amounts of these radioactive elements may be injected by the explosion into the interstellar gas. As far as we know, no other mechanism can create the special conditions required for production of fissionable nuclei.

We have firm evidence that a locally violent environment existed in our galaxy immediately before the birth of the Solar System. It is likely that the violence and the origin of the Sun and the Earth were part of the same sequence of events. The evidence for violence is the existence in certain ancient meteorites of xenon gas with an isotopic composition characteristic of the products of spontaneous fission of the nucleus plutonium 244. Supporting evidence is provided by radiation damage in the form of fission-fragment tracks that can be made visible by etching. The meteorites do not contain enough uranium or thorium to account for either the xenon or the fission tracks. They must have contained plutonium at the time that they solidified. Plutonium 244, although it is the longest-lived isotope of plutonium, has a half-life of only 80 million years, which is short compared with the age of the Earth. Therefore, the meteorites must be as old as the solar system, and the plutonium must have originated close, in both time and space, to the event that gave birth to the sun.

We are only beginning to understand the way stars and planets are born. It seems that stars are born in clusters, a few hundred or a few thousand at a time, rather than singly. There is perhaps a cyclical rhythm in the life of a galaxy. For 100 million years the stars and the interstellar gas in any particular sector of a galaxy lie quiet. Then some kind of shock or gravitational wave passes by, compressing the gas and triggering gravitational condensation. Various hang-ups are overcome, and a large mass of gas condenses into new stars in a limited region of space. The most massive stars shine brilliantly for a few million years and die spectacularly as supernovas. The brief blaze of the clusters of short-lived massive stars makes the shock wave visible, from a distance of millions of light-years, as a bright spiral arm sweeping around the galaxy. After the massive new stars are burned out, the less massive stars continue to condense, slightly contaminated with plutonium from the recent supernovas. These more modest stars continue their frugal existence for billions of years after the spiral arm that gave them birth has passed by. In some such rhythm as this, 4.5 billion years ago, our solar system came into being.

Whether some similar rhythms, on an even more gigantic scale, are involved in the birth of the radio galaxies, the quasars and the nuclei of Seyfert galaxies, we do not know. Each of these objects pours out quantities of energy millions of times greater than the output of the brightest supernova. We know nothing of their origins, and we know nothing of their effects on their surroundings. It would be strange if their effects did not ultimately turn out to be of major importance, both for science and for the history of life in the universe.

The main sources of energy available to us on the Earth are chemical fuels, uranium, and sunlight. In addition, we hope one day to learn how to burn in a controlled fashion the deuterium in the oceans. All these energy stores exist here by virtue of hang-ups that have temporarily halted the universal processes of energy degradation. Sunlight is sustained by the thermonuclear, the weak-interaction, and the opacity hang-ups. Uranium is preserved by the surface tension hang-up. Coal and oil have been buried in the ground and saved from oxidation by various biological and chemical hang-ups, the details of which are still under debate. Deuterium has been preserved in low abundance, after almost all of it was burned to helium in the earliest stages of the history of the universe, because no thermonuclear reaction ever runs quite to completion.

Humanity is fortunate in having such a variety of energy resources at its disposal. In the very long run we shall need energy that is unpolluting; we shall have sunlight. In the fairly long run we shall need energy that is inexhaustible and moderately clean; we shall have deuterium. In the short run we shall need energy that is readily usable and abundant; we shall have uranium. Right now we need energy that is cheap and convenient; we have coal and oil. Nature has been kinder to us than we had any right to expect. As we look out into the universe and identify the many accidents of physics and astronomy that have worked together to our benefit, it almost seems as if the universe must in some sense have known that we were coming.

Since the Apollo voyages gave us a close-up view of the desolate landscape of the moon, many people have formed an impression of the Earth as a uniquely beautiful and fragile oasis in a harsh and hostile universe. The distant pictures of the blue planet conveyed this impression most movingly. I wish to assert the contrary view. I believe the universe is friendly. I see no reason to suppose that the cosmic accidents that provided so abundantly for our welfare here on the Earth will not do the same for us, wherever else in the universe we choose to go.

Ko Hung was one of the great natural philosophers of ancient China. In the fourth century he wrote: "As for belief, there are things that are as clear as the sky, yet men prefer to sit under an up-turned barrel." Some of the current discussions of the resources of mankind on the Earth have a claustrophobic quality that Ko Hung's words describe very accurately. I hope that with this article I may have persuaded a few people to come out from under the barrel, and to look to the sky with hopeful eyes. I began with a quotation from Blake. Let me end with another, Blake this time echoing the thought of Ko Hung: "If the doors of perception were cleansed every thing would appear to man as it is, infinite. For man has closed himself up, till he sees all things thro' narrow chinks of his cavern."

Carbon Dioxide in the Atmosphere and the Biosphere

.....

1 9 9 0

I. THE MYSTERY OF THE MISSING CARBON

Sir Crispin Tickell, freshly retired from his demanding service as Her Britannic Majesty's ambassador to the United Nations in New York, where he had been effectively orchestrating the United Nations response to the Iraqi invasion of Kuwait, became warden of Green College in Oxford and invited me to talk there about carbon dioxide. He also happens to be an expert in his own right on the subject of this chapter. He became seriously interested in climate long before it was politically fashionable, wrote an excellent book with the title *Climatic Change and World Affairs,* and played a major role in pushing the problems of carbon dioxide and climatic change onto the political agenda of mankind.

Fifteen years ago Sir Crispin went to Harvard to study climate and I went to Oak Ridge, Tennessee. He was attached to the Center for International Affairs at Harvard, a good place for a diplomat whose primary interest is the political dimension of the climate problem. I was attached to the Institute for Energy Analysis at Oak Ridge, a good place for a scientist whose primary interest is facts and figures. In this chapter I shall be mainly concerned with facts and figures. If you want an authoritative discussion of the politics of climatic change, you will find it in Sir Crispin's book.

The main theme of this chapter is a scientific puzzle which I call "The Mystery of the Missing Carbon." I was shocked to discover, when I went to Oak Ridge in 1975, that nobody knew what happened to half the carbon that we were burning. Under the leadership of my late friend Ralph Rotty, Oak Ridge had collected a meticulously accurate data base concerning the quantities of carbon dioxide dumped into the atmosphere by coal burning, oil burning, gas burning, wood burning, and cement production in various countries. Rotty's numbers were, and still are, accepted worldwide as the most reliable. It is convenient when discussing these numbers to use the unit "gigaton of carbon," meaning a billion metric tons of carbon. The quantity of carbon dumped into the atmosphere was running close to 5 gigatons per year in 1975 and is now running close to 6. These numbers, unlike most of the numbers in the carbon cycle budget, are accurately known, with an error that does not exceed 1 gigaton.

The other reliable number in the carbon budget is the observed rate of increase of carbon dioxide in the atmosphere. The atmospheric carbon dioxide has been measured for thirty-two years by Charles Keeling, a scientist as meticulous and as dedicated to accuracy as Ralph Rotty. Keeling began in 1958 with a single measurement site on the mountain Mauna Loa in Hawaii. He now has ten sites extending down the Pacific Basin from Point Barrow in northern Alaska to the South Pole. The records from all his sites show a steady increase of carbon dioxide from year to year. The rate of increase for the entire atmosphere was 2½ gigatons of carbon per year in 1975, 3½ gigatons per year today. Roughly half of the carbon burned appears in the atmosphere. The other half has somehow disappeared. This is the mystery of the missing carbon. It is preposterous to claim any ability to predict the future of the carbon cycle so long as we lack a rudimentary understanding of what has happened to the carbon in the past.

There are other items in the carbon budget besides fuel burning and the growth of the atmospheric reservoir. In particular, there is the intensive destruction of forests and the accompanying erosion of topsoil and peat. Both these processes add carbon dioxide to the atmosphere. The quantities are difficult to measure, but there is a rough agreement among the experts that destroyed trees are worth about 2 gigatons and eroded soil about 1 gigaton per year. The true figures might be considerably larger, as some of our environmental activists believe. In any case, the additional 3 gigatons from deforestation and erosion only deepen the mystery. Taking fuel burning and environmental destruction together, human activities are putting 9 gigatons of carbon per year into the atmosphere. More than half of the carbon is missing. At this point it may be helpful to look at the overall carbon budget presented in the table.

CARBON BUDGET
(Gigatons of Carbon)

Capital Account		Annual Flow
7,000 B	Fossil Fuels	−6 A
700 A	Atmosphere	+3½A
40,000 A	Ocean	+1½ C
1,500 B	Topsoil and Peat	−1 C
800 B	Plants and Forests	−2 C
	Spring & Summer Growth	+50 B
	Autumn & Winter Decay★	−50 B
	Total "Missing Carbon"	−4 C

A—Well measured (error ± 20 percent)
B—Roughly known (error ± factor of 2)
C—Highly uncertain (sign may be wrong)

★This includes consumption by animals and humans.

The left side of the table shows the sizes of the various reservoirs that are actively involved in the carbon cycle. I have omitted the biggest reservoir of all, the carbon in chalk and limestone rock, because it does not contribute significantly to the cycle on a short time scale. If we were looking at processes on a geological time scale, the limestone reservoir would dominate the others. But on a time scale of years or decades, the weathering and deposition of limestone is comparatively unimportant. The essential fact which emerges from the left side of the table is that the three smallest and most active reservoirs, the atmosphere, the plants, and the soil, are all of roughly the same size. This means that large human disturbances of any one of these reservoirs will have large effects on all three. We cannot hope either to understand or to manage the carbon in the atmosphere unless we understand and manage the trees and the soil too.

The right side of the table shows the annual increases and decreases of the various reservoirs, estimated for the year 1990. A plus sign means that a reservoir is increasing, a minus sign means that it is decreasing. Here the most important things to notice are not the numbers but the letters attached to them. Letter A means that a quantity is known with an error less than 20 percent, which in this context is considered high accuracy. B means that a quantity is known within a factor of two up or down. C means that the quantity is highly uncertain, a mere guess. For a quantity labeled C, we are not sure that even the sign is correct. The essential fact on the right side of the table is that the B's and C's outnumber the A's. The uncertainties dominate the certainties. The bottom line of -4 gigatons is the missing carbon, the annual deficit, which is obtained by adding all the flows together. If the numbers were correct, the flows would necessarily add up to zero. The size of the deficit indicates the size of the errors in our estimates of the flows. We need to find an additional sink of carbon equal to 4 gigatons per year.

The easy way to explain the disappearance of the missing carbon is to say that it has gone into the ocean. We might simply proclaim that the annual flow into the ocean is 5½ gigatons instead of 1½ gigatons. The problem with this explanation is that oceanic measurements do not support it. The surface layer of the ocean is almost saturated with carbon dioxide and cannot absorb much more. Any large flux of carbon into the ocean must somehow be transported from the surface into the deep cold layers below. There are two known mechanisms for moving carbon into the deep ocean. Either it is carried down as dissolved carbon dioxide in the sinking currents that flow downward from the Arctic and Antarctic seas. Or it is carried down as particulate organic carbon, a rain of little corpses and fecal pellets produced by creatures proliferating and dying in the ocean surface. When oceanographers compute the quantities of carbon carried down by both these routes, they arrive at estimates in the range of 1 or 2 gigatons, and not 5½ gigatons. When I asked some famous oceanographers whether they might be able to transport 5½ gigatons, they protested vigorously. They said it was impossible.

The only other explanation of the missing carbon is that it is absorbed in trees and topsoil. If this is the true explanation, it means that the trees and topsoil, where they are not being destroyed by human activities, are growing in volume at a rate large enough to outweigh the destruction. The rapid growth, if it exists, must be a response to the worldwide fertilizing effect of the increased carbon dioxide in the atmosphere. This hypothesis of a growing biospheric reservoir of carbon is implausible for two reasons. First, it sounds absurdly optimistic to claim that Nature herself is able to repair more than half of the damage that we are inflicting upon her. Second, the experts on trees and soil reject the idea of a large biospheric sink of carbon just as vehemently as the oceanographers reject the idea of a large oceanic sink. I spoke recently on this subject at Duke University in North Carolina, which happens to have a first-class department of botany, with some of the world's great experts on trees and soil. Boyd Strain the tree expert and William Schlesinger the soil expert were in the audience. Boyd Strain said he is sure the missing carbon is not going into trees, and William Schlesinger said he is sure it is not going into soil.

So the mystery remains. Either the oceanographers are wrong or the botanists are wrong. Perhaps both are wrong. What we need in order to solve the mystery is more observations. Rotty spent his life making careful and meticulous analyses of fossil fuel burning. Keeling spent his life making careful and meticulous observations of carbon dioxide in the atmosphere. We need another Rotty and another Keeling to spend their lives making equally meticulous observations of oceans, trees, and soil. That is the only way to convert the C's in our carbon budget into A's. When the C's become A's, we shall know who was right and who was wrong.

We have recently seen some new evidence that supports the hypothesis that the missing carbon goes into the biosphere. If the new evidence is to be trusted, then the oceanographers were right and the botanists were wrong. I will come back to the new evidence later. It is indirect and not conclusive. Until we have direct measurements of all channels in the carbon cycle, the fate of the missing carbon will remain in doubt.

2. THE OAK RIDGE MANIFESTO

Everything I have said so far in this chapter is old stuff, well known to the experts. From this point on, I shall be saying things that contradict the accepted wisdom. Where I diverge from the experts, the disagreement is not a matter of fact but a matter of emphasis. I do not say that the experts are giving us wrong answers. I say that they are frequently not asking the right questions. In the view of the majority of experts, the central question is the prediction of climatic change caused by carbon dioxide, and the problem of the missing carbon is a peripheral issue of no great consequence. In my view the fate of the missing carbon is central, and the question of climatic change is only one of many important questions that cannot be answered satisfactorily until the missing carbon is understood.

My work at Oak Ridge was part of a big program of research into the carbon dioxide problem directed by the U.S. Department of Energy. In 1978 I found myself in disagreement with the management of the program. I expressed my disagreement in a one-page manifesto addressed to my Oak Ridge colleagues. The manifesto disappeared into the dustbin of history without producing any response. I resurrect it today because it raises an issue that is as vital in 1990 as it was in 1978. So here it is:

In the May 1978 Comprehensive Plan for Carbon Dioxide Effects Research and Assessment of the Department of Energy, the direct effects of carbon dioxide increase on plant growth and interspecific competition receive little attention. The plan is drawn up as if climatic change were the only serious effect of carbon dioxide on human activities. The programs for monitoring the biosphere on land and in the oceans are mainly aimed at measuring the effect of the biosphere on atmospheric carbon dioxide rather than the effects of carbon dioxide on the biosphere.

I submit that this distribution of emphasis is wrong. To indicate the crucial nature of the nonclimatic effects of carbon dioxide, it is sufficient to mention the fact that a field of corn plants growing in full sunshine will completely deplete the carbon dioxide from the air within one meter of ground in a time of the order of five minutes.

In a comparison of the nonclimatic with the climatic effects of carbon dioxide, the nonclimatic effects may be:
1. more certain,
2. more immediate,
3. easier to observe,
4. potentially at least as serious.

The nonclimatic effects are primarily effects on plant growth and physiology, including effects on the utilization by plants of water and nitrogen. The effects of the present 10 percent enrichment of atmospheric carbon dioxide by human activities may already be large, both in changing agricultural yields and in changing the balance of natural ecosystems. The effects of a future larger increase of atmospheric carbon dioxide may change the conditions of agriculture and plant ecology quite radically, long before any climatic effects become apparent. Our research plan should address these issues directly, not as a mere sideline to climatic studies.

End of manifesto.

Twelve years have gone by since these words were written, and nothing much has changed. The 10 percent enrichment of atmospheric carbon dioxide has grown to 15 percent. The financial resources of government research programs investigating the carbon dioxide problem have grown even more rapidly. But the increased funds have mostly been poured into computer simulations of the global climate, rather than into observations of the real world of roots and shoots, trees and termites. I do not blame only the government bureaucrats for the excessive emphasis on computer simulations. We scientists must share the blame. It is much more comfortable for a scientist to run a computer model in an air-conditioned supercomputer center rather than to put on winter clothes and try to keep instruments correctly calibrated outside in the mud and rain. Up to a point, the computer models are useful and necessary. They are only harmful when they become a substitute for real-world observation. In the twelve years since 1978 the results of computer models have tended to dominate the political discussion of the carbon dioxide problem. The computer results are simpler and easier for politicians to understand than the vagaries of the real world. The computer results say nothing about nonclimatic effects. The advent of the supercomputer has accentuated the neglect of nonclimatic effects about which I complained in 1978.

Let me give a simple example of a nonclimatic effect of carbon dioxide on the biosphere. Owners of commercial greenhouses discovered long ago that seedlings grow faster when the air in the greenhouses is enriched with carbon dioxide. Many experiments have been done in growth chambers designed so that the carbon dioxide can be accurately controlled and the response of plants accurately measured. A typical experiment was done in 1975, measuring the effects of carbon dioxide on the growth and transpiration of leaves of the American poplar, *Populus deltoides*. Experiments on other plant species usually give similar results. The poplar experiment used atmospheres ranging from one-tenth to three times the present outdoor concentration of carbon dioxide. The growth rate is zero at one-tenth of the outdoor level, rises rapidly as the carbon dioxide is increased up to the outdoor level, then rises more slowly as the carbon dioxide is increased to twice the outdoor level, then becomes constant as the carbon dioxide increases beyond twice the outdoor level. The saturation value of growth rate is one and a half times the rate at the outdoor level, and is reached at three times the outdoor level. So far, the results are unsurprising.

More surprising and of greater practical importance are the measurements of water transpiration in the poplar experiment. Transpiration means the loss of water by evaporation from the leaves. The rate of transpiration falls steadily as carbon dioxide increases, and is reduced to about half its present value when the carbon dioxide is enriched threefold. How is this decrease of transpiration to be explained? The essential point is that carbon dioxide molecules are rare in the atmosphere. They are hard for a plant to catch. The only way a plant can catch a carbon dioxide molecule is to keep open the little stomata or pores on the surface of its leaves, and wait for the occasional carbon dioxide molecule to blunder in. But the air inside the stomata is saturated with water vapor. On the average, about two hundred water molecules will stumble out of the hole for every one carbon dioxide molecule that stumbles in. The poplar experiment measured the water loss and the carbon gain of the leaves simultaneously, and found that the loss is a hundred times the gain when the carbon dioxide is at the outdoor level. The plant is forced to lose a lot of water in order to collect a little carbon dioxide. When the carbon dioxide in the atmosphere is enriched, the plant has a choice. The plant may either keep its stomata open and lose water as rapidly as before while increasing photosynthesis. Or it may partially close its stomata and reduce the loss of water while keeping photosynthesis constant. Or it may make a compromise, closing the stomata only a little, so that water loss is decreased while photosynthesis is increased. The poplar leaves in the experiment chose the compromise strategy. Plants will in general choose whatever strategy they find optimum, depending on local conditions of temperature, humidity, and sunlight.

The moral of this story is that for plants growing under dry conditions, enriched carbon dioxide in the atmosphere is a substitute for water. Give a plant more carbon dioxide, and it can make do with less water. Since the growth of plants, both in agriculture and in the wild, is frequently limited by lack of water, the effect of carbon dioxide in reducing transpiration may be of greater practical importance than the direct effect in increasing photosynthesis. It is easy to measure both these effects of carbon dioxide in greenhouses and growth chambers. It is difficult to measure them in the real world out-of-doors. Here then is the crucial task for understanding the human dimensions of the carbon-dioxide problem. Our research programs must come to grips with the responses of crop plants and grasses and trees all over the world to increased carbon dioxide. To measure these responses, experiments in growth chambers are inadequate and computer simulations are useless. There is no substitute for field observations, widely distributed in place and extended in time.

If we can establish research programs, putting as much money and time and talent into the measurement of ecological responses to carbon dioxide as we are now spending on climatic effects, we may be able within a few years to answer the politically crucial questions. Is the direct effect of increasing carbon dioxide on food production and forests more important than the effect on climate? Is the human species already hooked on carbon dioxide, needing a continued increase of fossil fuel burning to fertilize our crops? When the coal and oil are all gone, shall we be burning limestone to keep the atmosphere enriched in carbon dioxide at the level to which the biosphere will have become addicted? I am not saying that the answers to these questions should be yes. But we must be aware that we do not have the knowledge to answer them with a confident no.

3. OXYGEN

I now turn to another important aspect of the real world that our climate research programs have neglected. I shall talk about oxygen. As every schoolchild is supposed to know, the burning of fuels uses up oxygen from the atmosphere and the growth of plants puts oxygen back. You might imagine that one of our busy scientists might have measured the rate at which the oxygen in the atmosphere is being used up. The reservoir of oxygen in the atmosphere is large but not infinite. It amounts to 1.2 million gigatons. Since 8 tons of oxygen are used up for every 3 tons of carbon burned, and we are burning 6 gigatons of carbon per year, we might expect that the oxygen is being used up at a rate of about thirteen parts per million per year. Thirteen parts per million should be measurable. The measurement is not easy, but with modern precise instruments it should be about as difficult to measure the oxygen today as it was for Charles Keeling to measure the carbon dioxide when he began his work thirty-two years ago. All we need is an individual scientist willing to dedicate her life to the oxygen measurements as Keeling has dedicated his life to carbon dioxide. Ten years ago a panel of scientists recommended to the U.S. Department of Energy that a program of oxygen measurements be started. Nothing happened. Again, it is not only bureaucrats who are to blame. We scientists are also to blame for not practicing what we preach. It is easy to give advice, and not so easy to follow it.

I am surprised that the general public all over the world is not clamoring to know how fast we are using up the oxygen. You might imagine that ordinary citizens would want to know. The public is now aware that we have a serious problem with the depletion of ozone. I wish we could arouse the same public interest in the depletion of oxygen.

Whether or not the general public is concerned, there are important scientific reasons for measuring the oxygen. The oxygen cycle and the carbon cycle are coupled together. If we had an accurate measurement of the oxygen depletion, this would give information about the fate of the missing carbon. Roughly speaking, the oxygen depletion must balance the increase of carbon dioxide in the atmosphere and ocean, but will not be affected by the carbon that is absorbed in the biosphere. An accurate measurement of oxygen depletion will tell us how much carbon is going into the ocean and how much into the biosphere.

To achieve this result we have to measure depletion of oxygen not only in the atmosphere but also in the ocean. The measurement of oxygen in the ocean is in some ways easier and in some ways more difficult than in the atmosphere. The ocean is easier because the reservoir of dissolved oxygen is much smaller, a mere 8,400 gigatons compared with 1.2 million in the atmosphere. The expected decrease is of the order of one part per thousand per year in the ocean, compared with thirteen parts per million in the atmosphere. On the other hand, the ocean is more difficult because the water is not well mixed. The global atmosphere, as Keeling's measurements have shown, is well mixed on a time scale of a few years. Measurement of oxygen in the atmosphere at a single site such as Mauna Loa would determine the rate of atmospheric oxygen depletion for the whole earth. In the ocean the mixing times are of the order of thousands of years. To determine the depletion of oxygen for the whole ocean, the whole ocean would need to be sampled. Oxygen would have to be measured with an accuracy of one part per thousand at many thousands of places and at many depths. In the process we would learn other important facts about the ecology of the oceans.

There is a remarkable symmetry between the atmosphere and the ocean so far as carbon and oxygen are concerned. In the atmosphere oxygen is abundant and carbon dioxide is scarce; in the ocean, carbon dioxide is abundant and dissolved oxygen is scarce. Because carbon dioxide in the atmosphere is scarce, the disturbance of the natural ecology by human activities appears most prominently in the increase of carbon dioxide. In the oceans, since oxygen is scarce, the disturbance of the natural ecology will appear most prominently in a depletion of oxygen. It is possible that the depletion of oxygen in the oceans presents as serious a long-term threat to the ecology as the buildup of carbon dioxide in the atmosphere. Reducing oxygen by 50 percent will cause more drastic damage to more species than increasing carbon dioxide by 50 percent. A doubling of carbon dioxide would be for the majority of species a tolerable insult; a reduction of oxygen in the ocean to zero would be a catastrophe.

If we take the total inventory of 8,400 gigatons of oxygen in the ocean and divide it by a plausible rate of depletion, say 10 gigatons per year, we obtain a comfortably long time of the order of eight hundred years before the ocean is asphyxiated. Since the ocean is not well mixed, this estimate is misleading. Catastrophe may come to parts of the ocean long before the entire oxygen reservoir is exhausted. The Pacific Ocean as a whole is already seriously depleted. It contains 50 percent of the planet's water but only 40 percent of the dissolved oxygen. So long as we are not measuring the rate of depletion year by year, we have no basis for guessing how soon the asphyxiation of parts of the ocean might begin. A program of measurement of the oceanic oxygen would help us to preserve the life of the ocean, as well as helping us to understand the fate of the missing carbon.

4. GROWING TREES AND TOPSOIL

I now turn from questions of science to questions of public action. Newspaper writers often describe the political argument concerning what they call "the greenhouse" as a debate over priorities, with science on one side and action on the other. "The greenhouse" means the climatic effect of carbon dioxide and other atmospheric gases which are warming the earth. "Science" means the computer models of global climate which predict the warming. "Action" means the imposition of drastic restrictions on fossil fuel burning in order to hold the warming in check. The debate is supposed to go like this. The "action first" people say we should restrict fuel burning immediately without waiting to see whether the science is right. The "science first" people say we should concentrate first on getting the science right, finding out whether the global warming has really begun, before deciding what action to take. In the popular press, the "action first" people are usually the good guys and the "science first" people are the bad guys. This caricature of the political debate may contain some elements of truth.

But to me the words have different meanings. To me the greenhouse is not the main issue. The main issue is the management of the earth's ecology, with primary emphasis on trees and topsoil rather than on the atmosphere. To me "action" means mobilizing international efforts on a grand scale to plant trees and improve soil. If trees and topsoil are nurtured, as for a variety of ecological and economic reasons they ought to be nurtured, the growth of carbon dioxide in the atmosphere will be slowed down or halted incidentally. To me "science" means not computer models but detailed understanding of the carbon and oxygen cycles in the real world, especially as they are seen in the growth of plants and the circulation of oceans. With these meanings of "action" and "science," I am firmly on the side of "action first." Science cannot be hurried. It will necessarily take a long time, before all the uncertainties in the movements of carbon and oxygen are resolved. Science does not require that action be postponed until the science is complete, if the action is for other reasons beneficial. I am opposed to drastic restrictions on fuel burning, because such restrictions are not beneficial in the short run and may not be necessary in the long run. Planting of trees, increase of wetlands, and enrichment of soils are beneficial in the short run and will probably be necessary in the long run. My friend Gregg Marland at Oak Ridge is my main source of information about these matters, although he does not always agree with my opinions.

The essential facts concerning the carbon reservoirs are clear. The reservoirs of carbon in forests and soil are large enough to allow control of the growth of carbon in the atmosphere. There is enough land, mostly unproductive grassland and scrub forest, to allow a massive increase of the biospheric carbon reservoirs without taking any land away from agriculture. There is enough available nitrogen and phosphorus and potassium to balance the increase in the carbon reservoirs, to fertilize new forests and new topsoil. All that is lacking to make these things possible is a large amount of money and an international consensus. If the political will existed to drive such a program forward all over the world, the economic costs would not be prohibitive. I estimate that the costs could be paid by a tax of a few percent on all forms of energy. The costs of a total shift away from fossil fuels to renewable sources of energy would be much greater.

The proposal for massive renewal of forests and soil pleases neither side in the ongoing debate over the greenhouse. The conservatives reject it because it says that large-scale action by governments is necessary. The gloom-and-doom environmentalists reject it because it says the situation is not hopeless. But perhaps the time is now ripe for action. The recent success in achieving an international agreement to limit the production of chlorofluorocarbon gases in order to protect the ozone layer, a success in which Sir Crispin played an important part, gives encouragement to all of us who hope for international action to protect the biosphere as a whole. But I do not presume to tell the world how to achieve a political consensus. Achieving a political consensus is Sir Crispin's trade, not mine. I can only tell some of the facts with which a political consensus must deal.

The behavior of carbon dioxide is more complicated than the behavior of stratospheric ozone. The chemistry of stratospheric ozone was only recently disentangled and turned out not to be simple. The interactions of carbon dioxide with the biosphere are still largely unexplored. One important factor is the root-to-shoot ratio. The phrase "root-to-shoot ratio" is botanists' jargon for the quantity of biomass that a plant puts into its roots divided by the quantity that it puts into stem and leaves and flowers and fruit. Generally speaking, biomass that goes into roots contributes more to the buildup of the carbon reservoir in soil. Biomass that goes into shoots, except in the case of long-lived trees, mostly decays and returns its carbon to the atmosphere within a year or two. A change in the root-to-shoot ratio of grasses and other soft plants can shift the balance between the soil reservoir and the atmospheric reservoir of carbon.

Conversely, it is known from growth-chamber experiments that a common response of plants to an enrichment of carbon dioxide in the air is an increased root-to-shoot ratio. The effect is similar to the decrease in water transpiration that I discussed earlier. When a plant is given more carbon dioxide, it needs less leaf area to maintain its metabolism. The optimum strategy for the plant is then to put less effort into growing leaves and more effort into growing roots. We know that this response occurs in growth chambers. Whether it occurs, or how much it occurs, in the world outside, we do not know. But it is at least plausible that the 15 percent increase of atmospheric carbon dioxide due to human activities has produced a worldwide shift in root-to-shoot ratios and a consequent growth of the carbon reservoir in soil. This, rather than accelerated growth of trees in undestroyed forests, may be the process that accounts for the bulk of the missing carbon.

What then are we to do? Should the international community, following the pattern of the Montreal and London ozone agreements, try to regulate the carbon dioxide cycle by imposing drastic limits on the burning of fossil fuel? Some form of international regulation of fuel burning is certainly desirable. But the regulation of fossil fuels is not a sufficient response to the world's ecological problems. I would prefer to see action applied more directly to the preservation of the biosphere. In large parts of the Earth, where the chief source of energy is the burning of firewood, increased burning of fossil fuels seems to be the only way to save what is left of the forests. Which is more important, to save fossil fuel or to save the forests? I believe the forests should come first. For the action that is needed, the ozone agreements are not the best model. A better model is the international action, led by the World Health Organization, to eradicate the smallpox virus. The smallpox campaign, involving the coordinated action of thousands of people at the local level in every country, reached its triumphant conclusion in Somalia in 1977. We need the same kind of operation, centrally financed but locally administered and executed, to deal effectively with the health of the biosphere.

An example on a small scale of the action that is needed is a project undertaken by an electric power company, Applied Energy Services, that is building a coal-fired power station in Connecticut. The station will burn about 150,000 tons of carbon per year. The company decided, as an experiment in good citizenship, to plant about 50 million trees in Guatemala to remove an equal quantity of carbon from the atmosphere. Guatemala was chosen because the Guatemalan Forestry Service, the American Peace Corps in Guatemala, and a large number of Guatemalan smallholder farmers, are already engaged in a successful reforestation program. The power company is merely supplying some extra cash and some extra motivation to an existing enterprise. The cost of this outlay to the company amounts to a little less than 1 percent of the cost of electricity. If one includes the outlays of the other participants in the project, the Guatemalan government, the Peace Corps, and CARE, the total costs amount to about 6 percent of the cost of electricity. The Guatemalan government and the Peace Corps considered the reforestation to be worth paying for, quite apart from its effect on the global atmosphere. No matter how one apportions the costs between local and global benefits, the project appears to be cost-effective.

The Guatemalan experiment is on a small scale. To halt the increase of carbon dioxide in the atmosphere, to absorb 4 gigatons of carbon per year rather than 150,000 tons, the experiment would have to be multiplied by a factor of 20,000. The total costs would be measured in hundreds of billions of dollars per year rather than in millions. We do not know whether such experiments could be successful on a worldwide basis. The essential requirement will be, as it is in Guatemala, that the action be seen as beneficial by the people who carry it out at the local level. That was why the smallpox eradication campaign was successful. It was not seen by the local populations as imposed on them by a remote and alien authority. In Guatemala the farmers cooperate with the reforestation project because they are allowed to chop and use for their own purposes a fraction of the trees that they grow. In all such projects, it is wise to follow the rule enunciated long ago in the twenty-fifth chapter of Deuteronomy: "Thou shalt not muzzle the ox when he treadeth out the corn."

5. THE NEW EVIDENCE

The last part of this chapter goes back from action to science. I shall describe two new lines of evidence that recently appeared, both supporting the hypothesis that the missing carbon is mainly going into the biosphere rather than into the ocean. This evidence strengthens the case for action concentrated upon the building-up of forests and soil. If nature, without our help, already by natural processes counteracted half of the damage we are doing to the biosphere, this encourages us to believe that by intelligent cooperation with nature we may be able to counteract the other half. Cooperating with nature means doing things that nature does well, covering the land with trees and making soil out of roots.

The first new line of evidence comes from Charles Keeling himself. Keeling's record from Mauna Loa of the carbon dioxide in the atmosphere is the longest of his records and extends over thirty years, from 1958 to 1988. It shows a steady rise from 315 to 350 parts per million, superimposed upon an annual cycle of about 7 parts per million up and down. The annual cycle results from the springtime growth and autumn decay of vegetation which lives mainly in the Northern Hemisphere. Records in the Southern Hemisphere show a much smaller annual cycle. The record from Point Barrow in the Arctic shows a cycle twice as large.

Keeling remarks that if you look carefully at the Mauna Loa record, you see that not only the total quantity of carbon dioxide but also the amplitude of the annual cycle has increased over the thirty-year period. The record seems to show an overall increase of the annual cycle by about 10 percent between the decade of the sixties and the decade of the eighties. If we believe that the increase is real, it gives us direct evidence of an increase in the activity of the biosphere. It means that the northern biosphere must have been increasing its activity over this period at a rate of about .5 percent per year.

We cannot argue that the sizes of the biospheric reservoirs of carbon must be increasing in proportion to their increased annual activity. It is not clear whether the observed increase in activity should be attributed mainly to trees or to soft plants. All we can say is that if either the volume of the tree reservoir or the volume of the soil reservoir were increasing at .5 percent per year, the rate observed for the annual cycle, then the increase would be of the right magnitude to account for the missing carbon. Keeling's evidence shows that something in the biosphere has been growing. It may be the trees or it may be the soil. Either way, the growth would be large enough to absorb the 4 gigatons per year of missing carbon.

The second piece of new evidence comes from Pieter Tans at the University of Colorado in Boulder. Pieter Tans is a geochemist who started his career in the Netherlands trying to disentangle the distribution of the isotopes of carbon in Dutch trees of various ages. He is well acquainted with the difficulties of studying carbon in the real world rather than in computer models. He knows how to use computer models on occasion without putting too much faith in them.

Tans's new argument begins with the observation of Keeling that the annual average concentration of carbon dioxide in the Arctic is three parts per million greater than it is at the South Pole. This difference of three parts per million between North and South remains steady from year to year. It is easy to understand roughly why the difference exists. The fossil fuel sources of carbon dioxide are mainly in the North, and the carbon takes a few years to travel from North to South. Tans makes this explanation quantitative by using a computer model of the global circulation of carbon. The computer model takes as a given the known sources of carbon from fuel burning and deforestation. The purpose of the exercise is to find the location of the unknown sinks. Apart from the known atmospheric sink of carbon, the possible sinks are the biosphere and the ocean. If the unknown sink is in the biosphere, it must be mainly in the North, since that is where the bulk of the trees and soil are situated. If it is in the ocean, it must be mainly in the South, for two reasons. First, the Southern Hemisphere contains most of the ocean, just as the Northern Hemisphere contains most of the land. Second, the carbon dioxide fluxes into the northern and tropical oceans are comparatively well measured and are known to be small. In fact, the warm tropical ocean is a net source of carbon dioxide and probably outweighs the northern oceanic sink. Therefore, if there is a large oceanic sink at all, it can only be in the South. The choice between biospheric and oceanic sinks for carbon is reduced to a choice between North and South.

Tans finishes the argument by allowing the computer model to make the choice. Since the carbon is carried along passively by the global circulation, the difference in atmospheric carbon abundance from North to South is proportional to the average flow from North to South. If the sinks, except for the atmosphere itself, are in the North, the North-South flow is small and the North-South difference is small. If the major sink is in the South, the North-South flow is large and the difference is large. The computer model confirms these commonsense arguments. When

Tans puts the main sink of carbon into the southern ocean, the model predicts a concentration difference between North and South poles of seven parts per million. When he puts the main sink into the northern biosphere, the model predicts a North-South difference of three parts per million. Keeling's measurements, which are much more reliable than the computer model, give a difference of three parts per million. The argument of Tans is convoluted and indirect, but the result is a clear decision in favor of the biosphere.

If we believe these arguments of Keeling and Tans, the missing carbon is absorbed by the northern biosphere, and the main question remaining is whether it is going into trees or into soil. This question cannot be resolved by computer models. To answer it will require long, painful, and expensive observations. But action to preserve the biosphere need not wait on detailed understanding. Understanding is not a prerequisite for action, and action is not a substitute for understanding. While we act, the quest for a deeper understanding must continue.

[*Postscript, December 1991*] Since this chapter was written, some important new programs of field observation of atmosphere and ocean have begun. The U.S. Department of Energy has established the Atmospheric Radiation Measurements program, which will study intensively the behavior of clouds, rain, convection, and radiation in local regions of the atmosphere. A brilliantly successful experiment led by Walter Munk in the Indian Ocean has demonstrated the feasibility of monitoring climatic change in huge volumes of ocean with modest equipment. Keith Bonin, a young physicist at Princeton, has taken up the challenge of measuring the rate at which the oxygen in the atmosphere is decreasing.

PART III

Institutions

oooo

RECOGNIZE THE CONNECTIONS OF THINGS AND THE

LAWS OF CONDUCT OF MEN, SO THAT YOU MAY KNOW

WHAT YOU ARE DOING.

LEO SZILARD,

"TEN COMMANDMENTS"

CHAPTER 13

The Future of Physics

.....

1970

I. BRAGG'S RULES

I was asked to talk about the future of physics. Since we are here to dedicate a new building, I talk about things that people now in the building may have a chance to do during their working lives. I look at the next thirty years of physics, concentrating on practical questions that already face us today. The choice of fields of research ought to be biased in favor of projects that will attract students and allow students to participate actively. This bias is implicit in the choices that I advocate.

I begin with an example from the past which shows that foresight over a time scale of thirty years is sometimes possible and can be enormously fruitful. When I came as a graduate student to the English Cambridge twenty-four years ago, most of my physicist friends were cursing the name of Sir Lawrence Bragg, the director of the Cavendish Laboratory. Bragg had become director in 1938, one year after the death of Rutherford. During the brief interregnum the Cavendish had disintegrated with extraordinary speed. Under Rutherford it had been the world center of high-energy physics, high-energy in those days meaning anything over a hundred kilovolts. When Bragg took over the wreckage, most of the brilliant younger men who had worked with Rutherford were gone. They had accepted chairs at other universities where they were busy establishing research schools of their own. The leadership in high-energy physics had decisively passed to Berkeley. To the consternation of those who remained in Cambridge, Bragg made no effort to rebuild. He was not seriously interested in plans for a new accelerator. He sat smugly in his office at the Cavendish and said, "We have taught the world very successfully how to do nuclear physics. Now let us teach them how to do something else."

The people Bragg was supporting in 1946 when I arrived were a strange bunch, doing things that the high-energy crowd would hardly recognize as physics. There was Martin Ryle, who had come back from the war with truckloads of battered electronic junk, and was trying to use this stuff to find radio sources in the sky. There was Max Perutz, who had already spent ten years on an X-ray analysis of the structure of the hemoglobin molecule and remarked cheerfully that in another fifteen years he would have it. There was a crazy character called Francis Crick who seemed to have lost interest in physics altogether. Like most of my theoretical friends, I decided that I had nothing to learn from this bunch of clowns, and I came to America to be in a place where real physics was still being done.

Seven years later Bragg retired from the Cavendish. By that time it was clear to everybody that when he said he was going to teach the world how to do something else he was making no idle boast. He left Cambridge a center of furious activity and first-class international standing in two fields of research which are probably at least as important as high-energy physics in the over-all scheme of things, radio astronomy and molecular biology. Neither of these two new sciences had even a name when Bragg was appointed in 1938. By 1953 when Bragg retired, Ryle's careful mapping of the radio sky was providing a system of reference for astronomers all over the world. The most gigantic and mysterious energy sources in the universe, the radio galaxies and quasars, now usually have names like 3C9 or 3C273, where C stands for Cambridge. Also in 1953 the molecular biologists in Cambridge were not doing badly. Anybody who is interested in what it felt like to be a molecular biologist in Cambridge in 1953 can read Jim Watson's book *The Double Helix*. Cambridge in 1953 was certainly not suffering from intellectual stagnation.

Unlike Rutherford, Bragg did not leave behind him a disintegrating empire. In the seventeen years since Bragg retired, the world standing of Cambridge both in molecular biology and in radio astronomy has been maintained in the face of increasingly intense competition. I have lost count of the number of my old friends in Cambridge who have won Nobel prizes. And two years ago Ryle's radio astronomy group showed that they were still ahead of the world by discovering the first pulsars. I am happy that Bragg at eighty is in good shape physically and intellectually, and can enjoy this latest triumph of his protégés.

This history of the last thirty years in Cambridge is a little over-simplified. It is perhaps too much of a Horatio Alger success story. But it has important lessons for us today. What are the lessons? How did Bragg manage to do so well with what looked in 1938 like a disastrous situation? Broadly speaking, he did well by following three rules. The rules are: (1) Don't try to revive past glories. (2) Don't do things just because they are fashionable. (3) Don't be afraid of the scorn of theoreticians. Besides following these prohibitions, Bragg had also some other more positive advantages. He lived in the old European system which gave the director of a laboratory power to do what he liked and to disregard the objections of his colleagues. He was operating much of the time in a wartime environment, which removed some of the normal bureaucratic constraints. And above all, he had a great deal of luck. But luck of this magnitude does not come to a man twice in a lifetime unless he deserves it.

It is fair to say that in Princeton over the last thirty years we have not done as well as Bragg did in Cambridge. This criticism is not aimed at my friends at Princeton University. I speak only about what happened at my own place, the Institute for Advanced Study. On rule one, not trying to revive past glories, we score high. We have not since 1946 had a professor working in the field of general relativity. It seemed unlikely that we could find anybody in that field quite as good as Einstein. On rule two, not doing just the fashionable things, we score middling. We have always had room for a few unfashionable people like Joe Weber with his gravity wave detector, but a distressingly high percentage of our output of paper is in the fashionable part of particle physics and is to me indistinguishable from the paper produced by twenty other institutes of theoretical physics. On rule three, not being afraid of the scorn of the snobs, we score extremely low. The most original, unfashionable, and worthwhile thing that the Institute did since Einstein retired was the design and construction of von Neumann's prototype electronic computer. In the ten years after World War 2, the group around von Neumann led the world in ideas concerning the development and use of computers. In its way, this was as big a thing as molecular biology or radio astronomy. But the snobs at our Institute could not tolerate the presence of electrical engineers who sullied with their dirty hands the purity of our scholarly atmosphere. Von Neumann was like Bragg, strong enough to override the opposition. But when von Neumann tragically died, the snobs took their revenge and got rid of the computing project root and branch. The demise of our computer group was a disaster not only for Princeton but for science as a whole. It meant that there did not exist at that critical period in the 1950s an academic center where computer people of all kinds could get together at the highest intellectual level. The field which we abandoned was taken over by IBM. Although IBM is a fine organization in many ways, it cannot be expected to provide the atmosphere of intellectual fertility that von Neumann had created at the Institute. We had the opportunity to do it, and we threw the opportunity away.

So much for the past. How about the future? I was sorry when our computer project was destroyed because it was unique and ahead of its time. I have to confess that I am not equally sorry at the news that the Princeton-Pennsylvania accelerator is to be abandoned next year. The loss of the accelerator puts Princeton into a position similar in some respects to that of Cambridge in 1938. The leadership of accelerator physics now passes to Fermilab as then it passed to Berkeley. And Princeton has an opportunity to do something different.

What else is there for physicists to do? One possibility is to jump onto the antipollution bandwagon. I have done a little of this myself, sharing an office for a month with a professor of sanitary engineering who taught me about biological oxygen demand and activated sludge. This was great fun, and my office mate was brighter than most of the physicists I know. I would advise any physicists who have a genuine concern for the environment to take the time to find out what the problems are in the field of activated sludge. They will also find out whether they have anything useful to contribute toward solving these problems. Individual physicists, working in close collaboration with engineers and chemists and biologists, may well be able to make important contributions. However, they should not expect that what they do in the environmental field will be mainly physics. If they are any good, they will use their physics only as a cultural background in thinking about problems that are primarily chemical, biological, or political in nature. It would be a mistake for a physics department of a university to become heavily involved as a department in environmental work. Antipollution work is fine for individual physicists as members of interdisciplinary groups, but not for the central activity of a physics department. A department which rushes into environmental work just because it is fashionable is violating the second of Bragg's three rules.

2. NEW WAYS OF SEQUENCING DNA

I will talk in detail about another new direction in which physics may move and flourish during the next thirty years. This is a half-baked idea of my own which may be important for the future. If I were an experimental physicist, it is the line I would be trying to follow. I take it as self-evident that physics will not flourish in isolation from the rest of science. In particular, physics should keep in close touch with biology, since biology rather than physics is likely to be the central ground of scientific advance during the remainder of our century. Bragg understood this in 1946 when he put his money on Perutz and the X-ray analysis of hemoglobin in preference to a new accelerator. A tremendous opportunity exists now, just as it did in 1946, for making major advances in microbiology by means of physical techniques. If any of you are still young enough and have your eyes on the Nobel Prize, I advise you to think hard whether this might not be your best chance.

What I have in mind is this. The biochemists have discovered that the large molecules which dominate the basic processes of life have a simple structure. These molecules are of two kinds, proteins and nucleic acids, and both kinds are linear chains. A protein is a long string of units, each unit being one of twenty amino acids. A nucleic acid is a string of units, each being one of four nucleotides. Although the protein and nucleic acid chains are twisted and wound up in complicated ways when they are inside living cells, it seems to be true that their properties are uniquely determined by the sequence of units along the chain.

Until now we had two ways to determine the structure of these molecules. One way is X-ray crystallography, the method which Perutz used on hemoglobin and which led Crick and Watson to the double helix. The other way is wet chemistry, cooking the molecules with various reagents until they break into fragments, analyzing the fragments by chromatography, and finally deducing the sequence of the original molecule from the way the various fragments overlap. Both these methods have been used successfully on proteins and on small nucleic acids. Both methods have been brilliantly improved in recent years, so that a protein molecule like hemoglobin, which took Perutz twenty-five years to crack, can now be sequenced in less than a year. However, both methods have two basic defects which seem difficult to surmount. First, both methods require macroscopic quantities of molecules in purified form, whereas the majority of biologically important molecules occur in minute traces in a soup of similar molecules from which they can hardly be separated. Second, both methods fail on the large nucleic acids which are fundamentally the most interesting of all since they are the genetic material.

We have here an intriguing situation for a physicist. On the one hand, there is an enormous harvest of biological discoveries waiting to be reaped by the first person who can sequence an individual protein or nucleic acid molecule without going through the miseries of chemically purifying a macroscopic sample. On the other hand, the technical problem of sequencing an individual molecule, when the molecule is known to be a linear chain, is a job which modern physical methods are well suited to handle. Basically, the problem is to sort and count the units out of which the molecule is built. Sorting and counting are precisely the things that particle physicists know how to do.

Here is a possible way in which the problem might be attacked. One is trying to discover the exact sequence of nucleotides in the DNA molecules that constitute the genetic material in a living cell. One needs first to have some way of fishing out one DNA molecule at a time. One needs to separate the molecule from its watery surroundings and to support it in a vacuum without damaging it. One needs to attach the molecule firmly at one place to a solid support, while the rest of the molecule is stretched into a straight line by an electric field and hangs freely in vacuum. One needs to detach the nucleotide units, one by one in sequence, from the loose end of the chain; this is the crucial and no doubt the most difficult step. One needs to ionize the detached units so that they can be steered into a mass spectrometer. Finally, there is the easiest part of the whole operation, when the mass spectrometer sorts the ionized units into four channels labeled adenine, cytosine, guanine, and thymine, and the counters in each channel automatically record the sequence in which the units arrive.

The key to this style of analysis is to develop a technique for handling large molecules in a vacuum in such a way that one knows exactly where they are. I do not know how this can be done, but I will not be surprised if somebody learns how to do it within the next ten years. It will most likely be done by a physicist who is broad-minded enough to master the chemical idiosyncrasies of nucleotides in addition to the physics of partially wet surfaces.

If the sequencing of individual molecules by physical methods turns out to be possible, either in the way that I described or in some other way, the consequences will be startling. It will not only mean that a much wider variety of important molecules will be sequenced. The process will also be an extremely rapid one if it is feasible at all. By either of the two existing methods, the sequencing of one protein is a major project which keeps a team of talented people busy for a year or more. In contrast to this, one can envisage a physical sequencing apparatus that detaches and sorts nucleotide units at a rate of many per second, so that a giant DNA molecule would be completely analyzed in an hour. It is hard to imagine, in a process which handles individual molecules, that there could be any advantage in doing the job slowly. The increase in speed of analysis would cause a major revolution in microbiology. A single laboratory could sequence thousands of big molecules in a year instead of two or three. It would make sense to think of attacking a complete living cell and sequencing all of its protein and nucleic acid constituents. I cannot pretend to foresee what the biologists will do with all this information. At the very least, one should learn something interesting about cancer if one could compare in detail the constituents of a cancer cell with those of a normal cell from the same animal.

Some of you may object to this style of research, saying that it may be good biology but it is not physics. That is what many of us were saying about Bragg and Perutz in 1946. I believe we were profoundly mistaken. The idea that physics has to be pure in order to be good, that work on the borderline between physics and biology is beneath the dignity of a true physicist, was wrong in 1946 and is still wrong today. The surest way to save physics from stagnation or decline during the next thirty years is to keep young physicists working on the frontiers where physics overlaps other sciences such as astronomy and biology.

I described one possible example of such work, the analysis of big molecules by physically pulling them apart. It is easy to imagine other examples. One possibility which has been much discussed among molecular biologists is the development of electron microscope technology to the point at which the structure of individual molecules becomes directly visible. It might be possible in this way to achieve a nondestructive analysis of large molecules, as versatile and rapid as the destructive analysis achieved by feeding bits and pieces of the molecules into a mass spectrometer.

It would be pointless to try to make a list of important things that physicists will do in the coming decades. Inevitably, the most exciting things will be those that I did not think of. To me the most exciting part of physics at the present moment lies on the astronomical frontier, where we have just had an unparalleled piece of luck in the discovery of the pulsars. Pulsars turn out to be laboratories in which the properties of matter and radiation can be studied under conditions millions of times more extreme than we had previously available to us. We do not yet understand how pulsars work, but there are good reasons to believe that they are the accelerators in which God makes cosmic rays. Besides providing cosmic rays for particle physicists, the pulsars will during the next thirty years provide crucial tests of theory in many parts of physics ranging from superfluidity to general relativity.

It augurs well for the future of physics in Princeton that we have a first-rate group of astronomers and physicists working together on their common frontier. Some of them are making optical observations of the Crab Nebula pulsar on the Princeton campus, and I am proud to say that the Institute for Advanced Study is also contributing to their success by switching off our library lights while they observe.

I am not gloomy about the future of physics. There are only two really disastrous possibilities. One is to have solved all the major unsolved problems. That would indeed be a disaster, but I am not afraid of its happening in the foreseeable future. The other disastrous thing would be to become so pure and isolated from the practical problems of life that none of the brightest and most dedicated students want any longer to study physics. The second danger is a real one. It will not happen if we stay diversified, if we emphasize work that has important applications outside of physics, and if we follow Bragg's third rule: "Do not be afraid of the scorn of theoreticians."

CHAPTER 14

Unfashionable
Pursuits

.....

1 9 8 1

1. FASHIONS IN SCIENCE

I am delighted to be talking as a representative of the Institute for Advanced Study to an audience of Humboldt Foundation alumni, since the Institute and the Foundation are both supporting science on an international scale and are facing similar dilemmas and difficulties. We are both carrying on the tradition established by Alexander von Humboldt 150 years ago. Wanting to learn a little about von Humboldt, I went to the eleventh edition of the *Encyclopaedia Britannica,* printed in 1910, and found a splendid article written by the historian of science Agnes Clerke. If you go to later editions, you find Clerke's account only in shreds and tatters. In her article she describes the work of von Humboldt in setting up the first international network of meteorological and magnetic observation stations, and concludes with this resounding sentence: "Thus that scientific conspiracy of nations which is one of the noblest fruits of modern civilization was by his exertions first successfully organized." So that is what we are trying to do, the Institute and the Foundation, following the good example of von Humboldt. We are trying to strengthen and extend in our own era the scientific conspiracy of nations.

I decided to speak about the problem of fashions in science, since this is a problem of serious and growing importance for science generally and for the Institute and the Humboldt Foundation in particular. I shall speak first about the problem of fashion as we see it here at the Institute, then about lessons we may learn from the history of science on a longer time scale, and finally I shall explore how we may try to deal more wisely with the problem in the future.

It has always been true, and it is true now more than ever, that the path of wisdom for a young scientist of mediocre talent is to follow the prevailing fashion. Any young scientist who is not exceptionally gifted or exceptionally lucky is concerned first of all with finding and keeping a job. To find and keep a job, you have to do competent work in an area of science that the mandarins who control the job market find interesting. The scientific problems that the mandarins find interesting are, almost by definition, the fashionable problems. Nowadays the award of jobs is usually controlled not by a single mandarin but by a committee of mandarins. A committee is even less likely than an individual to break loose from the fashionable trends of the day. It is no wonder that young scientists who care for their own survival tend to keep close to the beaten paths. The leading institutions of higher learning offer security and advancement to those who skillfully follow the fashion, and only a slim chance to those who do not.

Our Institute here is no exception. When I first came here as a visiting member thirty-four years ago, the ruling mandarin was Robert Oppenheimer. Oppenheimer decided which areas of physics were worth pursuing. His tastes always coincided with the most recent fashions. Being then young and ambitious, I came to him with a quick piece of work dealing with a fashionable problem, and was duly rewarded with a permanent appointment. That is the way it was at the Institute then, and that is the way it still is now. Somebody who knows the history of the Institute may object at this point, saying that, after all, the Institute also gave a permanent appointment to Kurt Gödel. That is true. Gödel was one of the few indubitable geniuses of our century, the only one of our colleagues who walked and talked on equal terms with Einstein. Gödel worked in profoundly unfashionable areas of mathematics and became even more unfashionable as he grew older. Our institute can justly be proud of having made room for him on its faculty. There is only one fact that must temper our pride. It took the Institute fourteen years to make Gödel a professor, measured from the year he came to live and work here as an ordinary member. Gödel was such an independent and recalcitrant spirit that I suppose we deserve some credit for making him a professor at all, even after fourteen years of hesitation. Better late than never.

The young physicists who come to the Institute as members today are under much stronger pressure than I was thirty years ago. To begin with, they mostly come with money from government contracts which legally oblige them to work in a definite area of science for a definite length of time. We do not take the wording of the contracts too literally. The officials of the National Science Foundation and the Department of Energy who administer the contracts are reasonable people and allow us to interpret our obligations with some flexibility. If some of our members on contract money decide to work in areas which have nothing to do with the contracts, we are not obliged to turn them out onto the street. People whose interests do not fit into the contracts can usually be supported with Institute funds. But the contracts are a serious constraint. The contracts define in a general way the areas of work within which the visiting members of the physics school at the Institute will be active. The contracts define where the mainstream of physics is supposed to be. Inevitably, the people we invite to come here as members tend to be people whose work fits smoothly into one or another of the contracts.

I am now, after thirty years, one of the mandarins. I try in a vague and feeble way to encourage young physicists to work outside the fashionable areas. I try to keep alive a few areas of research which are not supported by contracts. I try to keep the Institute open to independent and recalcitrant spirits. I try to keep a door open in case another Kurt Gödel should one day come knocking. But I have to admit that my efforts to hold back the tide of fashion are about as effective as the efforts of my illustrious predecessor King Canute to hold back the tide of the Atlantic Ocean. The young people are compelled nowadays to follow the fashion by forces stronger than the wording of contracts and the authority of mandarins. The forces which drive the young people toward fashionable pursuits are peer pressure and the excitement of the chase itself. They know where the action is, and they want to be part of it. They know that they have only a short time to prove themselves as scientists. They know that their best chance of achieving something worthwhile in the short span of time allotted to them is to go with the crowd, to grab the scientific fruit quickly where it is ripe for picking.

The running of young scientists after quick success and quick rewards is not in itself bad. The concentration of their efforts into narrow areas of fashionable specialization is not necessarily harmful. After all, the fashionable problems become fashionable not by the whim of some dress designer but because a substantial majority of scientists judges them to be important. As a general rule, the judgment of the majority is well founded. The fashionable areas are often those in which crucially important discoveries are made. There is nothing wrong in a young scientist rushing into these areas in the hope of making a sensational discovery. Indeed, the joy and excitement of daily life at the Institute are greatly enhanced by the gregarious nature of research in the fashionable areas. When you are exploring in a fashionable area, every petty success and every ephemeral triumph can be shared with friends at the lunch table or the seminar. Without this communal interest in fashionable problems, without this sharing of news and rumors, our life here would be much the poorer.

Why then am I dissatisfied? Why am I grumbling at the young people for doing what I myself did when I was their age? I am grumbling because I do not think the fashionable stuff ought to be a hundred percent of what we do here. The fashionable stuff is useful and important and exciting. We can be proud that our young people do the fashionable stuff and do it well. We can expect that a majority of them will always prefer to do the fashionable stuff, for reasons that I understand and respect. I am only saying that we ought to have room here also for a minority who do not do the fashionable stuff. We ought to seek out and encourage the rare individualists who do not fit into the prevailing pattern. We ought to bias our admission of members a little toward unorthodox and unconventional spirits. If we here do not give the practitioners of unfashionable science a home and a place to work, who will?

2. ANCIENT HISTORY

There are many kinds of unfashionable science. One of the main difficulties of supporting it is the problem of selection. Unfashionable science comes in a thousand different shapes without any unifying structure. Let me give an example. Last week I was walking across the Forrestal Campus of Princeton University and came upon two graduate students sitting quietly in the middle of a field. I thought at first they were just enjoying the sunshine and the silence of an August afternoon, but when I came closer I saw that they were working with intense concentration, performing some delicate manipulations which required steady hands and freedom from distracting interruptions. Coming closer still, I saw that they were busily gluing little lead weights to the backs of honeybees. I watched in silence until they were finished, then walked with them back to their experimental hive which is equipped with cameras and videotape recorders. They are refining and extending the classic experiments of Karl von Frisch on the dance communication system of bees. They have found that bees dance more vigorously and more accurately when they have found a source of honey at a considerable distance from the hive. Unfortunately, the majority of bees find honey close to the hive and make only a brief and perfunctory dance when they return. The students want to observe the dance with high accuracy, so they have found a way to trick the bees into dancing more vigorously. A bee weighed down with forty-five milligrams of lead thinks she has made a long flight when she actually made a short one. She measures the length of a flight by the effort it costs her to fly. So the bees which carry weights dance accurately after every find.

That is a typical example of unfashionable science, being done right here on our doorstep in Princeton. I am not suggesting that the Institute for Advanced Study ought to support a school of entomology. But the example of the bee experiments shows all the characteristic features that make unfashionable science difficult to support: small scale, diversity of objectives, idiosyncratic style, and a certain lack of superficial seriousness.

To make clear the real and lasting importance of unfashionable science, I return to the field in which I am expert, namely mathematical physics. Mathematical physics is the discipline of people who try to reach a deep understanding of physical phenomena by following the rigorous style and method of pure mathematics. It is a discipline that lies on the border between physics and mathematics. The purpose of mathematical physicists is not to calculate phenomena quantitatively but to understand them qualitatively. They work with theorems and proofs, not with numbers and computers. Their aim is to clarify with mathematical precision the meaning of the concepts upon which physical theories are built.

Mathematical physics has three qualities which make it peculiarly relevant to the present discussion. First, it is important. It supplies basic ideas and vocabulary to the more practical areas of physics. Second, it is slow, taking typically fifty or a hundred years to develop a new concept from its origin to its fruitful application. Third, it is almost always unfashionable, since its rhythms run about ten times slower than the rhythms of scientific fashion. And because it is unfashionable, it has always been more highly regarded and better supported in Europe than in the United States.

As an example of a great mathematical physicist whose work is of crucial importance to the development of physics at the present time, I mention the name of Sophus Lie. Lie has been dead for eighty years. His great work was done in the 1870s and 1880s, but it has come to dominate the thinking of particle physicists only in the last twenty years. Lie was the first to understand and state explicitly that the principles of physics have a group-theoretical origin. He constructed almost single-handedly a vast and beautiful theory of continuous groups, which he foresaw would one day serve as a foundation of physics. Now, a hundred years later, all the physicists who classify particles in terms of broken and unbroken symmetries are, whether they are aware of it or not, talking the language of Sophus Lie. But in his lifetime Lie's ideas remained unfashionable, little understood by mathematicians and not at all by physicists. Felix Klein was one of the few leading mathematicians who understood and supported him.

Lie was one of those people who seem to have more than their fair share of bad luck. He was wandering around France as a young man when the Franco-Prussian War of 1870 broke out. He was Norwegian and spoke French with what sounded like a Prussian accent. The patriotic citizens of Fontainebleau decided he was a Prussian spy and threw him into jail. Meanwhile, France lost the war and conditions became generally chaotic. Lie was sitting quietly in his cell, working out his new mathematical discoveries, when his French friends finally found out where he was and succeeded in getting him released. In Rouse Ball's history of mathematics, published around the turn of the century, the account of Lie's work ends on a melancholy note: "Lie seems to have been disappointed and soured by the absence of any general recognition of the value of his results. . . . He brooded over what he deemed was the undue neglect of the past, and the happiness of the last decade of his life was much affected by it."

Another great genius of mathematical physics, even more unfashionable in his own day than Sophus Lie, was Hermann Grassmann. As a high-school teacher in Stettin, he published in 1844 a work entitled *Die Lineale Ausdehnungslehre* (The Calculus of Extension), introducing for the first time the basic notions of a vector, of a vector space, and of an anticommuting algebra. All these notions have been of central importance for the physics of the twentieth century, but not of the nineteenth. In his own century, Grassmann remained an obscure teacher in Stettin, ignored by the academic mandarins of his time. But he had a greater resiliency of spirit than Sophus Lie. Instead of brooding like Lie over his lack of recognition among the mathematicians, Grassmann started a second career as a student of Sanskrit and achieved a modest fame as translator of the Rig-Veda into German. Perhaps, if it is your fate to be an unrecognized mathematical genius, it is better for your health to earn a living as a high-school teacher rather than to be a university professor.

While preparing my remarks for this meeting, I went to the Institute library and was happy to find there a copy of the 1878 edition of the *Ausdehnungslehre* with the name of Hermann Minkowski, teacher of Einstein and first among mathematicians to understand relativity, written on the front page in pencil. I conjecture that this copy came to us through the hands of Hermann Weyl, who had been a friend of Minkowski and was responsible for stocking our library with books when the Institute began. The 1878 edition has a preface by Grassmann, still writing from Stettin and cheerfully expressing the hope that the new edition will receive more attention from the learned world than the first edition had received thirty-four years earlier. At the end of the preface is a footnote saying, "The author died while this book was in press." It was only in the 1890s that Felix Klein, always generous in fighting for unfashionable causes, organized the official recognition of Grassmann and the publication of his collected works.

A more recent example of a great discovery in mathematical physics is the idea of a gauge field, invented by Hermann Weyl himself in 1918. This idea has taken only fifty years to find its place as one of the basic concepts of modern particle physics. The history of Weyl's discovery is unlike the history of Lie groups and Grassmann algebras. Weyl was neither obscure nor unrecognized, and he was working in 1918 in the most fashionable area of physics, the newborn theory of general relativity. He invented gauge fields as a solution to the fashionable problem of unifying gravitation with electromagnetism. For a few months gauge fields were at the height of fashion. Then it was discovered by Weyl and others that they did not do what was expected of them. Gauge fields were in fact useless for the purpose for which Weyl invented them. They quickly became unfashionable and were almost forgotten. But then, gradually over the next fifty years, it became clear that gauge fields were useful in a different context. The decisive step in the rehabilitation of gauge fields was taken by our Institute colleague, Frank Yang, and one of his students, Bob Mills, in 1954, one year before the death of Hermann Weyl. There is no evidence that Weyl ever knew or cared what Yang and Mills had done with his brainchild.

The story of gauge fields is full of ironies. A fashionable idea, invented for a purpose which turns out to be ephemeral, survives a long period of obscurity and emerges finally as a cornerstone of physics. Such ironies are not unusual in the long history of mathematical physics. Another example is Gauss's invention of differential geometry, originating as a by-product of his work on the practical problems of geodesy and mapmaking, transformed into a new world of abstract generality by the genius of Riemann, and finally emerging fifty years later as the conceptual basis of Einstein's theory of gravitation. Common to these examples are the long time scale, usually longer than a human lifetime from start to finish, and the totally unpredictable quality of the final outcome. In no case did the inventor of the crucial concept have the slightest inkling of the physical context in which his invention would find its ultimate fruition.

I have given enough examples to prove my point, that unfashionable people and unfashionable ideas have often been of decisive importance to the progress of science. The time has now come to talk about the present and the future. I see no reason to expect that the pattern of development of scientific ideas in the future will be different from what it has been in the past. We must expect unfashionable ideas to emerge into importance as frequently in the future as they have done in the past, usually after long periods of gestation and in unfamiliar contexts. The problems which we face as guardians of scientific progress are how to recognize the fruitful unfashionable idea, and how to support it.

3. THE MONSTER AND THE MORAL

For a start, we may look around at the world of mathematics and see whether we can identify unfashionable ideas which might later emerge as essential building blocks for the physics of the twenty-first century. If we are lucky, we may find some good candidates for future greatness. We cannot expect to know in our own lifetimes whether we picked the right ones.

The guardians of mathematical orthodoxy in this century are a cabal of mathematicians writing collectively under the French nom de plume N. Bourbaki. Roughly speaking, unfashionable mathematics consists of those parts of mathematics which were declared by the mandarins of Bourbaki not to be mathematics. A number of beautiful mathematical discoveries fall into this category. To be mathematics according to Bourbaki, an idea should be general, abstract, coherent, and connected by clear logical relationships with the rest of mathematics. Excluded from mathematics according to Bourbaki are particular facts, concrete objects which happen to exist for no identifiable reason, things which a mathematician would call accidental or sporadic. Unfashionable mathematics is mainly concerned with things of accidental beauty, special functions, particular number fields, exceptional algebras, sporadic finite groups. It is among these unorganized and undisciplined parts of mathematics that I would advise you to look for the next revolution in physics. They have a quality of strangeness, of unexpectedness. They do not fit easily into the smooth logical structures of Bourbaki. Just for that reason we should cherish and cultivate them, remembering the words of Francis Bacon which our director Harry Woolf used as theme song of the Institute's Einstein Centennial celebration two years ago: "There is no excellent beauty that hath not some strangeness in the proportion."

As an example of strangeness in the proportion, I speak briefly about sporadic finite groups. Their history begins with the French mathematician Emile Mathieu, who discovered the first of them in the year 1861 and the second in 1873. Mathieu, as is usual in such cases, did not know that he had invented sporadic groups. The word "group" does not appear in the titles of his papers. But he knew that he had found something beautiful and important. Using the language of geometry, we may say that he had found that there exist, in spaces of twelve and twenty-four dimensions, structures of a peculiar symmetry which do not occur in spaces with any number of dimensions different from twelve or twenty-four. His work was published, but remained for a hundred years unfashionable. It was, as orthodox mathematicians like to say, an isolated curiosity.

About seventy-five years later the Mathieu groups turned out to have some practical use in the business of code making. Each Mathieu group forms the basis for the design of a uniquely efficient error-correcting code. This mundane utility of the Mathieu groups did nothing to raise their status in the eyes of mathematicians whose tastes were formed by Bourbaki. Then rather suddenly, in the last twenty years, a magnificent zoo of new sporadic groups was discovered by a variety of mathematicians working with a variety of methods. Some of them were discovered by following the ideas of Mathieu, others by studying the peculiarly unfashionable problem of packing twenty-four-dimensional billiard balls as tightly as possible into a twenty-four-dimensional Euclidean space, others by testing permutations and combinations with big computers.

The only thing these various discoveries had in common was a concrete, empirical, experimental, accidental quality, directly antithetical to the spirit of Bourbaki. Altogether twenty-five sporadic groups, including those of Mathieu, were discovered. Meanwhile, the fraternity of professional group theorists, using more general and abstract methods, succeeded in proving that the total number of sporadic groups could not be larger than twenty-six. So we reached the situation two years ago that only one more sporadic group remained to be found. It was known that this last group, if it existed, would be the biggest and most beautiful of all. It was given the nicknames "Monster" and "Friendly Giant" by the people who were hunting for it.

The end of the story came last year when Bob Griess, visiting here at the Institute from the University of Michigan, found the way to construct the Monster. Just yesterday I received from Michigan the final installment of a long paper containing a complete and definitive account of his work. The Monster is now revealed in all its glory to those who take the trouble to understand the details of Bob Griess's construction. The last and greatest of the sporadic groups, it now stands forever, unique and unassailable, a monument more durable than bronze.

What has all this to do with physics? Probably nothing. Probably, the sporadic groups are merely a pleasant backwater in the history of mathematics, an odd little episode far from the mainstream of progress. We have never seen the slightest hint that the symmetries of the physical universe are in any way connected with the symmetries of the sporadic groups. So far as we know, the physical universe would look and function just as it does, whether or not the sporadic groups existed. But we should not be too sure that there is no connection. Absence of evidence is not the same thing as evidence of absence. Stranger things have happened in the history of physics than the unexpected appearance of sporadic groups. We should always be prepared for surprises. I have a sneaking hope, a hope unsupported by any facts or any evidence, that sometime in the twenty-first century physicists will stumble upon the Monster group, built in some unsuspected way into the structure of the universe. This is only a wild speculation. The only argument I can produce in its favor is a theological one. We have strong evidence that the creator of the universe loves symmetry, and if he loves symmetry, what lovelier symmetry could he find than the symmetry of the Monster?

The sporadic groups are only one example from the treasure-house of weird and wonderful concepts that unfashionable mathematicians have created. I could mention many others. Can you imagine a regular polyhedron, a body composed of perfectly symmetrical cells arranged in a perfectly symmetrical pattern, having a total of eleven faces? Last year my friend Donald Coxeter in Toronto discovered it. Is it possible that the zeros of the zeta function, whose properties were conjectured by Riemann a hundred and twenty years ago and still remain one of the central mysteries of mathematics, will turn out to have connections with the world of physics? Last year Andrew Odlyzko, a mathematician at Bell Laboratories working with a Cray computer, found some new and unexpected properties of zeta-function zeros. Is it possible that the incompleteness theorems of Kurt Gödel, proving that there are questions in pure mathematics which any given finite set of axioms and rules of inference are unable to answer, will one day give us a deeper understanding of the limitations of our knowledge of the physical universe? Wherever you look in the realm of ideas, you find hints of revelations still to come, whispers of hidden connections.

Now my time is up, and I must keep my promise to give you some practical advice about the support of science. I am saying, both to the Institute for Advanced Study and to the Humboldt Foundation, that it is our duty and our privilege as independent organizations to be less shortsighted than our governments. Our role should be to take a longer view of science than either politicians or postdoctoral students can afford. What does the longer view of science teach us? What moral is to be drawn from the various stories that I have told? The moral is a simple one. We ought to give greater attention and greater support to unfashionable research. At any particular moment in the history of science, the most important and fruitful ideas are often lying dormant merely because they are unfashionable. Especially in mathematical physics, there is commonly a lag of fifty or a hundred years between the conception of a new idea and its emergence into the mainstream of scientific thought. If this is the time scale of fundamental advance, it follows that anybody doing fundamental work in mathematical physics is almost certain to be unfashionable.

We should not stop supporting the fashionable research that

keeps most of our young scientists busy and happy. But we should set aside a certain fraction of our resources, perhaps a tenth or perhaps a quarter, for the support of unfashionable people doing unfashionable things. We should not be afraid of looking foolish or even crazy. We should not be afraid of supporting risky ventures which may fail totally. Since we are independent, we have the right to take risks and to make mistakes. Organizations which only support research where there is no risk and no chance of mistakes will in the end support only mediocrity. If we proceed with good sense and courage to support unfashionable people doing things that orthodox opinion considers irrelevant or crazy, there is a good chance that we shall rescue for science an occasional Sophus Lie or Hermann Grassmann, people whose ideas will still be famous long after our contemporary fashionable excitements are forgotten.

CHAPTER 15

Astronomy in a Private Sphere

.....

1 9 8 4

I. THE LEGACY OF GEORGE HALE

In the year 1897 a famous cartoon appeared in a newspaper in Chicago. Underneath it is the caption: "The Biggest in the World. A Contrast in Modern Civilization." The cartoon shows on the right an unflattering portrait of the old Queen of Prussia, standing in front of the giant siege gun Big Bertha, with a banner carrying the word "Destruction." On the left is a handsome young lady, representing America, standing in front of the new telescope that had been given to the University of Chicago by the millionaire Charles Yerkes. Around the tube of the telescope is wrapped a banner with the word "Instruction." The citizens of Chicago at that time were proud of their rapidly growing university and equally proud of their giant telescope. Another newspaper reported the dedication ceremonies of the telescope with the headlines: YERKES BREAKS INTO SOCIETY. STREET-CAR BOSS USES A TELESCOPE AS A KEY TO THE TEMPLE DOOR. AND IT FITS PERFECTLY.

So Charles Yerkes gave his money and had his rewards, an entrée to the intellectual elite of Chicago, and his name attached to an observatory of world class. The Yerkes Observatory brought about a revolution in observational astronomy. It was the first observatory specifically designed for doing astrophysics. That is to say, it was not just a telescope in a dome, but it included a well-

173

equipped physical laboratory where starlight could be analyzed with sophisticated optical and spectroscopic devices. It was the first observatory built in the modern style, with optical shops, computing rooms, and laboratories taking up more space than telescopes. It was the first observatory in which a modern professional astronomer would feel at home.

The building of the Yerkes Observatory was not only an important event in the history of astronomy. It was also a typical example of a pattern that was to be repeated many times in the century that followed. The pattern is a juxtaposition of two apparently discordant themes. On the one hand, astronomy as a public entertainment, promoted by newspaper cartoonists and other representatives of the mass media, catering to the civic pride and superficial curiosity of a naive and ignorant citizenry. On the other hand, astronomy as a highly specialized and esoteric field of research, pursued by trained professionals and published in journals that only trained professionals can read. How does it happen that these two themes, the vulgar and the arcane, not only do not clash but even make sweet harmony together? When we look to the future and see every branch of astronomical science continuing to grow more specialized and more remote from its origins, how can we expect that public support for astronomy will be maintained? The two questions are not unrelated. If the future of astronomy is bright, it is precisely because there is here a natural community of interest between the professionals and the public. It was this community of interest, and not any unusual personal commitment of Charles Yerkes to astronomy, that made it appropriate for him to choose a telescope as his key to the temple door.

The brain that conceived and designed the Yerkes Observatory was not the brain of Charles Yerkes. The brain belonged to George Hale. In 1892, when the plan for the new observatory came into his head, Hale was twenty-four years old and a newly appointed associate professor of astrophysics at the University of Chicago. He wasted no time. Thirty years later Hale described how he went about the job of fund-raising:

> I visited several men who might conceivably be willing
> to provide for the telescope. But no one had the money to
> spare. A few days later I made another fruitless round of

visits in the city. At noon, somewhat discouraged, I called
at the Corn Exchange Bank to see Mr. Charles Hutchin-
son. . . . After explaining my object, I asked for suggestions. "Why don't you try Mr. Yerkes?" he replied. "He has
talked of the possibility of making some gift to the University, and might be attracted by this scheme." So I went at
once to President Harper, then at the threshold of his tremendous task of building the University of Chicago. After
a few questions, he heartily approved of the attempt, asked
me to write out a statement of the plan, and sent it to Mr.
Yerkes. A reply came back asking us to call on him. We did
so, and before the interview was over, Mr. Yerkes asked us
to telegraph the lens-maker Alvan Clark, with whom he
made a contract for the forty-inch objective. I remember
with pleasure Dr. Harper's enthusiasm as we left the office.
"I'd like to go to the top of a hill and yell," he cried.

Hale now had Yerkes hooked but not yet landed. Hale needed
not just a forty-inch lens but a telescope mount and a dome and a
stellar spectrograph and an observatory building three hundred
feet long. Over the next three years, Charles Yerkes was persuaded to provide all these things, slowly and painfully, one at a
time. Five years passed before the observatory was finished and
Yerkes earned his reward of presiding over the dedication ceremonies. Meanwhile, George Hale had founded the *Astrophysical
Journal,* the leading professional astronomical journal in the
world, and had secured the mirror-blank for a sixty-inch reflect-
ing telescope to put into his next observatory.

The next observatory happened to be at Mount Wilson in California, to which Hale moved in 1904. He installed his 60-inch reflector there in 1908. This time the telescope and the buildings
were paid for by Andrew Carnegie, who was subjected to the
same treatment as Charles Yerkes and succumbed even more
quickly. The citizens of Pasadena were as proud of their big new
telescope as the citizens of Chicago had been of theirs. Andrew
Carnegie made the mistake of coming in person to visit Mount
Wilson two years after the 60-inch reflector was installed. He
spent a rainy night on the mountain with Hale and saw no stars.
As a result, he found himself paying for a large share of the 100-

inch telescope that went into operation alongside the 60-inch seven years later.

Hale afterward explained why he felt himself compelled to make such immodest demands on Mr. Carnegie's generosity: "I was thus bound to undertake the heavy task of raising funds or to forego the possibilities I seemed to see ahead. These were nothing less than an effective union of astronomy and physics, directed primarily toward the solution of the problem of stellar evolution, but with equal consideration of the advantages to be gained by fundamental physics from such a joint study." A fair and balanced verdict on Hale's career was pronounced long after his death by Hunter Dupree: "Hale was one of the first prototypes of the high-pressure, heavy-hardware, big-spending, team-organized scientific entrepreneurs. Would that all who followed him on this path had his technical competence, his clarity of scientific objective, and his breadth of view."

Hale's final adventure, the planning and building of the two-hundred-inch telescope on Mount Palomar, belongs to a more modern era. Instead of raising the funds from Mr. John D. Rockefeller personally, as he would have done in the old days, Hale had to deal with the administrative apparatus of the International Education Board of the Rockefeller Foundation. But the result was the same. Six million dollars flowed out of the Rockefeller coffers, and the telescope that bears Hale's name dominated observational astronomy for a quarter of a century.

George Hale was preeminent as organizer of the private support of astronomy. Yet astronomy today is supported by governments, not by millionaires. The era of private endowment of major scientific enterprises is generally believed to be past. How then can George Hale and his millionaire friends be relevant to the problems of the funding of science in the 1980s? George Hale is relevant to our present-day problems because the private support of astronomy was never really private. In the transactions between Hale and his millionaire friends, the public was involved in essentially the same way as the public is involved in the negotiations between a present-day scientific entrepreneur and his congressional appropriations committee. Charles Yerkes was not buying the Yerkes Observatory for himself but for the citizens of Chicago. He felt himself to be an agent of the public, and he would not have acted as he did if he had not been confident of public approval. The inauguration of the observatory was reported by another Chicago newspaper under the headlines: "FEAST OF WISE MEN. YERKES GIVES A BANQUET TO VISITORS AND CITIZENS. SCIENTISTS LAUD THE UNIVERSITY TELESCOPE. DONOR SAYS IT IS FOR ALL." A congressman inaugurating a national laboratory today would say exactly the same thing: "Donor says it is for all." Whether the donor is a millionaire, a private foundation established by a millionaire, or a committee of Congress, the gift is given because the donor believes it to be in the public interest. The task of the professional astronomer today is the same as the task that was performed so brilliantly by George Hale—namely, to persuade the donor that first-rate professional work in astronomy is what the public wants. If the astronomer succeeds in this task, he will be able to say, as George Hale said at the end of his life, "The truth is, of course, that I have been enjoying from boyhood the things I most liked to do, and why should one be praised for simply having a good time? If this has helped other men to enjoy themselves also, this has added to my pleasure."

The era of private endowment of astronomical observatories is not entirely at an end. It is true that the steady growth of major observatories during the last thirty years has been mainly funded by governments. The two big new American observatories at Kitt Peak in Arizona and Cerro Tololo, Chile, the Anglo-Australian Observatory in Australia, the European Southern Observatory in Chile, and the Soviet six-meter telescope at Zelenchukskaya— these were all paid for with public money. Simultaneously with this multiplication of optical telescopes, an equally impressive program of construction of radio telescopes, infrared telescopes, and X-ray telescopes has been going forward, likewise paid for by government funds. As a general rule, when public money moves into any area of human activity, private money is driven out. But astronomical research is an exception to the rule. While public support has been increasing, private money has not been entirely driven out. Alongside the two great publicly supported observatories in Chile, one American and the other European, a third observatory has recently been completed at Las Campanas, built and staffed by the private resources of the Carnegie Institution of Washington, D.C. In addition to the new Las Campanas Observatory, the old observatories of the Hale era are still vigorously active and still in private hands. In the quality of the equipment and in the professionalism of the work done, there is no noticeable difference between the publicly and privately funded observatories. Astronomers do not particularly care who signs their paychecks, provided that the paychecks continue to arrive regularly. But it is important that they still have a substantial source of funds independent of government. This insulates them to some extent from the rapidly fluctuating political constraints to which government funding agencies are subject.

It is not easy to keep alive the tradition of independent private funding in an era of big government and continuing inflation. The Carnegie Institution is the chief sustainer of that tradition; it runs the Mount Wilson Observatory in California and the Las Campanas Observatory in Chile and pays the salaries of their staffs. Unfortunately, the salaries are no longer paid, as they were until recently, entirely from private funds. I quote now from the 1978 report of James Ebert, president of the Carnegie Institution:

> Our catalogue for 1978–1979 reads, "All salaries of Staff Members and supporting technical and administrative staff are met from Institution funds. Funds from other suitable sources are accepted or administered by the Institution usually for the provision of equipment or for fellowship grants supplementing the Institution's own fellowship fund." This statement of policy reflects a rich and treasured tradition of the Institution. That tradition must now be breached. This decision, which has been long in coming, was not reached without soul-searching by all of us. My principal concerns are shared by Trustees and Staff Members alike: that our increasing dependence upon external support will reduce the degree of flexibility with which our Staff Members pursue inquiries of their own choice; that our research will be skewed toward questions for which external funding is most readily available; that our autonomy will be reduced; and that our Staff Members' identification with the Institution will be weakened. . . . Unfortunately, knowing all these pitfalls does not mean that we know how to avoid them.

Does this decision mean that the tradition of private support of astronomy is finally dead? I do not think so. The tradition is breached, but it is still alive. The Carnegie Institution is still supporting astronomy on a large scale. If ever the government should interfere unacceptably with scientific programs or abandon support of astronomical research altogether, the Carnegie Institution can always reassert its authority and keep its observatories running with its own resources. The future is unpredictable. Many people believe that we are on a one-way slide toward centralization and governmental control of scientific activities. But it is possible that the tide will turn the other way, that future economic and political trends will favor decentralization and a revival of influence of private institutions.

2. THE AMATEURS AND THE PROFESSIONALS

One great advantage of astronomy in the competition for public funds is that it is not yet completely professionalized. In almost every country of the world there is a large group of skilled and serious amateur astronomers forming a bridge between the professionals and the public. In 1979 three supernovas were discovered in external galaxies, two by professionals and one by an amateur. A mixed group of amateurs and semiprofessionals in California, calling themselves the Monterey Institute for Research in Astronomy, has built and equipped an observatory at which they do work of fully professional quality. Other groups of amateurs are less ambitious and only go outdoors occasionally for a brief look at the moon and the planets. But the widespread amateur activity gives the public a feeling of familiarity with the practice of astronomy. Astronomy is not a science like nuclear physics or biochemistry, remote and incomprehensible to ordinary mortals. Everybody has seen pictures of comets and galaxies. All of us can imagine ourselves sitting at the business end of a telescope and discovering a supernova, even if we are not quite sure what a supernova is. When a professional astronomer comes before a congressional committee to ask for funds, the committee does not need to be told what astronomy is. The committee members know approximately what the astronomer will be doing and why it may be exciting.

The great majority of professional astronomers are like professional physicists or professional chemists, products of a specialized academic training. They spend their young years at universities being stuffed full of specialized information, and finally emerge with a Ph.D., which they hope will entitle them to practice their trade of teaching and research in astronomy for the rest of their lives. These Ph.D. astronomers are the backbone of the profession. They are dedicated and capable people. They staff our observatories and universities and work night and day at the tough and demanding job of exploring the universe. They constantly push to extend the limits of sensitivity of their instruments, and they struggle to build coherent theoretical understanding out of faint signals hardly distinguishable from noise.

They are, in the best sense of the word, a priesthood, a group of people trained and dedicated to the pursuit of unworldly knowledge. They have the virtues and the defects of a priesthood. Their virtues are seriousness of purpose, intellectual integrity, and a practical willingness to help one another in spite of professional rivalries. Their defects are exclusiveness, one might even say arrogance, a deeply ingrained belief that the world owes them a living, and an inability to talk on equal terms with people outside who do not belong to the fraternity. The inability to talk informally is a grave weakness when astronomers come before congressional committees to ask for public support. It is no accident that George Hale, the most successful astronomical fundraiser in history, did not have a Ph.D. He had no lack of professional competence. He personally invented the spectroheliograph and used it to take the first detailed pictures of the sun's atmosphere. He discovered the magnetic fields in sunspots. But he was too busy building observatories to have time for a Ph.D. A bachelor of science degree from MIT was good enough for him. And this probably made it easier for him to talk to millionaires in a language they could understand.

Fortunately, there has always been room in the astronomical profession for a minority of unconventional spirits who do not fit into the normal academic mold. The two most famous examples of nonacademic astronomers in this century were Bernhard Schmidt and Milton Humason. Bernhard Schmidt invented the Schmidt telescope, which takes wide-angle pictures with sharp focus. The Schmidt telescope made possible the all-sky photographic surveys that observers use routinely to locate interesting objects. It is hard to imagine how modern observers could find their way around the sky if they did not have the sky survey prints handy in a convenient drawer at the observatory.

Bernhard Schmidt grew up on a farm on a small island in the Gulf of Finland, then belonging to the Russian empire. At the age of eleven he began doing experiments with homemade gunpowder and blew off his right hand. After that, working with his left hand, using a cigar box and the bottom of a beer bottle that he had ground into a lens in a saucer of fine sand, he built a camera and took pictures with it. When he was grown, he moved to Mittweida, a town in Germany, and lived there for twenty-five years, supporting himself by making mirrors and lenses. At the age of twenty-six he made a 16-inch mirror of higher quality than all the telescope mirrors then in use. That made him famous, and he was kept busy with orders from professional observatories. Finally, at the age of forty-seven, he accepted a semiprofessional position as a "voluntary colleague" at the Hamburg Observatory. There he invented and built the first Schmidt telescope. The astronomer Walter Baade describes how he appeared to his colleagues in Hamburg:

> A highly unusual man, this Bernhard Schmidt. He always worked in the claw-hammer cutaway coat and striped trousers of formal attire. He rebelled at any regular working hours. Money meant nothing to him. He liked his schnapps, and chain-smoked good cigars. His friends were few, for he was shy and retiring. He prized his independence above everything else.
>
> By the summer of 1930 he had completed his first 14-inch Schmidt. He called me one sultry Sunday afternoon to say it was ready. From an attic window of the observatory he trained it on a cemetery. "Can you read the names on the tombstones?" he asked. "Yes," I replied, "but I can see only one thing: the optics are absolutely marvelous."

Schmidt published only one paper in his life, at the age of fifty-two. It is three pages long.

While Schmidt was making his reputation as a lens grinder in

Mittweida, Milton Humason was living by himself on Mount Wilson in California. Humason was fourteen years old. He had dropped out of high school after finishing eighth grade because he liked living wild on Mount Wilson better than sitting in class. He was roaming around Mount Wilson when George Hale came by and decided to build his new observatory there. Humason did not meet Hale at that time. But when the construction of the observatory began and the mule trains began to wind their way up the trail to the top of the mountain, Humason took a job as a mule driver. He drove mules up and down the mountain for a couple of years and began talking to the people who were building the observatory. He began to be interested in what the observatory was for. When the building was finished, he took a job as a janitor and moved inside. Soon after that he married the daughter of the chief engineer. Soon after that he began helping the astronomers develop their plates in the darkroom. A little later he began helping astronomers expose their plates at the telescope. After a few years he was taken on as a regular night assistant, and at the age of twenty-nine he became a professional astronomer, a full member of the observatory staff. For the rest of his life he worked at the 100- and 200-inch telescopes, pushing ever further the art of measuring redshifts of remote galaxies, and thereby uncovering the large-scale architecture of the universe.

I tell these stories of Schmidt and Humason, not just to evoke a sentimental glow of nostalgia for the good old days when life was simpler than it is now. Schmidt and Humason were a part of modern astronomy. It was vitally important for the flourishing of astronomy in this century that people like Schmidt and Humason could be brought into the profession from the outside, without any academic credentials, and were even welcomed as colleagues by the people on the inside. The examples of Schmidt and Humason show that the astronomical fraternity is not after all a closed priesthood, jealously guarding its professional privileges. Or at least it was not so until recently.

What is the situation now? Would it be possible today for a mule driver with an eighth-grade education to become a staff member at a major observatory? Would it be possible for a one-armed lens grinder to be invited there as an honored guest? I do not know. I hope the answer to these questions would be yes, but

I am not sure. It is important, if the astronomical community is to maintain in the future the good public relations that it has had in the past, that the doors of the temple of science be kept open to outsiders. If under present conditions a high-school dropout like Humason or a self-taught optical genius like Schmidt has no hope of acceptance into the academic hierarchy, then the astronomical profession is likely to run into serious trouble. The public has a way of reacting strongly against any group of people who claim superior status and privileges for its members on the basis of paper qualifications. If astronomy has become a closed shop in which only people formally qualified with a Ph.D. are permitted to work, then science is hurt in two ways. Science is hurt immediately, because some of the most creative and inventive spirits are kept out of it. And science is hurt in the long run, because the public is intelligent enough to tell the difference between a challenging intellectual adventure and a welfare program for holders of the Ph.D.

Fortunately for the future of astronomy, the nature of the subject makes the atmosphere of a closed shop hard to sustain. New instruments and new objects of study are constantly emerging. Each new instrument and each new discovery bring new people with them into the astronomical profession. The old fraternity of optical astronomers is constantly rejuvenated by fresh influxes of radio astronomers, X-ray astronomers, plasma physicists, planetary geologists, and meteoritic chemists. And optical astronomy itself does not stand still, but brings in fresh crowds of electronic and computer experts to build the new optical detectors that are now replacing Humason's photographic plates.

One aspect of astronomy that does not change is a peculiar affinity between those who love to explore the sky and those who love to explore the natural beauty of the earth. I mentioned earlier the Monterey Institution for Research in Astronomy, a group of serious amateur astronomers who have proved that it is still possible to do work of professional quality with private funds. One of the chief patrons and supporters of the Monterey Institution was Ansel Adams, the great photographer of our western mountains. Ansel Adams was not the first nature lover to be favorably disposed toward astronomy. When George Hale welcomed Andrew Carnegie at the newly built Mount Wilson Observatory in 1910, he stood with Carnegie and a group of friends for an official photograph. There in the photograph, between Hale and Carnegie, stands the tall and dignified figure of John Muir.

3. ENTERTAINMENT, INSTRUCTION, AND MONUMENTS

In 1979 the late Philip Handler, then president of the National Academy of Sciences, put up a big statue of Einstein on the grounds of the academy building in Washington. He thought it would be a good idea to bring Einstein, the most famous scientist, and with the possible exception of Charlie Chaplin the most famous person in twentieth-century America, to his rightful place on the tourist circuit, where he could be seen in the company of his peers Jefferson and Lincoln. Handler tackled this project as George Hale would have tackled it, moving swiftly and decisively to override any possible opposition. He commissioned the statue at a cost of $1.5 million from the sculptor Robert Berks, raised half of the money in a hurry from private donors, and borrowed the rest from a bank. Immediately, there arose a storm of protest from the academic community. Academy members and scientists protested because they had not been consulted about the design and the financing of the monument. Professional artists protested because the sculptor had not been selected in proper fashion by a jury of artists and connoisseurs. Intellectual snobs of all kinds protested because the statue is a vulgar realistic portrait rather than an abstract composition conforming to the prevalent fashions in academic art. Handler was shocked and amazed by the bitterness and intensity of the protests. But he went ahead boldly and put up the statue in time for the Einstein centennial in 1979. You can see it for yourselves whenever you go to Washington. If you are brave, you may even admit that you like it. I like it myself, although I do not dare to say so in Princeton.

Two years later I happened to meet Philip Handler in Washington, and I asked him whether he felt the statue had been worth all the abuse he had had to take from his academic colleagues. Would he do it again if he had the choice? Handler replied emphatically, yes. He first knew for sure that the statue was right when it came to graduation time in the spring of 1980. He watched out of his office window and saw group after group of kids, mostly black, come from the high schools of Washington in their caps and gowns on graduation day to have their graduation photographs taken in front of Einstein's statue. When Handler saw that, he knew the struggle had not been in vain. With this statue, the academy has for the first time given the people of Washington something they can feel and touch, something they can be proud of, something they can in some sense possess.

The story of the Einstein statue carries a lesson for any scientist or astronomer seeking public support. The public has a soul. The public can usually tell the difference between real greatness and academic pretension. The public responded warmly to Einstein because it saw in him a truly great man without pretensions. The public supported George Hale for the same reason. The public does not expect much in return from the people it supports. It expects honest work, professional competence, and the opportunity to participate to the extent possible in the processes of scientific discovery. The telescope with the banner labeled "Instruction" symbolized in 1897 the desire of the public for participation. Under the conditions of modern scientific research, public participation must often be limited in scope or only symbolic in nature, but it is nonetheless important for that. Public participation may take the form of entertainment, instruction, or the enjoyment of public monuments. Entertainment today means mainly television. No astronomer should underrate the value of the services done for astronomy by our colleagues Fred Hoyle and Carl Sagan, who happen to be gifted as television stars. Instruction means popular science magazines, lectures, and books. Those of us who are not television stars can still contribute to public participation in science, by teaching and writing for as wide an audience as we can reach.

Last but not least, the public can participate in science by sharing our public monuments, taking the kids for a picnic and walking through the dome of the Hale telescope in the peace of a summer afternoon on Mount Palomar, driving up Mount Hamilton by moonlight for a visitors' night at the Lick Observatory and looking at the glory of Saturn's rings through the Crossley refractor, or standing tall and proud in cap and gown in front of

Einstein's statue on a spring morning in Washington. Astronomers are lucky, because their places of work are also places of pilgrimage for members of the public who go to the mountains in search of natural beauty. The heavens too are full of beauty unfolding before us as our knowledge increases. So long as astronomers take the trouble to share with the public as much as possible of the grandeur and the beauty of their discoveries, the public will see to it that their work will continue.

Edwin Hubble was the astronomer who came after George Hale, using the telescopes that Hale had built, and discovering with their help the law of expansion of the universe. Hubble also followed the good example of George Hale in explaining to the public in simple words the substance of his discoveries. "For I can end as I began," Hubble wrote. "From our home on the Earth, we look out into the distances and strive to imagine the sort of world into which we are born. Today we have reached far out into space. Our immediate neighborhood we know rather intimately. But with increasing distance our knowledge fades, and fades rapidly, until at the last dim horizon we search among ghostly errors of observation for landmarks that are scarcely more substantial. The search will continue. The urge is older than history. It is not satisfied and it will not be suppressed."

CHAPTER 16

To Teach or Not to Teach

.....

1990

I. THE VIEW FROM ENGLAND

I dedicate this chapter to the memory of a great American mathematician, my friend and colleague Hassler Whitney, who devoted the last years of his life to the reform of the teaching of mathematics in elementary schools. Whitney died at the age of eighty-two on May 10, 1989. He was actively engaged in talking with schoolchildren a few days before his death. He shared my concerns about the teaching of science, although I do not claim that he agreed with my remedies. Two months before Whitney died, Erich Bloch, the head of the National Science Foundation, came on a site visit to the Institute for Advanced Study in Princeton to learn what our mathematicians had been doing with his money. To Bloch's astonishment, Whitney barged into the room and told him that what the National Science Foundation ought to be doing is making sure that third-graders know how to add and subtract. Whitney also demonstrated in vivid detail how to get the kids' attention. But there I must leave Hassler Whitney and turn to Willard Gibbs.

A year and a half ago I gave an after-dinner talk at Yale University on the occasion of the 150th birthday of Josiah Willard Gibbs, the greatest American physicist of the nineteenth century. Since I was talking in a relaxed mood at the end of a strenuous day, I took the opportunity to be provocative. I was trying to keep a tired

187

and well-fed audience from falling asleep. I said it was lucky that Willard Gibbs was not taught physics in school. I said the reason he did so well as a physicist was that he spent most of his class-room hours learning Latin. I was pricking the sacred cows of the science education establishment and challenging the accepted wisdom.

After I came back to Princeton from Yale, the physicist Chiara Nappi, who is also a colleague at the Institute for Advanced Study, gave me the text of a different talk about science education. Her talk was published in abbreviated form in the May 1990 issue of *Physics Today*. It is full of good sense, and it says things that had not been said before. I found Nappi's statement completely convincing. Everything in the statement is true. There is only one little problem. The things Nappi says in her statement are diametrically opposite to the things I said in my talk at Yale. She says the kids need to be taught more science in schools. I said they need to be taught less. How can we both be right?

My task in this chapter is to explain how it can happen that two opposite statements can both be true. The key to the explanation is Niels Bohr's principle of complementarity, which Bohr liked to apply to situations in ethics and philosophy as well as in physics. Complementarity says that nature is too subtle to be described from any single point of view. To obtain an adequate description, you have to look at things from several points of view, even though the different viewpoints are incompatible and cannot be viewed simultaneously. Statements that are true when seen from one point of view may be false when seen from another. There is no logical contradiction here, because the behavior of the object you are observing changes as you change your point of view. Here is a quotation from Niels Bohr:

> In the Institute in Copenhagen, we used often to comfort ourselves with jokes, among them the old saying of the two kinds of truth. To the one kind belong statements so simple and clear that the opposite assertion obviously could not be defended. The other kind, the so-called "deep truths," are statements in which the opposite also contains deep truth.

The minds of children, and the interactions between children and teachers, are subtle and dynamic enough so that deep truth can be expected to prevail. We may be surprised by Bohr's assertion that the principle of complementarity applies to an object as simple as an electron. We have no reason to be surprised by the discovery that the principle applies to something as complicated as a child. I now put my Yale talk and Nappi's article side by side, to see how they can both be true.

Nappi and I are both immigrants in America, she from Italy, I from England. Both of us base our arguments on childhood experiences that we brought from our homelands. It is not surprising that the viewpoints of an Italian child and an English child are complementary. You cannot look through Italian and English eyes simultaneously. Here, first, is my view of science education, seen through English eyes.

Throughout the nineteenth century and the first quarter of the twentieth, very little science was taught in English schools. This began to change in the 1920s and 1930s. Various committees of learned men declared that the English were a nation of scientific illiterates and that something had to be done about it. What had to be done was to push Latin and Greek out of the schools and bring in science. By the time I reached high school, we had some excellent science teachers and some serious science was taught. I was lucky. When I was halfway through high school the war began and the system began to fall apart. In my last year of high school I spent a total of seven hours a week in class. That was the best time I could have chosen to get an education. After the war was over, the teachers came back and the system was tightened up, and now nobody dreams any more of spending seven hours a week in class. Now the kids are kept chained to their desks and are pumped full of predigested science, just as they are in America.

If you look back and see what effect the reform of the schools had on the output of science in England, you can see that the effect was substantial. All through the nineteenth century and well into the twentieth, so long as the schools were heavily concentrated on Latin and Greek, England produced an amazing number of first-rate scientists: Darwin, Faraday, Maxwell, Joule, Kelvin, Dirac, Crick, and so on. You do not need to count up the number of Nobel prizes to prove that England was doing well. It is more difficult to make an objective assessment of science in England during the later period, beginning about 1950, since all young scientists have had to go through O-levels and A-levels, which are the English jargon words for a formal scientific education. Many of the younger English scientists are good, but I see only one, Stephen Hawking, that I would put in the same class with Maxwell and Dirac. Somehow or other, the shift in the schools from Latin and Greek to physics and chemistry has been successful in keeping the most original minds away from science.

We all know that the decisive years for turning young minds away from science are the years before they reach high school. The damage is mostly done in elementary and middle schools. Again, I use my own experience to show how apparently unfavorable circumstances may lead to favorable results. Here is what happened to me. I spent the years from eight to twelve at an establishment known in England as a prep school, which corresponds roughly to an American middle school. The school did not teach any science. The wave of reform, which by that time had brought science to the high schools, had not yet penetrated down to the prep schools. At the prep school we were still taught the classical nineteenth-century curriculum, plenty of Latin, a good deal of mathematics, no science. The school was similar to that splendid educational institution Dotheboys Hall, as Dickens describes it in his novel *Nicholas Nickleby*. The headmaster was a sadist who reserved for himself the pleasure of teaching Latin to the upper forms. His method of teaching was to keep a riding whip handy and apply it zealously to anybody who made mistakes in grammar. Since I was good at Latin grammar, I mostly escaped the whip. So far as I was concerned, the cruelty of the headmaster was less oppressive than the brutality of the boys. The boys were at their most barbarous age, and they redressed the balance of injustice by torturing those who had escaped whipping. Their favorite instrument of torture, sandpaper applied to the face or to other tender areas of skin, was more to be feared than the headmaster's whip.

So it happened that I belonged to a small minority of boys who were lacking in physical strength and athletic prowess, interested in other things besides football, and squeezed between the twin oppressions of whip and sandpaper. We hated the headmaster with his Latin grammar and we hated even more the boys with their empty football heads. So what could the poor helpless minority of intellectuals, later and in another country to be known as nerds, do to defend ourselves? We found our refuge in a territory that was equally inaccessible to our Latin-obsessed headmaster and to our football-obsessed schoolmates. We found our refuge in science. With no help from the school authorities, we founded a science society. As a persecuted minority, we kept a low profile. We held our meetings quietly and inconspicuously. We could do no real experiments. All we could do was share books and explain to each other what we didn't understand. But we learned a lot. Above all, we learned those lessons that can never be taught by formal courses of instruction, that science is a conspiracy of brains against ignorance, that science is a revenge of victims against oppressors, that science is a territory of freedom and friendship in the midst of tyranny and hatred.

Perhaps my experience in that prep school between the ages of eight and twelve was not exceptional. Perhaps there were others in similar circumstances who found in science a beacon of freedom and hope. Perhaps that is why, during all those years when the schools were teaching Latin and Greek and totally neglecting science, England produced so few great classical scholars and so many great scientists.

The historian Ann Koblitz has described how the young women of Russia seized upon science as their road to liberation, even more ardently than the young gentlemen of England. The decade of the 1860s produced the first great flowering of women's liberation in Russia and, not coincidentally, the first large contingent of women scientists. As Koblitz describes it in a recent article in *Isis,* "Science was perceived as virtually synonymous with truth, progress and radicalism; thus the pursuit of a scientific career was viewed as in no way a hindrance to social activism. In fact, it was seen as a positive boost to progressive forces, an active blow against backwardness." The same sentiment was expressed two hundred years ago by the great chemist and social activist Joseph Priestley: "The English hierarchy, if there be anything unsound in its constitution, has reason to tremble even at an air pump or an electrical machine."

2. THE VIEW FROM ITALY

That is enough about England and Russia. Now let us hear what Nappi has to say about the teaching of science in Italy.

Freeman Dyson

The approach in Europe is more systematic and steady in math and science, as in all other subjects. Students start studying math and science at an earlier age and proceed through high school at a more relaxed pace. In the lower grades, while basic math and problem-solving skills are mastered, concepts of higher mathematics are also introduced. In high school, there are no crash courses. For example, most American high school students study algebra intensively for a whole year, with daily classes on the subject, only to drop it the following year to concentrate on another subject, such as geometry, for another intense full year. But in Europe these subjects are studied in parallel over several years. Likewise, the physics that American students are supposed to learn in a year is spread over three or four years in Europe. Concepts in math and science need to be assimilated, and that takes time. European high school students study physics, chemistry, biology and mathematics every year. The amount that they study varies from one type of high school to another, but they all must take these subjects every year.

The point I want to make is the following: *If courses are unnecessarily tough, and moreover optional, students do tend to opt out.* The teenage years are particularly critical. Boys and girls undergo so many physical and emotional changes that it is unwise to place too much pressure on them then. It is the time when gender roles and stereotypes really sink in. Especially in the United States, there is a great deal of pressure on girls to concentrate on being socially successful. It is well known that these problems start in high school and that there is no significant difference between boys' and girls' performances in math and science up to eighth grade. Further, girls in European high schools do seem to perform better than their American counterparts. It is not that stereotypes or gender roles do not exist in Europe. They do. However, in more structured educational systems like those in Europe, there is much less room for stereotypes to have an effect. No matter how you envision your role in life, you still need to know a required amount of math and science before you get out of high school. And because courses are not made unnecessarily intense and demanding in European schools, all students can handle them better, in spite of some inevitable teenage crises.

The American educational system is actually very selective. It selects the very talented and self-motivated students, those who would do well in any system. It does not give a fair chance to the others; it simply neglects them. An educational approach based on difficult and elective courses tends to discriminate against lower-class children, who often do not have the supportive home environment that would channel them toward math and science and help them through these subjects. In Italy the same curriculum is used all over the country. Children of the same age study the same topics in all subjects at about the same time. The Italian system has proved to be a powerful social equalizer. During the course of one generation, it has leveled enormous cultural differences between north and south, men and women. A national curriculum has the advantage that results do not depend too heavily on the particular geographical area, school district or even the teachers' level of competence.

In conclusion, US students' performance in math and science could be highly improved by a more systematic approach to math and science teaching. One of the main problems at the moment is that US schools start teaching math and science too late, and therefore much too fast, with the result that teenagers are driven away from the optional math and science courses. This approach hurts everyone, but its most serious impact is on women and minorities. A change would represent an important step toward equality in education and society.

I apologize to Nappi for squeezing her eloquence down to a few abbreviated paragraphs. She also spoke of the shock she experienced when she came to the United States and everybody asked her how it happened that she became a professional physicist in spite of being a woman. In Italy this question did not arise, because girls and boys alike were exposed to physics, whether or not they liked it, and those who liked physics tended naturally to become physicists, whether or not they happened to be women. To be a woman physicist in Italy is, as Nappi says, no big deal. Her message to the United States, based on her Italian experience, is that formal education in science can be effective and can reach children at all levels of society, provided only that it is begun early and continued steadily through twelve years of schooling. My message is the opposite. I am saying that I was lucky not to be taught much science in school, that formal instruction in science is counterproductive, that a heavy science curriculum turns off more kids than it turns on. I am saying that if you want to turn children into scientists you must let them experience science as an escape from tyranny and not as another form of tyranny.

How can Nappi and I both be right? Here we must go back to Niels Bohr and the lessons of complementarity. Nappi is right when she says that science, impartially imposed on children by a centralized educational authority, can be a powerful force working for social justice and equality of opportunity, as it is in Italy. I am right when I say that a minority of children set free from the slavery of the classroom, as we were in wartime England, will pursue science with a passionate enthusiasm that a class of school-trained examination passers cannot match. We can both be right, because we belong to different cultures and we are speaking about different kinds of children. There is no such thing as a child in the abstract. There are only particular children, all of them different. Nappi's prescriptions are good for the great mass of children, mine are good for the elite. Hers are good for the law-abiding majority, mine are good for the rebels and outlaws. But it is not possible to divide children into a docile majority and a rebellious minority and deal with them separately. Each individual child, like each individual electron, has complementary qualities of docility and rebelliousness. Each child needs both discipline and freedom. Discipline and freedom are, like the position and momentum of an electron, complementary aspects of education that are both essential. Somehow or other, teachers have to supply both. That is the true vocation of a teacher, to start all the children learning with an equal dose of discipline, and then to know when it is time for discipline to stop and freedom to begin. That is a difficult, almost an impossible, vocation. That is why teachers deserve our deep respect.

3. THE PROBLEM OF THE PH.D.

Let me turn now from schoolchildren to the problems of higher education. The dilemmas that we encounter in high schools reappear in a similar form in colleges and graduate schools. We have again a clash of cultures, with Nappi upholding the virtues of the traditional European Ph.D. system while I am trying to destroy it. And again, both of us are right. The virtues of the Ph.D. system are real. It was invented in Germany as a way of giving official status to young people who wished to dedicate their lives to scholarly pursuits. The system worked well in nineteenth-century Germany, and made the German universities into models for the rest of the world and especially the United States to copy. The system worked well so long as the students were few in number, talented enough to do genuinely original research, and intending to make careers in academic institutions. The system still works well for the minority of students who are, like the German students of a century ago, budding professors or budding Nobel Prize winners. But the system does not work well for the majority of students in America today. A recent article by Susan Coyle with the title "The Long Haul to a Doctorate," explains why the system is failing. Students spend far too many years in school before they are finished. The average student emerges at the end of the Ph.D. program, already middle-aged, overspecialized, poorly prepared for the world outside, and almost unemployable except in a narrow area of specialization. Large numbers of students for whom the program is inappropriate are trapped in it, because the Ph.D. has become a union card required for entry into the scientific job market. I am personally acquainted with several cases of young people who became mentally deranged, not to speak of many more who became depressed and discouraged, their lives ruined by the tyranny of the Ph.D. system. It is no wonder that most of the best and the brightest of our young people, including my own daughters, decided to stay out of the trap. And unfortunately, now that the Ph.D. has become a union card for scientists, staying out of the trap means staying out of the scientific profession.

I was lucky, growing up in England at a time when the Ph.D. was not yet obligatory. Many of the leading scientists in England, like the surgeons, took pride in calling themselves Mister rather than Doctor. Soon after I left, the Ph.D. system tightened its grip on England as it did earlier on America. I have been fighting the system in America for forty years, with absolutely no success. Nobody comes now to work at the Institute for Advanced Study, as George Kennan and I did in the good old days, with only a bachelor's degree.

Politicians and business leaders are wondering why American graduate schools are filled with foreign students and not with Americans. Susan Coyle answers their question. "Getting a doctorate takes about seven years, followed by up to three years in a postdoctoral appointment. For students, this means more debt, less income and perhaps postponing the start of a family." For the rare spirits who are genuinely in love with science, a seven-year vow of poverty may not be a deterrent. For ordinary bright Americans who are choosing a career, the deterrent is strong enough to keep most of them out of science.

What can we do to limit the damage that the Ph.D. system is doing to our young people? Our problem is in many ways similar to a problem that existed in England a hundred years ago. At that time in England, the mathematical tripos examination distorted the whole structure of mathematical education. The tripos was an absurd and artificial contest that gave the students no exposure to modern mathematical ideas and little incentive to try their hand at research. The tripos system, in the opinion of my teacher Professor G. H. Hardy, set back the progress of mathematics in England by about a century. When Hardy came to Cambridge as a young radical, he decided that the only way to save English mathematics was to abolish the tripos completely. But he soon found that his attempts to abolish the tripos united against him all the vested interests of Cambridge, with the result that even modest reform of the system was stymied. Hardy then changed his tactics. Instead of trying to abolish the tripos, he started a campaign to trivialize it. Trivializing the tripos meant making it so easy that students could get it out of the way and still have time to go on and learn some real mathematics. The decisive step was to forbid any public announcement of the tripos order of merit, so that the students were no longer competing like racehorses for the position of senior wrangler. The tactic of trivialization achieved most of Hardy's objectives, although Hardy himself remained sorry that the tripos virus remained alive in attenuated form. He remained to the end of his life an abolitionist.

The Ph.D. system is distorting and damaging American science today, just as badly as the old tripos was distorting English mathematics a hundred years ago. Like Hardy, I am forced to recognize that abolition is politically impossible. Too many vested interests are entrenched in the system. The best we can hope for is to trivialize the Ph.D. as Cambridge trivialized the tripos. I would like to give everybody a Ph.D. at birth, or on the day they enter graduate school, so that the Ph.D. would no longer be an obstacle either to education or to scientific employment. If such a rational solution of the problem is judged to be too radical, we could envisage a compromise solution in which the time required to obtain a Ph.D. is drastically shortened. Sitting through graduate courses and writing a thesis could be alternative options, instead of both being required for every student. The time it would take to finish the degree would then be cut in half, and the damage to the students reduced in proportion. Some students need formal course work. Others do not. Some students are capable of significant original research. Others are not. It is cruel and destructive to force them all into the same mold. The poet William Blake told us two hundred years ago: "One law for the lion and ox is oppression." Even worse than one law for the lion and ox is the attempt of Doctor Moreau in H. G. Wells's story to chop both lion and ox by plastic surgery into a tortured semblance of human beings. Sometimes, when I am visiting graduate schools of physics and listening to the heart-rending complaints of the students, I am unhappily reminded of Doctor Moreau's island.

Perhaps I exaggerate the miseries of our graduate students. But I do not exaggerate the harm that the Ph.D. system is doing to the pursuit of science in this country. Drastic changes are long overdue.

4. BACK TO SCHOOL

After the digression into higher education, I return to the schoolroom, which most experts agree is at the root of our difficulties. I said that our children need both Nappi's suggested remedies and mine. What then is the educational establishment to do? Should we give to each child, or to each teacher, or to each school, or to each district, the choice of learning in a structured Italian-style environment or of running wild and free? Is it possible in the real world of 1990 to offer such a choice? My answer to these questions again goes back to the experiences of my childhood.

I learned little science, except for mathematics, in school, but I learned plenty of science in other ways. I learned mostly from two sources, books and museums. The enormous advantage of books and museums is that a child comes to them freely, not under compulsion. Even if a child is forced to visit a museum as a member of a supervised group, there is a chance to run around and it is not as bad as sitting in class. Most of the children one sees, either in public libraries or in museums, seem to be enjoying themselves. So my first recommendation to people in charge of science education is, more money for public libraries and museums. Public libraries and museums ought to be as common as schools. Then we could have, side by side with Nappi's regular classroom instruction, an alternative for children who learn better on their feet than on their behinds.

Besides libraries and museums, children also need to be exposed to laboratories and computers. Here again the essential problem is to make sure that the exposure results in attraction rather than repulsion. Being forced to chop up a frog in a laboratory is worse than being forced to learn the periodic table of elements in a classroom. Children who enjoy chopping up frogs should do it in their own time, with their own frogs. Children who enjoy optics or electronics should be given the materials to build microscopes or radios. If materials are available and children are given enough free time, they will learn more from one another than they learn from teachers. Children who enjoy computers should be let loose, to play with as large a variety of hardware and software as we can afford to give them. Computers should be a part of the landscape which children are free to explore, not a required course that they have to take for credit.

The generation that is now young has three good reasons for turning away from science. Science is presented to our young people as a rigid and authoritarian discipline, tied to mercenary and utilitarian ends, and tainted by its association with weapons of mass murder. These three reasons for hating science are real and serious. It is useless to pretend to our children that these three ugly faces of science do not exist. Children will not be fooled. If we try to fool them, they will turn away from science even more. Our task as educators is to show our children that science is a hexagonal mountain with six faces, with three beautiful faces in addition to the three ugly faces. The three beautiful faces of science are science as subversion of authority, science as an art form, and science as an international club. The way to attract young people into science is to show them all six faces and give them freedom to explore the beautiful and the ugly as they please.

Science as subversion has a long history. There is a long list of scientists who sat in jail and other scientists who helped get them out and incidentally saved their lives. The finest moment in the history of the Institute for Advanced Study where I work came in 1957 when we appointed the mathematician Chandler Davis a member of the Institute, with financial support provided by the National Science Foundation. Chandler was then a convicted felon because he refused to rat on his friends when questioned by the House Un-American Activities Committee. After his Institute fellowship was over, he sat for six months in jail. He is now a distinguished professor at the University of Toronto and is still actively engaged in helping people in jail to get out. If science ceases to be a rebellion against authority, then it does not deserve the talents of our brightest kids. I was lucky to be introduced to science as a rebellion against Latin and football. We should try to introduce all our children to science as a rebellion against poverty and ugliness and militarism and economic injustice.

Another face of science that children should explore is science as art. The physicist Niels Bohr and the poet Robert Frost got to know each other at Amherst in 1923. This was not a mere social encounter but a genuine meeting of minds. One can find many traces of Bohr's ideas, and even of quantum mechanics, in Frost's poetry. Another writer who knew how to turn science into art was Loren Eiseley, equally gifted as poet and as paleontologist. The immense popularity of Maurits Escher shows how fruitful an educational tool the marriage of science and art might be.

Finally, the sixth face of science is the most beautiful of all, science as an international club. Instead of being tied to weaponry and narrow patriotism, science is and always has been an international enterprise. If you are a scientist, you have friends in every corner of the globe. Scientists in every country are linked by personal contacts with the world outside. Scientists in good and bad situations are fighting as best they can for open communications and international collaboration. Little by little, one step at a time, the international commonwealth of science is growing in strength. Slowly, that great dream with which Niels Bohr tried in vain to inspire Franklin Roosevelt and Winston Churchill, the dream that the international commonwealth of science might be a model for a peaceful international commonwealth of nations, is coming closer to reality. In the international eradication of smallpox, in the Montreal convention for the preservation of the ozone layer, and in the burgeoning of environmental movements all over the world, we see examples of Bohr's dream coming true. When international science takes the lead, the diplomats and the politicians cautiously follow. To be a scientist means to take a hand in pushing Bohr's dream along toward its final goals, the open world, the abolition of weapons of mass murder, the obsolescence of war. What the kids in the ghetto need, to open their minds to science, is not more hours of physics and chemistry, but a vision of a future that will be different from the past. A dream of a better future; that is what our kids need. And that is what science, if we don't confuse science with SAT scores, can give them.

PART IV

Politics

oooo

LET YOUR ACTS BE DIRECTED TOWARD A WORTHY

GOAL, BUT DO NOT ASK IF THEY WILL REACH IT; THEY

ARE TO BE MODELS AND EXAMPLES, NOT MEANS TO AN

END.

LEO SZILARD

"TEN COMMANDMENTS"

CHAPTER 17

Pugwash 1962

.....

1 9 6 2

1. THE MEETINGS

Two Pugwash conferences on Science and World Affairs were held in England in 1962. The ninth conference was held in Cambridge in August, the tenth in London in September. The two meetings were different in purpose and character. The ninth conference followed the tradition set by earlier meetings. It was small, informal, and concentrated on a particular subject, in this case "Problems of Disarmament and World Security." The tenth conference broke with tradition in every respect. It was large, formal, and scattered over a variety of topics. The people who attended both meetings said that the ninth was not only pleasanter but more useful. However, there was a reason for making the tenth conference big and formal. It was intended that the tenth conference should guide the international continuing committee which organizes Pugwash meetings. The continuing committee reported to the tenth conference on the work the committee has done over the last five years, and the conference elected a new committee representing a wider group of countries than the old one. The tenth conference performed a necessary function in enabling a larger group of people to take formal responsibility for the future of the Pugwash movement. Apart from this, the high point of the tenth conference was the personal appearance of Bertrand Russell, who opened the proceedings with a wise and witty speech and received a standing ovation.

Freeman Dyson

The real business of Pugwash meetings is getting Western and Soviet scientists together in small groups. The purpose is not to reach formal agreements but to get to know each other individually and to understand the divergent mental processes that underlie our political disagreement. Judged by this criterion, the tenth conference was inevitably a failure. No personal intimacy or understanding can be expected to grow in meetings of three or four hundred people sitting in rows in a lecture hall. On the other hand, the ninth conference provided excellent opportunities for getting to know Russians as people. I acquired a vivid and immediate impression of the ways of thinking of several Russian scientists upon political questions. This account will deal only with the ninth conference, leaving the tenth to the official historians to whom it rightly belongs.

The ninth conference was held in physical surroundings that were ideal for the purpose. All delegates were housed in the new block of Caius College, a brand-new building that combines the eternal beauty of Cambridge with such new-fangled luxuries as central heating and hot and cold running water. Caius College fed the entire conference three times a day, and every evening we were invited to the home of one or other of the Cambridge participants. Each home that we visited had behind it a large and idyllic garden, where sherry and soft evening light made conversation flow freely in broken English and ungrammatical Russian.

For the working sessions the meeting was divided into five groups, each containing ten or fifteen people. The working sessions were held in undergraduate sitting rooms in the old part of Caius College. Each little group was crammed in cozy informality into aged leather sofas and armchairs around an aged fireplace. For the most important part of the conference, the nonworking sessions of two or three delegates taking an afternoon stroll together between meetings, the quiet college gardens, and the punts on the river were always available.

The following topics were assigned to the five working groups: (1) Problems of reduction and elimination, under international control, of weapons of mass destruction and of their means of delivery. (2) Problems of balanced reduction and elimination of conventional armaments. (3) Political and technical measures contributing to the lessening of international tensions. (4) Problems

204

of security in a disarmed world. (5) Economic aspects of disarmament. I chose to work in group 4 for two reasons. First, the subject is remote from the area of current negotiations at Geneva, and therefore allows discussion unhampered by rigid official positions of the two sides. Second, it is my opinion that the subject of group 4 must be thought through and understood in detail before any decisive action on the more immediate issues of disarmament will be possible. My choice of group 4 was justified by the outcome. I afterward learned that few of the participants in the other groups were as happy as I was in group 4. Group 1 especially suffered from the baneful effects of the Geneva negotiations, and degenerated into a dogged defense of official positions.

The situation in group 4 was particularly favorable, because Leo Szilard belonged to it. Szilard, who drafted the famous letter from Einstein to Roosevelt to get the United States involved with nuclear energy in 1939, and who drafted the famous Franck report trying to stop Truman from using the bomb on a Japanese city in 1945, has also been from the beginning one of the leading spirits of Pugwash. In our group, whenever positions were becoming rigid and the atmosphere threatened to become sticky, Szilard would put forward some idea sufficiently outrageous to unite Russians and Westerners in opposition to it. Our most bellicose Westerner was an Englishman, and he too had the effect of pushing Russians and Americans closer together. Finally, our group was fortunate in containing on the Russian side Khozhevnikov, a distinguished international lawyer who had served for seven years as a judge of the International Court. He spoke with great precision and good humor, and understood better than anybody the problems of establishing uniform legal procedure in a world of divergent legal traditions.

Broadly speaking, the debate in group 4 centered around the question of how the U.N. Security Council could be enabled to do the job for which it was originally intended. The Russians mostly took the view that, in a disarmed world with a veto-free inspection system, the existing Security Council would be sufficient for enforcing disarmament and resisting aggression. The Westerners were prepared to accept the Security Council as the basic instrument of international security, but wished to establish in addition a subsidiary organization having the power to move police forces rapidly into disputed areas when required. Both sides accepted the existence of the veto, in the hands of the two major powers at least, as a legal recognition of the fact that a police action of the international organization against a major power is impracticable. The Westerners wished the international organization to be empowered to take certain clearly defined and limited actions, for which promptness and reliability are essential, without waiting for the Security Council's approval.

We had four full days for the meetings of our working group. The time was divided sharply into two phases. In the first phase, which lasted for three of the four days, discussion was free and ranged over all kinds of hypothetical situations which we could imagine as creating threats to peace in a disarmed world. We discussed specifically the various stubborn animosities, such as the Israeli-Arab, the Pakistani-Indian, and the German-Polish, that will persist and create trouble in a disarmed world. These animosities provided us with examples against which to test the adequacy of various proposed forms of international peacekeeping machinery. On the fourth day the discussion changed abruptly in tone; instead of arguing about matters of substance, we argued about pieces of paper. The reason was that the Russians desired to take home with them an agreed written statement from each of the working groups. The purpose of these agreed statements was never made clear; the Russians assured us that they would circulate them at a high level within their government. Inevitably, the negotiation of an agreed statement generated the mental atmosphere that has made the Geneva negotiations sterile. We wasted the fourth day haggling over words and phrases, and the statement that emerged from our labors was a summary of those uncontroversial issues to which nobody had any serious objection. At the beginning of this day of haggling, Szilard wisely remarked, "Now I am going to help you to write your statement," walked out of the door, and did not return. To me the fourth day was of interest in two respects. First, it showed dramatically how a Russian will transform himself from an amiable intellectual companion into a hard bargainer as soon as he feels himself to be speaking officially for his country. Second, the ironing out of the agreed draft, sentence by sentence in two languages, provided a splendid lesson in the fine points of Russian semantics.

All in all, looking back on the friendly first three days of working group 4 and on the slightly acrimonious fourth day, one over-whelming impression remains. I lived for four days mentally in a disarmed world, with all its difficulties, and the longer I was there the better I liked it. At the end of the four days I did not feel happy to return to the present-day world of deterrence and counterforce, missiles and megatons. I would seriously recommend that all military experts and political leaders who have learned to take our present world for granted should from time to time be exposed to an experience like mine. It would refresh their imaginations and enlarge their hopes.

2. THE LESSONS

Here are the general conclusions that I reached from talking with Russians, inside and outside the working sessions. The dominant note was a tremendous sincerity and urgency in the desire of each Russian for drastic disarmament. The feeling of personal sincerity cannot be communicated at second hand, but everybody who was talking to the Russians at Cambridge was impressed by it. For these Russians quick and savage disarmament is a passionate concern. They see no other escape from the ever-increasing arms race and the final catastrophic war. They do not accept any half-measures, such as stabilized deterrence or disarmament by gradual stages. Their feelings against half-measures arise partly from a rational belief that the world requires a sudden major perturbation to shake it off its present disastrous course, and partly from the irrational and traditional Russian impatience with gradual methods.

It is important that the public should understand the basic cause of the disagreement between Russian and Western positions on disarmament. Our newspapers mostly write as if inspection were the main problem. In fact, inspection is a problem, but a comparatively minor one. The wiser heads in East and West are now fairly close together in their views of how much inspection is feasible and necessary. The major issue separating the two sides is the issue of speed. All our discussions tended to become stuck on the question of speed, and on this issue even an informal meeting of minds was difficult to reach.

The divergence of views on the proper speed of disarmament

arises in the following way. A Russian looks at disarmament as a problem for heads of state. The heads of state must decide upon a logical method of disarmament. The process of decision may take much time and long negotiations. But once the decision is made and the treaty signed, it is a simple matter to carry out the terms of the agreement. It is safer and more convenient to make the physical process of disarmament as rapid as possible, in order to minimize the special difficulties that might arise during the intermediate stages. The Russians chose eighteen months as a reasonable length of time in which to complete the major act of disarmament, the elimination of the means of delivery of weapons of mass destruction. A Russian sees any desire to prolong the carrying out of disarmament, after the agreement is signed, as a desire to cheat or to frustrate the agreement.

A Westerner looks at disarmament as a political process in which the public and the recalcitrant sections of the government must be coaxed and persuaded to acquiesce as the process continues. The start must be gradual so that it can begin at all. Drastic political decisions, such as the final elimination of long-range missiles, cannot possibly be made until the process of disarmament has been in operation for several years and the public has begun to feel at home with it. For a Westerner many of the political difficulties of disarmament only emerge after the agreement is signed, and a time scale shorter than ten years for the complete carrying out of an agreement seems quite unrealistic.

At Cambridge I learned that it is almost impossible for a Russian, even a Russian with wide knowledge of the Western world, to grasp the idea of a government being unable to do whatever it decides to do. In vain I argued that we cannot disarm rapidly for the same reason that we cannot desegregate our schools rapidly. A Russian thinks of both these problems in terms of his own experience. He assumes that if a government has decided upon a policy, opposition to that policy can only come from a conspiracy of evil individuals whose influence must be fought and overcome. In the case of the schools the evil individuals are the Ku Klux Klan; in the case of disarmament they are the Pentagon generals. A Russian cannot imagine a state of affairs in which the opposition to government policy comes from a group of responsible political leaders without whose cooperation the government cannot function. Still less can a Russian understand that this internal opposition is not regarded by us as evil, but is deliberately built into our system in order to make it impossible for the government to take hasty and drastic actions against the will of a minority.

At the meetings in Cambridge and London the Russians were happy to find that their government's policy of rapid disarmament was supported by a large majority. The official American plan, with its slow beginning, indefinite duration, and numerous escape clauses, was generally regarded as so unsatisfactory that it was hardly even discussed. The personal sincerity of the Russians, together with the logical directness and sharpness of their ideas, had a strong effect in winning support for the Soviet plan. The public statement of the tenth conference went far toward endorsing the official Soviet proposals on disarmament. This was primarily a victory of a policy of speed over a policy of caution.

I personally agree with the majority in preferring speed to caution. I consider that, if we should sign the Soviet draft treaty on general and complete disarmament tomorrow, we should significantly improve our chances of preserving our world and our constitutional system intact. However, the hard fact is that no treaty as abrupt and revolutionary as the Soviet draft could ever be implemented by our slow-moving political machinery. It should be our task at future Pugwash meetings to convince the Russians that they must learn to live with our slowness, just as we have to learn to live with their secretiveness. Our slowness and their secretiveness are facts of history which must be understood and tolerated, but which cannot be arbitrarily overridden.

CHAPTER 18

Death of a Project

.....

1 9 6 5

I. A BRIEF HISTORY OF PROJECT ORION

In January 1965, unnoticed and unmourned by the public, Project Orion died. The men who began the project in 1958 and worked on it through seven strenuous years believe that it offers the best hope, in the long run, of a reasonable program for exploring space. By a reasonable program they mean a program comparable in cost with our existing space program and enormously superior in promise. They aimed to create a propulsion system commensurate with the real size of the task of exploring the Solar System, at a cost which would be politically acceptable, and they believe they have demonstrated the way to do it. Now the decision has been taken to follow their road no further. The purpose of this article is neither to bury Orion nor to praise it. It is only to tell the public for the first time the facts of Orion's life and death, and to explain as fairly as possible the political and philosophical issues that are involved in its fate.

First, a brief technical summary. Orion is a project to design a vehicle which would be propelled through space by repeated nuclear explosions occurring at a distance behind it. The vehicle may be either manned or unmanned; it carries a large supply of bombs, and machinery for throwing them out at the right place and time for efficient propulsion; it carries shock absorbers to protect machinery and crew from destructive jolts, and sufficient shielding to protect against heat and radiation. The vehicle has, of course, never been built. The project in its seven years of existence was confined to physics experiments, engineering tests of components, design studies, and theory. The total cost of the project was $10 million, spread over seven years, and the end result was a rather firm technical basis for believing that vehicles of this type could be developed, tested, and flown. The technical findings of the project have not been seriously challenged by anybody. Its major troubles have been, from the beginning, political. The level of scientific and engineering talent devoted to it was, for a classified project, unusually high.

The fundamental issue raised by such a project is: why should one not be content with alternative means of propulsion that are free from the obvious biological and political disadvantages of nuclear explosions? The answer to this question is that, on the purely technical level, an Orion vehicle has capabilities that no other system can approach. All alternative propulsion systems that we know how to build are either temperature-limited or power-limited. Conventional rocket systems, whether chemical or nuclear, are temperature-limited. They eject gas at an exhaust-velocity V limited by the temperature of chemical reactions or of solid structures. The upper limit for V appears to be about four kilometers per second for chemical rockets, eight kilometers per second for nuclear rockets. For missions involving velocity changes many times V, multiple-staged rockets are required, and the initial vehicle size needed in order to carry a modest payload soon becomes preposterous. The initial weight is multiplied by about a factor of three, whenever an amount V is added to the velocity change of a mission. It is for this reason that programs based on conventional propulsion run into a law of heavily diminishing returns as soon as missions beyond the moon are contemplated.

The other class of propulsion systems at present under development is the nuclear-electric class. These systems use a nuclear reactor to generate electricity, which then accelerates a jet of ions or plasma by means of electric or magnetic forces. The velocity of the jet is no longer limited by considerations of temperature, but the available thrust is limited to very low values by the power of the electric generator. Vehicles using nuclear-electric propulsion accelerate slowly and require long times to achieve useful velocities. They have undoubtedly an important role to play in long-range missions, but they offer no hope of transporting men or machines rapidly around the solar system.

The Orion propulsion system is neither temperature-limited nor power-limited. It escapes temperature limitations because the contact between the vehicle and the hot debris from the explosions is so brief that the debris does no more than superficial damage. It escapes power limitations because the nuclear engine (bomb) is outside the vehicle and does not depend on coolants and radiators for its functioning. An Orion vehicle is unique in being able to take full advantage of the enormous energy content of nuclear fuel in order to achieve, simultaneously, high exhaust velocity and high thrust.

Let me give a specific example of the performance that would be achieved by first-generation Orion vehicles. Designs were worked out in detail for vehicles that could carry eight men and a payload of a hundred tons on fast trips to Mars and back. The vehicles were small enough to be lifted into space by Saturn chemical rockets, and the cost of the Saturn boosters turned out to be more than half the estimated cost of the whole enterprise. These designs do not prove that a manned expedition to Mars is a worthwhile undertaking; they indicate only that if you wish to go to Mars, then Orion will take you there more rapidly and cheaply than other vehicles that are now being developed.

So much for the technical background of Orion. Next comes the political history. The idea of a bomb-propelled vehicle was first described by Stanislaw Ulam and Cornelius Everett in Los Alamos in 1955. It was transformed into a serious and practical proposal by a group of physicists and engineers at the General Atomic Division of General Dynamics Corporation in San Diego, under the leadership of Theodore Taylor. Work at General Atomic started in the spring of 1958, as a direct response to the first Sputniks. The initial group at General Atomic, including Taylor, were old weaponeers from Los Alamos. They seized happily upon this opportunity to make their knowledge of nuclear explosions serve a loftier purpose than weaponry. Within a few months they had worked out the basic theory of the Orion system, and found that it worked even better than they had supposed.

The problem then arose of obtaining government sponsorship and money for the project. The National Aeronautics and Space Administration (NASA) did not yet exist. There was only one government agency which could logically take responsibility and fund the project—namely the Advanced Research Projects Agency (ARPA) of the Defense Department. It was a thoroughly anomalous situation to have a group of weapons experts in a private company working on a space project. It took many months of negotiation to obtain the first contract from ARPA. At that early date in its history, ARPA did not insist that anything which it supported must have a military justification. The terms of the first contract permitted peaceful interplanetary exploration to be designated as the major goal of the project. Nevertheless the project was administered through Defense Department channels, and military influences were inevitably at work upon it.

Soon after Orion officially began, NASA was established with legal responsibility for all nonmilitary space activities. NASA quickly began to annex parts of ARPA's nonmilitary functions, and the air force responded by annexing ARPA's military space projects, so that the situation of ARPA was reminiscent of the partition of Poland between Prussia and Russia in the eighteenth century. In the end, Orion was left as the only space project in the hands of ARPA, largely because neither NASA nor the air force considered it a valuable asset. Taylor's efforts to interest NASA in Orion during this period met with no success.

In 1960 ARPA decided to drop Orion, and Taylor was compelled to go to the air force for sponsorship. According to the law, the air force may handle only military projects, and must apply a rigid definition of the word "military." A project is defined as military only if a direct military requirement for it exists. There is no military requirement for interplanetary exploration. Thus Taylor paid a high price for his air force contract. Although the technical substance of the work was not changed, the project became in name a military enterprise directed toward real or imagined military requirements. This arrangement continued in force until the end of the project in 1965.

The effect of the military sponsorship of Orion was, in the end, disastrous. The air force officials administering the project were sympathetic to the long-range and nonmilitary aspects of the work, but they were compelled by their own rules to disguise their sympathies. Each year, when they applied to the high authorities in the Defense Department, Harold Brown and Robert McNamara, for more money to expand the project, they had to argue in terms of immediate military requirements. Men as wise and critical as Brown and McNamara could easily see that the military applications of Orion are either spurious or positively undesirable. So the requests for expansion were turned down. The air force was told that if it wished to continue the project for nonmilitary reasons it should enlist the cooperation of NASA.

In 1963 NASA finally showed some official interest in Orion. Jim Nance, acting first as assistant director of the project under Taylor and later as director in his own right, established friendly relations with the Marshall Space Flight Center in Huntsville, Alabama. Within NASA, Orion's possibilities appealed particularly to the Office of Manned Space Flight, where people are beginning to worry about what they should do after the Apollo mission is over. NASA awarded Orion a small study contract, which resulted in the design of ships for specific interplanetary missions. Also in 1963 the test-ban treaty was signed, and nuclear explosions became more than ever politically questionable.

In 1964 the shadows began to close in. The air force grew tired of supporting a project that McNamara would not allow to grow, and announced that further support would be forthcoming only if NASA would make a serious contribution. At the eleventh hour, in October 1964, Nance succeeded in getting the basic technical facts concerning Orion declassified, so that it became possible for the first time to discuss the issue publicly. A certain interest in Orion belatedly developed within the engineering community but did not extend to the scientific community. In December 1964 the question of the support of Orion came to a final decision within NASA, with the result that was announced in January 1965.

2. CONCERNING THE VERDICT

As is proper in conducting an inquest, we have first assembled the historical evidence, and now we come to the question of a verdict. Who killed Orion, and why? And was the murder justifiable?

Four groups of people were directly responsible for the death of Orion. These are the Defense Department, the heads of NASA, the promoters of the test-ban treaty, and the scientific community as a whole. Each group encountered Orion within the context of a larger struggle in which Orion appeared to them as a relatively minor issue. In each group a negative attitude toward Orion was dictated by general principles which, in the wider context, were wise and enlightened. In each group the men who killed Orion acted from high and responsible motives. And yet their motives were strangely irrelevant to the real issues at stake in this highly individual case. I will examine the four groups in turn and describe how the problem of Orion presented itself to them.

The Defense Department chiefs have been waging for many years a successful battle to stop the air force from embarking upon a great variety of technically interesting projects whose military importance is questionable. The nuclear-propelled airplane was one such project, which was stopped only after large sums of money had been wasted on it. More recently, as in the cases of the B-70 bomber and the Dynasoar orbital airplane, McNamara has been strong enough to call a halt before the big money was spent. There is little doubt that, when the air force asked for more money for Orion, the authorities in the Defense Department mostly thought of it as one more in the long series of air force extravaganzas which it was their duty to suppress. The way in which the money was requested made it difficult for them to view it otherwise. Within this context their decision was unquestionably right.

The heads of NASA were not interested in Orion at the time NASA began, for the simple reason that it was a classified project supported by the Defense Department and therefore outside their terms of reference. They were explicitly enjoined by Congress not to trespass upon military ground, and they had no wish to become gratuitously involved with a project encumbered by all the bureaucratic nuisances of secrecy. The established policy of NASA is to conduct as many as possible of its operations openly and without requiring all its employees to be cleared for security. Few will question that this policy is wise as a general rule, and indeed essential to the maintenance of a healthy scientific atmosphere within NASA.

215

When the heads of NASA came to their final decision concerning Orion, in 1964, the jurisdictional issue was no longer central. The air force had officially appealed to NASA for a declaration of support, and participation in a future development of Orion would not have compromised the nonmilitary status of NASA. In 1964 the dominating concern at the top levels of NASA was the search for political stability. The heads of NASA have learned that their first duty to the space program is to keep it politically popular. Without consistent support from the public and from Congress, there would be no possibility of an effective program. It is therefore wise to sacrifice technical improvements if technical improvements carry risks of failure that may be politically upsetting to the entire program. Above all, spectacular and public failures are to be avoided. When a responsible public official thinks of Orion, he inevitably envisions a shipload of atomic bombs all detonating simultaneously and wiping out half of Florida. Though it is technically easy to make such an accident impossible, it is not possible to exorcise the fear of it. The heads of NASA know that fear is the most potent force in politics, and they have no wish to be feared.

The promoters of the test-ban treaty are a heterogeneous group of people, including the Arms Control and Disarmament Agency, the State Department, a large segment of Congress, the White House staff, and the President's Science Advisory Committee (PSAC). About the only thing that all the people working for the treaty had in common was a total unconcern for the welfare of Project Orion. Most of them had never heard of Orion, and most of those few who had heard of it (for example, some influential members of the PSAC) had met it only in a context in which they were committed to oppose it. They had met it within the context of a continuing battle to stop the military arm of the U.S. government from expanding the arms race into arenas where no arms race yet existed. The PSAC had been successful in opposing a race to build bigger bombs than the USSR was building, and had also successfully opposed the idea of placing offensive nuclear weapons in orbit. The members of the PSAC have developed a deep commitment to the policy of military restraint, of deploying new weapon systems only when a military need exists and not just for the sake of technological novelty. Their commitment to this goal has served their country well, and has borne fruit in many other wise decisions besides the decision to negotiate the test-ban treaty. Seeing Orion from this viewpoint, as an air force project ostensibly aimed at large-scale military operations in space, they felt no qualms in crushing it.

Lastly, the scientific community as a whole is responsible, in a negative sense, for the death of Orion. The vast majority of scientists have consistently refused to become interested in the technical problems of propulsion, believing that this is a job for engineers. A clear illustration of their point of view is provided by the report on National Goals in Space for the Years 1971–1985, recently published by the Space Science Board of the National Academy of Sciences. This report describes in detail a recommended program of space activities, based on the assumption that the propulsion systems available until 1985 will be those now under development. The Space Science Board does not concern itself with the question of whether a scientific effort might bring radical improvements in the art of propulsion before 1985. To somebody familiar with the potentialities of Orion, the Space Science Board program seems both pitifully modest and absurdly expensive.

Here again the disinterest of scientists in problems of propulsion arises from attitudes which in a wider context are wise and healthy. In their dealings with NASA and with the public, scientists have constantly preached that the payload is more important than the rocket, and that what you do there is more important than how you get there. They have argued repeatedly, and usually without success, that ten dollars spent on unmanned vehicles are scientifically more useful than a hundred spent on manned vehicles, and that often one dollar spent on ground-based observations is scientifically more useful still. They have been alienated from the field of propulsion by the spectacle of NASA officials claiming a scientific justification for space propulsion developments that have little or nothing to do with science. They have, after long years of listening to the pseudoscientific propaganda of the manned space program, learned to confine their attention to that small part of the NASA empire within which they have some real influence—namely, the Office of Space Science and Applications (OSSA). Within OSSA they have created an atmosphere of scientific sanity, which has allowed excellent and many-sided programs of unmanned scientific exploration to be carried out with the eighth of the NASA budget that is allotted to this purpose.

The Space Science Board of the National Academy, in its consideration of future activities, was mainly concerned with preserving the quality and the scientific integrity of these existing unmanned programs. The board rightly sees as its primary task the definition of the ends, rather than the means, of the space science enterprise.

What then is the attitude of a scientist, who is actively engaged in scientific space activities, toward a project such as Orion? He has perhaps just been denied by NASA a half-million-dollar ground-based telescope with which to observe planets. Or he has designed an experiment which was excluded, because of space limitations, from the next orbiting solar observatory. And then he hears that a wonderful new propulsion system has been invented which might allow him, fifteen years later, to make high-quality nearby observations of Jupiter and Saturn. The price of the new system is quoted as only a few billion dollars. He is understandably not enthusiastic.

This brief summary of Orion's history has shown that every one of the four murderers had good and laudable motives for killing the project, or, in the case of the scientific community, for not lifting a finger to save it. Orion had a unique ability to antagonize simultaneously the four most powerful sections of the Washington establishment. The remarkable thing is that, against such odds, with its future never assured for more than a few months at a time, the project survived as long as it did. It held together for seven long years a band of talented and devoted men, and produced in that time a volume of scientific and engineering work which in breadth and thoroughness has rarely been equaled.

The story of Orion is significant, because this is the first time in modern history that a major expansion of human technology has been suppressed for political reasons. Many will feel that the precedent is a good one to have established. It is perhaps wise that radical advances in technology, which may be used both for good and for evil purposes, be delayed until the human species is better organized to cope with them. But those who have worked on Project Orion cannot share this view. They must continue to hope that they may see their work bear fruit in their own lifetimes. They cannot lose sight of the dream which fired their imaginations in 1958 and sustained them through the years of struggle afterward—the dream that the bombs which killed and maimed at Hiroshima and Nagasaki may one day open the skies to mankind.

CHAPTER 19

Human Consequences
of the Exploration
# of Space

.....

1 9 6 8

I. LITERARY ANTECEDENTS

When Columbus set sail into the Atlantic, he knew he was going
to do something great, but he did not know what. This remark
about Columbus has been repeated many times by people discussing human activities in space; and still it is the truest thing that can
be said. I shall describe a personal view of the human situation in
which the exploration of space appears as the most hopeful feature
of a dark landscape. Everything I say may be as wrong and irrelevant as Columbus's reasons for sailing west. The important thing
is that he did sail west and we do go into space. The true historical
consequences of these events can only be known much later.

In recent months thoughtful voices have been heard question-
ing the wisdom of pursuing big space projects at a time when so
many human problems remain unsolved on Earth. Just now,
when the direction of space activities after the Apollo missions is
still to be decided, it is important for us to think seriously about
the value of such enterprises. This chapter is an attempt to think
ahead, to sketch a possible future for man in space. My intention
is not that my readers should believe everything I say, but that

they should be provoked into forming their own judgments, their own visions of human needs and purposes.

We do not need to have an agreed set of goals before we do something ambitious. No philosopher-king or hierarchy of committees can dissolve the causes of human discord and give us a universally accepted order of priorities. On the contrary, it is natural and right that we shall continue to stumble ahead into space without knowing why. The ultimate strength of the space program derives from the fact that it unites in a constructive effort a crowd of people who are in it for diverse reasons. I am in it partly because I am a scientist interested in astronomical problems. But many scientists are indifferent or hostile to the program, and I was enthusiastic about space travel long before I became a scientist.

I am writing here about matters that are more human than scientific, about social problems that have little to do with science or with space. At the end I will argue that the exploration of space offers remedies to some of our social diseases, but my argument will remain on the level of literature rather than of science. When I discuss human affairs, I like to deal in individual people rather than in abstract principles. I find science fiction more helpful than sociology in suggesting probable futures. Like anybody who is concerned with the long-range future, I owe a great debt to the ideas of H. G. Wells. Wells was an unsuccessful biologist who became a successful novelist. He understood better than most of us the comedy of the individual human being, and yet he never lost sight of our biological background, of the human species emerging from dubious origins and groping its way to an even more dubious destiny. He was no physicist, and he never took space travel seriously, although he used it on occasion as a stage property for his stories. His visions of man's future are Earth-bound, pessimistic, and quite different from my vision as I shall describe it. But I do not need to agree with Wells in order to acknowledge the greatness of his influence. His contribution to human thought is not the description of particular futures, but the awareness of the future as an object of intellectual study, having a depth and breadth as great as the study of the historic past. I am a child of Wells in so far as I cannot think of human destiny beyond the year 2000 as lying outside the scope of my responsibilities.

As an example of the insight into human character that I find

more illuminating than sociological analysis, I mention the
Artilleryman who appears briefly in Wells's *War of the Worlds*. This
is an insignificant man who becomes convinced, as civilization
collapses around him, that he can keep everything under control.
He has unlimited self-confidence and a fine flow of words, quite
out of touch with reality. Recently, I met a United States diplomat
who serves in a country where our policies might charitably be
described as being on the point of collapse. At first, I wondered,
"Now where have I met this man before?" and then I remembered
Wells's Artilleryman. If you listen carefully, you will hear the voice
of the Artilleryman wherever human society is facing problems
of overwhelming difficulty.

Another splendid example of Wells's insight is the General
Intelligence Machine which appears in his story "When the
Sleeper Wakes," written in 1899. It did not take much wisdom to
foresee in 1899 a machine which would sit in a living room and
speak upon request, giving up-to-date news reports concerning
the events of the day. Wells's insight is shown in the nature of the
information that the machine provides. It puts out a continuous
stream of commercial advertising and political propaganda at such
a level of imbecility that the characters in the story refer to it only
by the name of "Babble Machine." To convey the flavor of the
thing, I quote from Wells: "Babble Machines of a peculiarly rancid
tone filled the air with strenuous squealing and an idiotic slang,
'Skin your eyes and slide,' 'Gewhoop, bonanza,' 'Gollipers come
and hark.'" I find it comforting, when the drivel put out by our
contemporary Babble Machines drives me to fury or despair, to
reflect that even the worst television commercials are not as bad as
Wells imagined they would be.

2. FACTS OF LIFE

Here is a short list of facts central to the human situation. Like
Wells and other social analysts, I select my facts to make my
theory plausible. One fact of human life is nationalism. In all parts
of the world nationalism is the strongest political force. In most
places it is the only effective force making possible the organization of people's efforts for peace or war. Where nationalism is

weak, as in Nigeria or Belgium, it is usually because a smaller political unit, a tribe or a province, has usurped the place of the nation in people's minds. The strength of nationalism in the world as a whole has steadily increased during recent centuries, and is probably still increasing.

Another fact of life is race. The events of the last years have made it clear, if it was not clear before, that the problem of race runs deep in American society. No society with a substantial racial minority is free from problems. Some societies are more tolerant than others, but tolerance is fragile. For most of us it is pleasanter to live segregated than to face the frictions of racially mixed housing. In the pure white English society into which I was born, having at that time no racial problems to worry about, we developed our famous class system instead. As a middle-class child, I was unable to communicate with most of the children of my neighborhood, since they were "Oiks" and spoke a different dialect.

A third fact of life is drugs. By this I mean not the harmless legal drugs but the illegal ones, LSD, marijuana, and so on. Many people have more experience with these than I do. But I have not brought up a couple of teenagers without learning that drugs are an important part of the landscape. And the existing drugs are only the first wave of an ever-increasing series of problems that come under the name of biological experimentation. As biochemistry advances, there will be more and more varieties of drugs, illegally available, offering strange adventures to reckless young people. To make these things legal will never be acceptable to anxious parents and neighbors; to make them illegal will never effectively stop their abuse. Later on, when biology and genetics have advanced a little further, even more serious problems of medical experimentation will arise. Our young people may be able to induce dreams and hallucinations in each other, programmed to order, by gadgetry feeding directly into their brains. What reality would be able to compete with this dream world for their minds? Ultimately, perhaps a hundred years from now or perhaps sooner, humanity will be faced with the possibility of deliberate programming of the genetic makeup of children. Either a government using its paternalistic authority, or a group of individuals in defiance of authority, may cause children to be born differing radically from the norm in moral or intellectual power. Such experimentation may be of immense value from certain points of view. What a grand and terrible thing it would be to call into being a child with the endowments of Einstein or of Martin Luther King! And yet, which of our existing social institutions is strong enough to withstand the stresses that a generation of genetic experimentation would produce?

I listed three disagreeable facts that confront the human species: nationalism, racism, and biological engineering. Under the heading of biological engineering I include the whole range of problems of which LSD gives us a foretaste. These three facts are usually regarded as separate problems, each to be handled as best we can in its own context. I instead concentrate attention on the features common to all three, to see if there is an underlying pattern.

The underlying pattern is the propensity of human beings to function best in small groups. Most of us have experienced the happiness that comes from a communal effort. Goethe has described it imperishably in the death scene of his *Faust*. Our teenagers are disoriented because they are no longer involved in the communal activities of family and village, sowing and harvesting, hedging and ditching. It was not only in the country that communal work used to keep children happy and out of mischief. My grandmother grew up in the 1860s, a working-class girl in the notorious industrial north of England, which was still the classic capitalist hell that Friedrich Engels had described twenty years earlier. She went to work in the local wool factory when she was eight. She loved it. It was not a huge anonymous affair like a General Motors assembly line. Her father and her mother and her sister were all working there together. She became a skilled weaver and made good money. She would have hated to be left at home or stuck in school doing nothing useful.

Our pot-smoking teenagers are unanimous in saying that the great thing about pot is not the drug itself but the comradeship that it creates. And to make the comradeship real, there must not only be a group of friends inside the circle but enemies outside, police and parents and authorities to be defied. Just as, in the old Yorkshire wool factory, the spirit among the workers was warm and intimate, the comradeship strengthened by their shared hostility to the millowner and his managers. This is human life the way it is, my son wearing his hair odiously long because I dislike to be seen together with it in public, and we of the older generation fulfilling our duty as parents by keeping our hair short and marijuana illegal.

The strength of nationalism and racism derives ultimately from the same source as the tension between the generations. We all have a psychological need to feel identified with a group, preferably not too large a group, with a common purpose and a common enemy. Countries as big as the United States are already far too big to fulfill this need satisfactorily. Countries as small as Holland or Switzerland generally handle social problems better than big countries do. Nationalism is most genuine and spontaneous in countries which are both small and threatened, such as Finland or Israel.

It is easy to theorize, as many paleontologists have done, that the human species has built-in instincts of tribal exclusiveness, frozen into our inheritance during the hundreds of thousands of years that our ancestors spent roaming in small nomadic bands. Such a theory is plausible as an explanation of present-day nationalism, racism, and teenage gang warfare, but it cannot be proved. For my purpose it is not important to decide whether exclusiveness is an inherited instinct or a culturally acquired characteristic. The essential fact is that tribal exclusiveness exists in our species and has been essential to our rapid evolution.

Rapid evolution in any species depends largely on a phenomenon known as "genetic drift." Genetic drift is the random drifting of the average genetic endowment in a small inbreeding population. The speed of drift varies inversely with the square root of the size of the breeding group. The direction of drift is somewhat influenced by natural selection, but drift occurs even in the absence of selection. The force that drove a group of apes to develop an aptitude for calculus, or symphonic music, or theological argument, could only be genetic drift and not natural selection. All the things that we prize most in human culture, our appreciation of art, poetry, holiness, and natural beauty, must be products of genetic drift.

I imagine, though this is pure speculation, that genetic drift has been of decisive importance to human progress even in historic times. When we make a list of the most creative periods in human history, confining ourselves to the Judeo-Christian tradition with which I am familiar, we think immediately of eighth-century Jerusalem, fifth-century Athens, and fourteenth-century Florence. In each case we have a city, hardly more than a village by modern standards, producing out of a small population within a hundred years an astonishing concentration of intellectual achievement. In each case the outburst of genius followed a long period during which the city existed with an even smaller population, rather isolated from its neighbors and quarreling with them incessantly. It seems plausible that the best recipe for human cultural progress would read roughly as follows: take a hundred city-states, each with a population between ten thousand and a hundred thousand; let each one hate its neighbors sufficiently to prevent substantial interbreeding; encourage priestly and aristocratic caste systems to reduce still further the size of breeding units; introduce an occasional major war or plague to keep the populations small; let the mixture simmer for a thousand years; and one of your hundred cities will be the new Florence, the new Athens, or the new Jerusalem.

Up to this point I have presented the case for human divisiveness, for insularity, exclusiveness, and intolerance. These human qualities, however evil their effects in our present society, are not easily to be eradicated. Throughout the long centuries of our prehistory and even until recently, these qualities have been beneficial to our species. In the self-sacrifice of a soldier, the fury of a mob, the loyalty of a teenager to his gang, the same qualities are still with us. We still function best in small groups.

But this is only half the story. We cannot go back to the Middle Ages or to classical Greece. Even if the ideal of universal human brotherhood may still be remote for most of us, the three great forces of modern technology, the forces of weaponry, population growth, and pollution, stand against the historic forces of tribalism. We are in danger of exterminating ourselves with our hydrogen bombs and the still worse horrors that biological engineering will soon put in our hands. We are in danger of exhausting our resources and ultimately reducing ourselves to a starvation diet through overpopulation. We are in danger of ruining all that is beautiful on this planet through our accumulations of poisonous mess. All three dangers demand that mankind unite. Each of them, and the problem of weapons above all, requires a world-wide authority to protect us from our own folly. Slowly and against stubborn resistance, practical necessities are driving us to forget our quarrels and accept peaceful coexistence with our enemies. For twenty-four years the nuclear physicists have been saying "One World or None," and there is no reason to doubt that in the long run they are right. The earth has grown too small for bickering tribes and city-states to exist on it. Our bombs are too big, our machines are too complicated, our smog and garbage is too pervasive, to be left much longer in the hands of tribal authorities.

As far into the future as anyone can see, the dangers of modern technology will continue to grow and will threaten mankind on this planet with the choice of political union or death. Political union will inevitably mean some degree of political oppression, government by remote bureaucracy, overcentralization. We will be lucky if we can succeed in organizing a world government that does not degenerate into a world police state. But the forces of tribalism and nationalism will probably remain for a long time strong enough to defeat attempts to impose world government. People will prefer to live in filth with the threat of annihilation hanging over their heads, rather than allow foreigners to tax them.

Unfortunately, the unifying force of technology, while not yet powerful enough to bind us into a worldwide brotherhood, is already strong enough to destroy the historic benefits that we once derived from tribalism. Genetic drift does not work anymore as a force for cultural uplift, when our cities contain millions of people instead of thousands. Statistical fluctuations will not transform Chicago into the Athens of Aeschylus and Socrates. No place on earth is any longer genetically or culturally isolated. The last group of people who seriously tried to get away from their neighbors, to conduct a large-scale social experiment under conditions of isolation, were the Mormons. It took less than fifty years for our beneficent government to catch up with them, to put an end to their dreams of independence. Anyone who has read the first and finest of the Sherlock Holmes mystery stories, *A Study in Scarlet,* will know what that meant. There is now no place on this planet where a group of dissidents, wishing to do their thing undisturbed by governmental authorities, can hide. Big Brother is watching us all from the skies. Never again on this planet will there be a Pitcairn Island for the *Bounty* mutineers, or a New England for the Pilgrim Fathers.

3. THE PROMISE OF SPACE

Now comes at last the hopeful part of my message. I have presented a gloomy view of our human predicament. On the one hand, we are historically attuned to living in small exclusive groups, and we carry in us a stubborn disinclination to treat all men as brothers. On the other hand, we live on a shrinking and vulnerable planet which our lack of foresight is rapidly turning into a slum. Never again on this planet will there be unoccupied land, cultural isolation, freedom from bureaucracy, freedom for people to get lost and be on their own. Never again on this planet. But how about somewhere else?

Space travel provides a possible answer to these grave human problems. The main question in my mind is "When?" Many people consider it ridiculous to think of space as a way out of our difficulties, when the existing space program is being rapidly cut down, precisely because it appears to have nothing to offer to the solution of social problems. It is true that the existing space program has nothing to offer. If one believes in space as a major factor in human affairs, one must take a very long view.

To avoid misunderstanding, it is important to make a sharp distinction between human affairs and scientific affairs. The existing space program consists of two unequal parts, the scientific program using unmanned vehicles and absorbing about one-tenth of the money, and the unscientific program including manned flights and taking nine-tenths of the money. The scientific program has already been of immense value to science. In the next two decades, if the economic ax has not chopped it to pieces, the scientific space program should be able to settle the question of the existence of life on Mars, and I cannot think of any question in the whole of science more important than that. In the long run, the discovery of alien life would undoubtedly have human as well as scientific consequences, but I do not include these in my discussion. I am looking for consequences of space travel that affect the mass of my fellow citizens and not merely my academic colleagues. The unscientific part of the existing space program affects the public more directly but only superficially. It is an international sporting event with the whole world serving as the stadium. I support the manned space program for reasons which I will presently explain, but I do not pretend that it yet offers benefits commensurate with its cost, either to science or to the general public.

How long it will take for space travel to become socially important is mainly a matter of economics, a field in which I have no competence. I will only put forward a few tentative remarks to suggest that the time should be measured in decades rather than in centuries. There is a prevalent view among the educated public that space travel is necessarily and permanently so expensive that it can never be made available to large numbers of people. I believe this view to be incorrect. An illuminating analysis of the economics of space operations was made by Theodore Taylor. He calculated the cost of running a commercial jet plane service from New York to Los Angeles under the following ground rules: (1) There shall be no more than one flight per month. (2) The airplane shall be thrown away after each flight. (3) The entire costs of Kennedy and Los Angeles airports shall be covered by the freight charges. Under these rules, which are the rules governing our present space program, the cost of freight between New York and Los Angeles is comparable to the cost of putting freight into orbit. The point of this calculation is that the economies of commercial airline operations are economies of scale and of efficient organization. There is no basic physical or engineering reason why it should be enormously cheaper to fly to Los Angeles than to fly into orbit.

This is not the place for a technical discussion of space propulsion. In order to make space travel cheap we need two things. The first is a reliable vehicle, preferably an air breather, which can take off from an airport, fly itself directly into orbit, reenter and land, and be ready to repeat the operation day after day. The second is a massive volume of traffic and a correspondingly massive sale of tickets. The second of these requirements will probably be met within a few decades after the first is achieved. There are formidable technical problems involved in producing a reusable orbital vehicle, but the problems are not likely to remain permanently unsolved. Few people in the existing space program have worked on these problems, because the policy has been to do things fast rather than cheaply. The cutback of the present program may encourage more long-range work on cheaper vehicles. I hesitate to predict the time scale of these developments, but I expect between fifty and a hundred years from now to have space travel with a volume of traffic and a cost to the passengers comparable with our present intercontinental jet flights. This prediction has the great advantage that if the reality exceeds my hopes I may be here to enjoy it, whereas if I am proved wrong the other way, I will never know it.

I will not say more about the economic aspects of space travel. The technical problems can be solved only by long and hard work, not by philosophical discourse. I am here discussing goals and purpose. Why should so many people want to rush around in space? What good will it do? One thing that emigration from Earth will not do is to solve the problem of the population explosion. Emigrants will always be a small minority, like the Spanish conquistadores rather than the Irish peasants of the Hungry Forties. Those who stay on Earth must solve their population problems, one way or another. Those who emigrate will have only postponed theirs.

The expansion of mankind into space will confer benefits on us in three main respects. I am here ignoring the scientific benefits and speaking only of social benefits. The three benefits are garbage disposal, invulnerability, and the open frontier, in increasing order of importance. I discuss each of them in turn.

If humanity were to be forever confined to the Earth, the problem of pollution could hardly be solved without an enforced economic stagnation. Many industrial processes are inherently messy, and the sum total of industrial processes threatens to heat the Earth's biosphere to an intolerable extent within a century or two at present rates of economic growth. If cheap space transportation were available, it would become socially desirable and economically advantageous to move many of the messier industries into space. The solar wind is a magnificent garbage disposal system, sweeping any dispersed matter in the solar system into the outer darkness where it will never be seen again. Prime candidates for the move upstairs would be the nuclear reactor and processing industries, with their large radioactive waste and thermal pollution problems. The migration of industry into space need not be directed by a grandiose governmental plan. It would occur spontaneously as a result of economic pressures, if polluting industries were forced to pay, for the privilege of remaining on Earth, the actual cost of their pollutions. I foresee a time, a few centuries from now, when the bulk of heavy industry is space-borne, with the majority of mining operations transferred to the moon, and the Earth preserved for the enjoyment of its inhabitants as a green and pleasant land.

If the problem of garbage disposal for an Earth-bound humanity is difficult, the problem of vulnerability is insoluble. How can we expect to go on living forever on this exposed planetary surface, armed with deadly weapons which year by year grow more numerous and more widely dispersed? The only way to make the Earth safe from these weapons would be to establish a supranational monopoly of military force, and even such a monopoly would not give us permanent security. The guardians of the monopoly would be men with their own national loyalties, and there would always be danger that the monopoly would break up in ruinous civil war, as happened on a smaller scale in 1861. We can hope to survive in a world bristling with hydrogen bombs for a few centuries, if we are lucky. But we have small chance of surviving ten thousand years if we stay stuck to this planet. We are too many eggs in too small a basket.

The emigration into distant parts of the solar system of a substantial number of people would make our species as a whole invulnerable. A nuclear holocaust on Earth would still be an unspeakable tragedy, and might still wipe out 99 percent of our numbers. But the 1 percent who had dispersed themselves could not be wiped out simultaneously by any man-made catastrophe, and they would remain to carry on the promise of our destiny. Perhaps some of them would come back to repopulate the Earth, after the radioactivity had cooled off. I find it a consoling thought that the human race will one day be invulnerable, that we have only to survive this awkward period of a century or two between the discovery of nuclear weapons and the large-scale expansion of our habitat, and then we shall be masters of our fate, freed from the threat of permanent extinction.

The third and deepest benefit which space offers to humans is the recovery of an open frontier. At this point we come back to the question: where will all these people go when they set out in their latter-day *Mayflowers*? It is conventional in science fiction to think of going to planets, to Mars in particular. But planets will probably not play the major role in man's future. They are mostly uninhabitable, and even if they are habitable they will not increase our living space very much. If we succeed in colonizing Mars, Mars will soon resemble the Earth, complete with parking lots, income tax forms, and all the rest. It will not be possible to hide on Mars any more than on Earth.

The real future of man in space lies far away from planets, in isolated city-states floating in the void, perhaps attached to an inconspicuous asteroid or perhaps to a comet. Comets are especially important. It is believed that between a billion and ten billion comets exist on the outer fringes of the Solar System, loosely attached to the Sun and only rarely passing close to it. Each of these comets is a mine of biologically useful materials—carbon, nitrogen, and water. Together they provide a thousand times as much living space as the planets. Above all, they provide an open frontier, a place to hide and to disappear without trace, beyond the reach of snooping policemen and bureaucrats.

This vision of comet-hopping emigrants, streaming outward like the covered wagons on the Santa Fe Trail, is perhaps absurdly romantic. Probably, it will never happen the way I imagine it. But something along these lines will ultimately happen. Space is huge enough, so that somewhere in its vastness there will always be a place for rebels and outlaws. Near to the sun, space will belong to big governments and computerized industries. Outside, the open frontier will beckon as it has beckoned before, to persecuted minorities escaping from oppression, to religious fanatics escaping from their neighbors, to recalcitrant teenagers escaping from their parents, to lovers of solitude escaping from crowds. Perhaps most important of all for man's future, there will be groups of people setting out to find a place where they can be safe from prying eyes, free to experiment undisturbed with the creation of radically new types of human being, surpassing us in mental capacities as we surpass the apes.

The ultimate benefit of space travel to mankind will be to make it possible for us once again to live as we lived throughout prehistoric time, in isolated small units. Once again our human qualities of clannish loyalty and exclusiveness will play a constructive role, instead of being the chief dangers to our survival. Our tribal instincts will move back from the destructive channels of nationalism, racism, and youthful alienation, and find satisfaction in the dangerous life of a frontier society. Genetic drift and diversification will again become important factors in human progress. Only in this way can the basic dilemmas of our age, arising from the discordance between our tribal loyalties and the necessities of a worldwide technological civilization, be resolved. And when the angry young men and rebels and racists have again a frontier to which they can go, perhaps we timid and law-abiding citizens who choose to stay quietly down here on Earth will find it easier to live together in peace.

CHAPTER 20

The Hidden Costs of Saying No

.....

1 9 7 4

> One Law for the Lion and Ox is Oppression.
>
> You never know what is enough unless you know what
> is more than enough.
>
> William Blake,
> *The Marriage of Heaven and Hell*
> (1790).

I. THE PAST

William Blake lived two hundred years ago, in a time of revolution and rapid change. He was considered crazy by his contemporaries. He stayed at home, patiently etching his poems on plates of copper, while Byron scribbled pages by the hundred and captured the attention of Europe. But everything I shall say in an hour was said long ago in two sentences by William Blake.

During the last ten years, in every industrialized country, the general public and the political authorities have become acutely aware of the existence of hidden costs. The economists have taught us that industrial and social innovations carry hidden costs that do not appear in the immediate profit-and-loss accounts of any individual enterprise. Flood control dams in California cause rivers to carry less sand to the ocean, with the consequence that

234

the width of swimming beaches is diminishing. High-intensity street lights, installed by highway authorities to reduce the frequency of accidents, destroy the quality of the sky over an astronomical observatory fifty miles away. Many examples of hidden costs have become notorious: the sinking of the city of Venice, the smog of Los Angeles, the poisoning of the American eagle by insecticides. The public has been awakened to the importance of hidden costs, mainly through the influence of a small number of books. Let nobody say that books have lost their power to persuade in the modern world of computers and television. A few writers gifted with common sense and eloquence, Rachel Carson with her *Silent Spring,* Fairfield Osborn with his *Plundered Planet,* Barry Commoner with his *Closing Circle,* persuaded the people and Congress of the United States of America to count the hidden costs of industrial development. A similarly small and gifted group of writers has done the same for northern Europe. As a result, we now have laws that prescribe a public accounting of hidden costs before any large public enterprise is undertaken.

Several proposed enterprises have come spectacularly to grief during the process of public accounting, and have as a consequence been discredited and abandoned. The most famous project killed by the public examination of hidden costs was the American supersonic transport plane (SST). But the most important effect of the new attitude toward technological innovation does not lie in the small number of big projects that have been exposed to public scrutiny and then stopped. Far more important is the larger number of projects that never come to the notice of the public but die unseen, their proponents discouraged by the expense, delay, and uncertainty that the procedures of public examination impose. For every one power station or oil refinery that is publicly killed, ten others are privately discouraged. The doctrine of deterrence, whether or not it is valid in the strategic sphere, certainly applies in the sphere of technological innovation. After a government kills one thorium-breeding reactor project, nobody has the heart to try to begin another. After one nuclear rocket program has been officially abandoned, young people with brains and imagination turn their attention elsewhere.

I am not saying that the counting of hidden costs is a mistake, or that the public indignation aroused by dead birds and dead fish was unjustified. We shall not turn the clock back to the time when everyone was free to dump soot upon his neighbor's garden. Rachel Carson's cry of anguish has made this planet a pleasanter place, not only for birds but also for people. The good that she has done shall not be undone. But it is not enough to count the hidden costs of saying yes to new enterprises. We must also learn to count the hidden costs of saying no. The costs of saying no may be high, although they are often uncertain and intangible. Our existing political processes introduce a strong bias into the consideration of new enterprises. The costs of saying yes can be calculated and demonstrated in a style that is familiar and congenial to lawyers, whereas the costs of saying no are a matter of conjecture and have no established legal standing. We must learn that costs may be tragically real even when they are legally unprovable. We must try to establish processes of decision making that give the costs of yes and no an equal voice. We need to know more accurately the costs of saying no, and we need procedures that allow a more realistic weighing of uncertainties when knowledge is lacking.

One case study, in which the costs of saying no were demonstrated in convincing fashion, was published by Carl Djerassi. Djerassi took the trouble to document his facts carefully, and his conclusions have not, so far as I know, been challenged. His study is concerned with the process of development of chemical birth-control agents. The presently existing birth-control agents are in various ways unsatisfactory, unsafe, or unsuited to the purposes for which they were intended. Djerassi analyzes in detail the costs in money and time which are imposed by government regulation upon anybody who wishes to develop a new agent. The costs apply equally, whether the project is undertaken by an industrial company, a government agency, or a private philanthropic organization. The cost in time turns out to be seventeen years, the cost in money $18 million dollars of 1970 vintage. These are minimum figures, based on the assumption that the various steps in the prescribed procedure follow one another smoothly and that no unforeseen difficulties arise. The figures are presented for work performed under United States regulations, but the conclusions would not be substantially different in other industrialized countries. The large expenditures of time and money are required in order to carry out long-term studies involving large numbers of animals and, in the later stages, human volunteers, to ensure that the product is safe and effective before it is made available for public use.

Djerassi was not arguing, and I am not arguing, that these strict regulations governing the introduction of new drugs should be abandoned. The regulations came into existence as a result of the public reaction to the Thalidomide tragedy, in which thousands of babies were crippled by a supposedly harmless sleeping pill. Nobody with responsibility for developing new drugs would wish to have another such tragedy on his conscience, and nobody with responsibility for formulating regulations would wish to leave open a chance that it might happen again. In this case the costs of saying yes are so high and so abominable that the regulations must be accepted as a permanent necessity. Djerassi is saying that the practical consequence of these regulations must also be accepted. The regulations mean in practice that no substantially new chemical birth-control agents will become available during the foreseeable future. No companies, and few individuals, will devote themselves to an expensive and elaborate project that will take at least seventeen years to complete and may at any stage be halted and come to nothing. Djerassi argues that it should still be possible to develop new agents under the existing regulations, if the government would give such projects long-term financial and administrative support. Needless to say, the government has done nothing in the meantime to bring such hopes to reality. I draw the following conclusion from Djerassi's study. In the development of new drugs, the price of safety is that large public expenditures are required to do a job that in the past could be done by private industry, and in the future may not be done at all. This is one of the rare cases in which the costs of saying no are not hidden but are almost calculable, as a result of one man's careful work in collecting the relevant facts.

I now return to the supersonic airliner. I do not say that the killing of the SST project was a mistake. There were some good reasons for killing it. Nevertheless, the decision was influenced by calculations of costs and benefits which bore little relation to reality. For example, it was argued that the SST would have a large adverse effect on the balance of payments of the United States, because it would stimulate a massive flow of American tourists to Europe, unbalanced by any comparable flow of Europeans to America. This argument may have had some merit, but the calculations that were used to support it have already been made obsolete by the world economic crisis. As often happens in such cases, a cost that could be calculated in dollars and cents was taken seriously by the politicians, even though the precision of the calculation was illusory. Almost all numerical estimates of the long-range costs of technological innovations are illusory. In the case of the SST, the most important cost of saying no was the discouragement of future enterprises in aeronautical engineering, many of which have not yet been conceived. This cost may in the long run heavily outweigh the costs that we should have incurred by saying yes. As always, the weighing of intangible costs is a matter of taste and of judgment.

2. THE FUTURE

I consider two problems of the future to be of central importance, namely, climate modification and genetic engineering. It is obvious that any further large expansion of the industrial activities of mankind will cause noticeable changes in the climate of the earth. This fact is often used by advocates of "limits to growth" as an argument for halting further expansion. I wish to argue the contrary view. I see no reason to believe that the present climate of this planet is in any sense optimal. The concept of an "optimal climate" is meaningless, since different people with different ways of life will always have different preferences in matters of climate. It is neither possible nor desirable to choose one particular climate, such as that of Mallorca or Hawaii, and impose it uniformly upon the whole world. But there are many large areas of the planet, for example the Sahara desert and the Siberian tundra, where some mitigation of the climate would produce substantial benefits. A warmer Siberia and a wetter Sahara would allow a richer life not only for human beings but also for wild animals and plants.

The idea that an artificially created ecology can be richer and aesthetically more pleasing than a natural one is at present highly unpopular. The fashionable belief is expressed by the writer Barry

Commoner when he states as a basic law of ecology: "Nature Knows Best." Commoner is able to present an impressive collection of horror stories to support his opinion that human alteration of a natural ecology leads inevitably to deterioration and disaster. But there are also some impressive examples to the contrary. I spent my childhood years in rural England, and I frequently return there for a few days of rest and spiritual renewal. At any season of the year you may find in rural England an ecological harmony of extraordinary richness, with a great variety of species of plants, birds, and animals. This ecology is unusually robust, surviving without obvious damage the assaults inflicted by a high density of human population and industry. It is a community of species in which ecologists and poets can equally rejoice. But nothing in the ecology of rural England is natural. The natural state of England was a rather uniform expanse of forest and swamp. Almost everything that now exists there is artificial, created by people who were not afraid to turn wilderness into village, cropland, and pasture. There are no laws of nature that forbid us to create an artificial ecology as varied and as beautiful as that of rural England, either in the central Sahara or on the shores of the Arctic Ocean. To do this will require a long time, great quantities of energy, and knowledge that we do not yet possess of the long-range consequences of our actions. When we have acquired the knowledge and power to modify climates according to our taste, we shall be exposed to great dangers at the same time as we reap great rewards. There is no reason why a prudent fear of the dangers should cause us to deny the possibility of the rewards.

A look at the past history of the earth's natural climate gives additional grounds for optimism concerning the feasibility of producing desired changes without disastrous side effects. It is known that about five thousand years ago the climate of northern Europe and Asia was milder than it is now, and the variety of indigenous plants and animals was greater. Mixed forests grew far to the north, where now only conifers can survive. In roughly the same period the rock paintings of the central Sahara show herds of giraffes, which are vivid evidence of a climate wet enough to support trees and grass over a wide area. We have no idea how and why the climate in these two widely separated areas deteriorated, or whether the changes in the two areas were causally linked. It is improbable that changes on this scale and at so early a date were strongly influenced by human activities. But our ignorance of the mechanisms of climatic change is so profound that all theories of causation are pure speculation. What we can say with some degree of certainty is that five thousand years ago a climatic regime existed which was in some parts of the Earth more hospitable to living creatures than the present regime. It is possible that some comparatively modest human intervention, applied with adequate understanding of the consequences, would result in the restoration of the regime that existed naturally in the past. This possibility should be a source of hope to mankind. A wetter Sahara and a warmer Arctic could mean a doubling of the area of the planet suitable for productive agriculture. A hungry world should count the cost before saying no to such possibilities.

The second big problem of the future is genetic engineering. The most important technological advances of the next fifty years are likely to come from biology and not from the physical sciences. Within less than fifty years I expect that we shall have achieved a mastery of the fundamental processes of living organisms, as complete as the mastery we now possess of the processes of physics and chemistry. A mastery of biological processes will imply, among other things, the ability to produce microorganisms with enzymatic machinery tailored to our needs. Chemical processes carried out by systems of enzymes generally proceed with higher efficiency, higher specificity, and lower wastage of material, than processes carried out by conventional industrial methods. We can expect that the development of microbiological technology will revolutionize the production of food, the conversion of coal and crude oil into clean fuel, the concentration and reduction of ores, and the handling and recycling of waste materials. Each one of these revolutions will have profound effects on the conditions of human life. All of them together will change the world in ways that we can hardly imagine. When I use the phrase "genetic engineering," I am referring to this future industrial revolution based on artificially produced microorganisms. I am not speaking about genetic engineering applied to human beings, since that is a separate problem with unique dangers and more dubious rewards.

The human rewards resulting from a massive development of microbiological genetic engineering may be very great. We can expect that almost any organic material, from sawdust to sewage, may be converted quantitatively into clean fuel and other useful chemicals. We can expect to evolve techniques of "indoor farming" that will allow abundant production of food in all parts of the globe. We can expect the overall style and appearance of industry to change in an aesthetically desirable direction. Oil refineries need not stink, mine dumps need not despoil the earth, and people who work in factories need not drive to homes twenty miles away to find clean air. A second industrial revolution, based on biological technology, may largely undo the evil effects of the first industrial revolution based upon steam and coal. These are some of the rewards that genetic engineering appears to offer to us.

These are the possible rewards. But there are also dangers. And in recent years my biologist colleagues have been thinking more about the dangers than about the rewards. A group of leading microbiologists under the chairmanship of Paul Berg recently issued a statement calling attention to the dangers involved in the use of newly discovered techniques of manipulating DNA molecules. Berg's group not only called attention to the dangers but called upon all biologists to abstain from certain types of experiment that were judged particularly hazardous. The hazardous experiments involve the grafting of alien genes into the genetic apparatus of bacteria that might afterward escape from control and infect human populations. I have no competence to assess the magnitude of the danger involved in these experiments. I accept the view of the experts that the danger is real and serious. Once again we must respect the caution of scientists who do not wish to take any risk that they might inflict a new Thalidomide tragedy upon babies yet unborn. But the tone of the Berg statement leaves me with a feeling of dissatisfaction. The statement is written as if the only factors to be considered were, on the one hand, the danger to society involved in certain experiments, and on the other hand, the professional interest of a few biologists in doing the experiments. The cost of saying yes to these experiments is a risk of a disastrous epidemic disease, the cost of saying no is a minor setback in the professional careers of a few scientists. When the balance of costs is presented in these terms, the inevitable conclusion is a negative one. Any biologist performing such experiments is automatically judged to be selfish and irresponsible.

Unfortunately, the experiments now judged dangerous lie close in technique and concept to experiments that would be required for the development of a genetic industrial technology. The prohibition of the dangerous experiments may imply the postponement of an industrial technology that is of crucial importance to mankind. This is the hidden cost of saying no, a cost that the Berg statement ignores. The Berg statement includes a proposal for an international meeting to be held next year to "further discuss appropriate ways to deal with the potential biohazards of recombinant DNA molecules." It is to be hoped that the international meeting will consider not only the hazards of these molecules but also their promise for human welfare. Not only the costs of saying yes but the costs of saying no. The most useful outcome of the international meeting would be the definition of two clearly separated classes of experiments, one class carrying danger to human populations, the other class carrying no visible danger but still promising to unravel the complexities of structure that must be understood before genetic engineering will become a reality. It is as important to encourage the second class of experiment as to discourage the first.

3. SUMMING UP

I have looked at four problems of the regulation of technological development, two from the past and two from the future. From the past came Djerassi's study of the regulation of chemical birth-control agents, and the downfall of the American supersonic airliner. From the future came climate modification and genetic engineering. These four examples suggest some general conclusions.

In each case two stubborn facts of life make it difficult for political authorities to reach wise decisions. The two facts are the unpredictability of technology and the inflexibility of bureaucratic institutions. Technology has always been, and always will be, unpredictable. Whenever things seem to be moving smoothly along a predictable path, some unexpected twist changes the rules of the game and makes the old predictions irrelevant. Quantitative factors that are predictable are outweighed by qualitative factors that are unpredictable. To take an example from the past, which I owe to Leon Cooper, a nineteenth-century development program aimed at the mechanical reproduction of music might have produced a superbly engineered music box or Pianola, but it would never have imagined a transistor radio or subsidized the work of Maxwell on the physics of the electromagnetic field which made the transistor radio possible. In the future, genetic engineering will have a major impact on agriculture and industry all over the world, but the impact will come in unexpected ways and will certainly not follow the path that I have predicted for it. Yet human legislators act as if the future were predictable. They legislate solutions to technological problems, and they make choices between technological alternatives before the evidence upon which a rational choice might be based is available. It often happens in technological development that one design turns out to be decisively better than its competitors, for reasons that could not have been predicted in advance. There is no way to find the best design except to try out as many designs as possible and discard the failures. The governmental authorities in all countries have to learn the lesson that Blake etched on a plate of copper 180 years ago: "You never know what is enough unless you know what is more than enough."

The other lesson that we have to learn is that bureaucratic regulation has a killing effect on all creative endeavor. No matter how wisely framed and well intentioned, legal formalities tend to become inflexible. Procedures designed to fit one situation are applied indiscriminately to others. Regulations, whose purpose was to count the cost of saying yes to an unsound project, have the unintended effect of saying no to all projects that do not fit snugly into the bureaucratic system. Inventive spirits rebel against such rules and leave the leadership of technology to the uninventive. These are the hidden costs of saying no. To mitigate such costs, lawyers and legislators should carry in their hearts the other lesson that Blake has taught us: "One Law for the Lion and Ox is Oppression."

PART V

Books

oooo

SPEAK TO ALL MEN AS YOU DO TO YOURSELF, WITH

NO CONCERN FOR THE EFFECT YOU MAKE, SO THAT

YOU DO NOT SHUT THEM OUT FROM YOUR WORLD;

LEST IN ISOLATION THE MEANING OF LIFE SLIPS OUT OF

SIGHT AND YOU LOSE THE BELIEF IN THE PERFECTION

OF THE CREATION.

LEO SZILARD,

"TEN COMMANDMENTS"

CHAPTER 21

Pupin

.....

1 9 6 0

I welcome the opportunity to write a foreword to this reprinting of *From Immigrant to Inventor*. Pupin's book has always fascinated me, because of the personality of the author and his ability to weave the history of his times into the drama of his life.

The book has two major themes. One is the experience of the European immigrant coming to the United States, with his gradually growing awareness that he belongs to two cultures whose ends are not always reconcilable. The other is the experience of a student of physics, breaking at an unusually mature age into the intellectual kingdom of Faraday and Maxwell. In describing these various experiences, Pupin makes the spirit and texture of a past age come to life. Especially his descriptions of the scientific atmosphere in the different countries that he visited have an absolutely authentic touch. He achieves this authenticity by recording in objective detail the confusions of his own mind and the slow growth of clarity and understanding. I have never seen anywhere else such an honest account of the struggles of a scientist to reach a clear vision of his subject. To record these struggles accurately a man needs unusual honesty and an unusual memory, and he must resist all temptation to be wise after the event. The fact that Pupin was twenty-six before he started the serious study of physics may have made it easier for him to view his experiences dispassionately.

I have special reasons to be interested in Pupin, because I am also a physicist and came to the United States as an immigrant from Europe. This does not mean that there has been the slightest

similarity between his experiences and mine. The most striking
impression that his book makes upon the modern reader is the
contrast between the nineteenth and twentieth centuries in the status and treatment of immigrants. I find it amusing to compare my
experiences as a twentieth-century immigrant physicist with
those of Pupin seventy years earlier.

In my case there was no question of arriving unannounced in
New York with five cents in my pocket. The first step in my pilgrim's progress to America was to go to be interviewed by a
Selection Committee. This committee, composed of Englishmen
with some experience of the American academic world, selects
each year a dozen or more young men to spend one or two years
in the United States. The successful applicants are supported during their time in America by a fellowship, paid out of a fund established for this purpose by a philanthropic American millionaire.
The committee takes great pains to be wise in making its selections. Their first requirement is that the applicant have a program
of study that could profitably be pursued at an American university. The second requirement is that the applicant have a suitable
character and background, so that he may function as an "ambassador of goodwill" between his native country and the United
States. The committee makes its selections well, according to
these criteria. I do not believe that any other committee could do
the job better. But I feel a little uncomfortable when I reflect that
they would certainly not have selected Pupin.

After the Selection Committee, my next hurdle was the American visa. This was for me no problem, since I was born with
good conservative political opinions, in a country with an unfilled
quota. If Pupin had had the misfortune to live in this century, he
would have had much more trouble. He had already at the age of
fifteen acquired a police record of open opposition to his country's
government, he had taken part in subversive demonstrations, and
he had associated repeatedly with revolutionary Czech national-
ists in Prague. It is unlikely that any American consul during the
last ten years would have run the risk of approving his visa.

After the bureaucratic preliminaries were completed, I took my
place on the ship that was to carry me across the Atlantic, in a
stylish second-class cabin paid for by my American sponsors.
When I arrived in New York, I was met at the pier by a represent-

ative of the sponsors, given an ample supply of pocket money, and taken for a tour of the city. When the time came for me to proceed on my way to Cornell University, the same carefully prepared welcome awaited me. At Cornell I was greeted by an advisor of foreign students who arranged, in the most friendly way possible, for me to do whatever I liked. Soon after this I was browsing in the library at Cornell and sat down to read *From Immigrant to Inventor*. The contrast between my pampered luxury and Pupin's robust independence was overwhelming.

If I compare the status of physics in Pupin's day and in mine, the difference is equally startling. Pupin, at the end of his struggles as immigrant and student, received an appointment as "Teacher of Mathematical Physics" in the Electrical Engineering Department of Columbia University. This was by the standards of the time an excellent position for a young man. But the teaching load was so heavy that any research work could only be done in the evenings after the students had departed. There was no provision of money for the purchase of research equipment. Pupin, with his colleague Francis Bacon Crocker, organized courses of public lectures outside the university; they managed to make enough money from these popular lectures to buy a modest amount of experimental apparatus. All their early work was done in this way, paid for out of their own pockets, with inadequate equipment, inadequate space, and inadequate time. That Pupin succeeded in carrying out a research program under these conditions is a tribute to his astonishing energy and devotion to science. And he not only carried out a program. He made important discoveries.

To turn to the other side of the picture, when I received a faculty appointment at Cornell University in 1951, I started with the enormous teaching load of three hours a week. I had at my disposal a huge laboratory devoted to pure research in physics, equipped with the latest and most refined research apparatus, and supported by government funds. If any theoretician like me had an interesting idea for an experiment, he would not even have to endure the tedium of doing the experiment himself, for there were plenty of competent experimentalists who would be glad to do it for him. This life of academic ease and plenty has now become so familiar to us that we almost take it for granted. It is good to be reminded that we enjoy it only because Pupin and others like him fought hard for the reform of the system under which they had to labor.

The development of physics in America came to full flower in the 1930s. This was the time when a whole generation of European refugees came to the United States, bringing with them in force the scientific renaissance that had begun a decade earlier in Europe. The contributions of this generation, which included Einstein and Fermi, were so tremendous that it often seems as if there had been no science worth mentioning in the United States before they arrived here.

In fact, however, the refugees coming to America had the ground well prepared for them. The tide of refugees from Germany flowed in all directions, to Latin America and the Soviet Union as well as to North America. It was only in the United States, and to a lesser extent in England, that the immigrants caused a decisive improvement in the scientific life of the country to which they came. The reason for this is undoubtedly that the United States was at that time the only country ripe and ready to respond to the stimulus of the refugees with a sharp increase in its own scientific activity. Without belittling the contributions of the refugees, one may say that they accelerated a process of scientific development in this country which would have occurred more slowly without them. The fact that the United States was ripe for such a development must be credited to the scientists of an earlier generation, and to Pupin not least.

There is a symbolic significance in the manner in which Pupin's name is commemorated at Columbia University, where he spent his working life. There is a big building on the campus which houses the Physics Department and is called Pupin. Few of the people who daily walk in and out of the building know or care who Pupin was. Their job is to do physics, and they do it well. Several of the most important experiments of the last twenty years were done in that building. This is for Pupin a particularly fitting memorial. The aim of his whole life was to imbue his fellowmen, and fellow Americans in particular, with his own deep love for pure scientific knowledge. The Pupin Building records the fact that he succeeded in this aim. He would have considered it all to the good that his personal fame has been eclipsed by the greater achievements of his heirs.

With characteristic honesty, Pupin called his book *From Immigrant to Inventor*, rather than *From Immigrant to Discoverer*. From the days of his childhood he had had dreams of being a great discoverer. Throughout his long years of apprenticeship and study, he was driven onward by the desire to understand and solve some basic problem in pure science. This aim he never achieved. The results of his researches, important as they were, should rightly be called inventions rather than discoveries. His greatest single brainchild was the electric transmission line that made the long-distance telephone possible. This transmission line was rapidly adopted by all the telephone systems in the world, and has been in constant use ever since. Pupin records in his book the story of how this idea came to birth. For him the outstanding lesson of his invention was that it was made, not by an engineer tinkering around with electrical gadgetry, but by a theoretical physicist pondering the implications of a mechanical problem posed by the eighteenth-century French mathematician Joseph-Louis Lagrange.

Wealth and fame came to Pupin as a result of his inventions. He soon understood that his own special talent lay not in the creation of new ideas but in the inspired application of old ones. However, he also believed with passionate intensity that the primary aim of science is the pure understanding of nature, and that useful applications must be considered of secondary importance. He used the prestige and influence that he derived from his inventions in an unceasing campaign to improve the standing of fundamental science in America. In this way the paradoxical situation arose that it was Pupin the practical inventor who did more than any other man of his time to convince the American public that great scientific discoveries are more important than inventions.

Pupin's triumph has been so complete that now, twenty-five years after his death, pure scientists have more prestige, more influence, and more financial support than he would have imagined to be possible. Perhaps, in this apotheosis of the fundamental researcher, some injustice has been done to the class of inventors to which Pupin himself belonged. We have reached the point where a first-rate inventor is rarer than a first-rate scientist. Inventors are no longer welcomed in most university departments, and even in industrial laboratories pure research is increasingly becoming the

251

fashionable thing to do. Perhaps the time will soon come when a group of pure scientists will be compelled to organize a campaign to prevent the permanent extinction of the inventor. This would be the final payment of the debt of gratitude that everyone in a comfortable academic position in America owes to Michael Pupin.

CHAPTER 22

Oppenheimer

.....

1 9 8 0

Robert Oppenheimer: Letters and Recollections reveals Oppenheimer through personal letters, through the recollections of his friends recorded by the editors, and through his own recollections recorded in 1963 by Thomas Kuhn. The text is half letters and half recollections. The editors have done a superb job in putting this material together and making it into a coherent narrative. Each of them is a distinguished historian. Alice Smith came to Los Alamos in 1943, lived through Oppenheimer's reign there, and afterward wrote *A Peril and a Hope,* a history of the postwar struggle of scientists to deal with the political consequences of nuclear weapons. Charles Weiner has been for many years active in recording interviews with scientists as raw material for historians of science who work on a more technical level. Together, Smith and Weiner have the knowledge and background to understand all aspects of Oppenheimer's correspondence. They have also the tact to fill out unobtrusively the many gaps in the documentary record.

The most important editorial decision made by Smith and Weiner was where to stop. They decided to stop in 1945. As they say in their preface, "In sharp contrast to the surviving letters that Oppenheimer wrote before the war, most of the later correspondence is voluminous, formal, and guarded. . . . Not only formal but cautious. . . . Therefore, we have chosen to present the less familiar Oppenheimer, learning, playing, making friends, doing physics, winning recognition, as yet unburdened by the actuality of the bomb, by fame, and by public responsibilities." Their decision allowed them to end their story with a wonderfully evocative letter, one of the few not written by Oppenheimer himself. The last letter was written in November 1945 by Edith Warner, who ran a little restaurant at the crossing of the Rio Grande where Oppenheimer used to relax with his friends. "Your hours here mean much to me and I appreciate, perhaps more than most outsiders, what you have given of yourself in these Los Alamos years. Most of all I am grateful for your bringing Mr. Baker [Niels Bohr]. I think of you both, hopefully, as the song of the river comes from the canyon and the need of the world reaches even this quiet spot."

The letters in this volume divide themselves into four periods, showing distinct phases of Oppenheimer's development. In the first period Oppenheimer is a Harvard undergraduate and his letters go mostly to his high-school English teacher Herbert Smith. To those of us who knew Oppenheimer as a public figure already wrapped in enigma and legend, these early letters come as a shock. The shock resembles the shock that we experienced in 1953 when Michael Ventris and John Chadwick deciphered the Linear B script of the Mycenaean tablets. We had been brought up on legends of the Mycenaean heroes preserved by oral tradition and distilled in the poetry of Homer. Here we had suddenly presented to us written documents, factual records of the Mycenaean age, hundreds of years older than Homer. And the documents turned out to be bureaucratic records, devoid of heroism and of poetry. So it is with Oppenheimer's Harvard letters. "Tiresome" is the best word I can find to describe them. I say this as a warning to the reader. Do not be discouraged if you find the early letters irritating. The quality soon improves. The first flash of real brilliance comes with a letter to Miss Limpet (alias Paul Horgan) from Celia (himself) describing the antics of Celia's son Henley (also himself). The letter ends with a parody by Henley of Eliot's recently published "Waste Land." The "Waste Land" is an easy poem to parody, but I have never seen it done better. In the second period, when Oppenheimer was starting his career as a physicist, he wrote a poem of his own with the title "Crossing." It describes with exquisite economy of language the landscape of New Mexico which he had come to love. Perhaps it was no coincidence that fifteen years later he persuaded Edith Warner to set up her restaurant by the bridge at the crossing of the Rio Grande.

The third period is the time of maturity, when Oppenheimer was teaching physics and building a first-rate school of research in California. To this period belong the finest letters, many of them addressed to his brother Frank. One of these, written in 1932, contains a paragraph on the subject of discipline, revealing something of the force that drove Oppenheimer to be the man he became. "But because I believe that the reward of discipline is greater than its immediate objective, I would not have you think that discipline without objective is possible: in its nature discipline involves the subjection of the soul to some perhaps minor end; and that end must be real, if the discipline is not to be factitious. Therefore I think that all things which evoke discipline: study, and our duties to men and to the commonwealth, war, and personal hardship, and even the need for subsistence, ought to be greeted by us with profound gratitude; for only through them can we attain to the least detachment; and only so can we know peace."

The fourth period is the time of sudden metamorphosis when Oppenheimer leapt into command of nuclear weapons research, founded and directed the Los Alamos Scientific Laboratory, and pushed the production of bombs to completion in time for Hiroshima and Nagasaki. Many of the letters from this period are still astonishingly warm and human. But they are more superficial than the earlier letters, and discuss the how of the bomb project rather than the why. Only one letter, to Rabi in 1943, deals explicitly with the why. At the end, immediately before Edith Warner's concluding letter, comes the text of the farewell talk given by Oppenheimer to the Association of Los Alamos Scientists. The talk is in Oppenheimer's postwar manner, impersonal and guarded. By November 1945 his metamorphosis from private to public person was complete.

This volume will be a mine of information for historians interested in Oppenheimer and his times. It gives much new insight into Oppenheimer's character. More clearly than before we can see the nature of the flaw which made his life ultimately tragic. His flaw was restlessness, an inborn inability to be idle. Intervals of idleness are probably essential to creative work on the highest level. Shakespeare, we are told, was habitually idle between plays.

Freeman Dyson

Oppenheimer was hardly ever idle. His restlessness appears already in the early Harvard letters, outpourings of words written by a young man unable to stop when he has nothing more to say. Restlessness was at the root of the craving for discipline that is revealed in his letters to his brother. Restlessness drove him to his supreme achievement, the fulfillment of the mission of Los Alamos, without pause for rest or reflection. Without his restlessness, the pace at Los Alamos would certainly have been slower. There would then have been at least a chance for the Second World War to have ended quietly in a Japanese surrender with Hiroshima and Nagasaki spared.

Oppenheimer was well aware of his own weakness. In later life he never spoke of himself directly, but he occasionally expressed his inner thoughts obliquely by quoting poetry. Especially from George Herbert, his favorite poet. In my Oppenheimer file there is a recent letter from an old friend who knew Oppenheimer better than I did. "It was another lunchtime," she writes. "This one was at the Oppenheimers' house, on a beautiful spring day, and Kitty had masses of daffodils about the house. The Kennans and we were invited. Robert was at his most charming and hospitable best. After lunch, over coffee in that old part of their living room on the lower level with Robert's favorite books in the black-painted bookcases at the back, somehow Robert discovered that George Kennan did not know George Herbert. Robert went to his bookcase and drew out a rather nice old edition of Herbert and read in that sympathetic voice of his "The Pulley":

> When God at first made man,
> Having a glasse of blessings standing by . . .

and ending as no doubt you recall with the lines:

> Yet let him keep the rest,
> But keep them with repining restlessnesse;
> Let him be rich and wearie, that at least,
> If goodnesse leade him not, yet wearinesse
> May tosse him to My breast.

256

CHAPTER 23

Heims

.....

1980

John von Neumann and Norbert Wiener: From Mathematics to the Technologies of Life and Death, by Steve Heims, is a joint biography of two great mathematicians who were deeply and passionately involved in the political and moral problems of our time. Heims has done an excellent job of historical research, interviewing the friends and colleagues of his subjects, collecting their letters and studying their writings. He brings them vividly to life as human beings. He explains lucidly in nontechnical language the main themes of their professional work. He describes the events of their public careers and the political opinions that they expressed in public and in private. Every fact and every quotation is carefully documented in 115 pages of bibliographical notes. So far so good. If Heims had been willing to stay in the background, to present his work as a historical narrative with the protagonists speaking for themselves, he would have made an important contribution to the understanding of the great moral dilemma of our age. Unfortunately, he stands at the front of the stage between his characters and the audience, making it difficult for us to hear their voices and to see the drama of their lives in historical perspective.

Wiener and von Neumann were admirably suited by temperament and circumstance to serve as spokesmen for the two opposing views that dominated the great debate over weapons and strategy after the end of World War 2. Wiener came to believe that modern weapons in the hands of modern governments are an absolute evil, and that a morally responsible person should have

257

nothing whatever to do with them. Von Neumann believed that
the old political realities of national power and the old tribal imperatives of fighting for survival would remain essentially unchanged even in a world of hydrogen bombs. The great tragedy
of our times lies in the fact that both these viewpoints contain a
large element of truth. Heims denies the existence of a moral dilemma by proclaiming repetitiously that Wiener was right and
von Neumann wrong. He robs the drama of its wider meaning by
describing von Neumann's beliefs as unfortunate side effects of a
bourgeois upbringing. He fails to understand the historical background of the 1940s and 1950s because his interpretations are
dominated by the ideological clichés of the 1960s and 1970s. I am
not saying that history ought to be morally neutral. I am saying
only that history ought to understand before it condemns. In the
remainder of this review I discuss the three essential points at
which a lack of historical insight leads Heims to condemn without
understanding.

First, there is the moral problem with which the nuclear age
began, the dropping of the bombs on Hiroshima and Nagasaki, a
decision that Wiener protested and von Neumann approved.
Heims says flatly, "The primary consideration in dropping the
atomic bomb on Japan in August 1945 had not been speeding the
end of the war—the bombs were not necessary for that purpose,
and the US government knew that." If that statement were true,
then there would have been no moral dilemma, and Truman
would stand condemned as a liar as well as a mass murderer.
Heims quotes several secondary sources in support of this statement. He does not, here or elsewhere, refer to the primary source,
Robert Butow's book, *Japan's Decision to Surrender.* Butow is an
American historian who spent several years in Japan soon after the
surrender, examining Japanese state papers and interviewing ex-
tensively the surviving members of the wartime Japanese government. He came closer than any later historian can come to
answering the crucial question, "Would Japan have surrendered if
the atomic bombs had not been dropped?" I asked Butow this
question explicitly when he was visiting Princeton. Butow replied, "The Japanese leaders themselves do not know the answer
to that question, and if they cannot answer it, neither can I."
Butow went on to explain that the Japanese government in 1945

was delicately balanced between the civilian leaders, who were trying to open peace negotiations through the Soviet Union, and the military leaders, who were preparing to defend every inch of Japanese soil with the same suicidal ferocity with which they had defended Okinawa. None of us can know, even with the advantages of hindsight, which way the balance would have tilted if the bombs had not been used. Truman in 1945, without hindsight, and with the carnage of Okinawa fresh in his mind, could know even less. It is reasonable to condemn Truman's action, as Wiener did, but it is not reasonable to deny the historical circumstances out of which his action arose.

Second, there is the fact that von Neumann in the late 1940s and early 1950s advocated a preventive war against the Soviet Union. The phrase "preventive war" conveys today an impression of militarism gone mad. But to the generation that lived and suffered through the 1930s, the phrase had another meaning. It was widely held, especially by liberal intellectuals, that the French and British governments had behaved in a cowardly and immoral fashion when they failed to march into Germany in 1936 to stop Hitler from remilitarizing the Rhineland. A preventive war in 1936, when Germany was still effectively disarmed and incapable of serious resistance against invading forces, might have overturned Hitler's regime in a few days and saved the 50 million human beings who were to die in World War 2. We cannot know whether a preventive war in 1936 would have been either feasible or effective. We know only that the idea of preventive war as a morally acceptable option was widely accepted by the people of von Neumann's generation, who looked back to 1936 as a tragically missed opportunity. To them the idea of forestalling a terrible catastrophe by a bold preventive action was neither insane nor criminal. Von Neumann argued in 1950 that America was facing the same choice that France and Britain faced in 1936. The Soviet Union was then just beginning to acquire nuclear weapons. Von Neumann saw 1950 as the last chance for America to overthrow the Stalin regime, as 1936 had been the last chance to overthrow Hitler, without a war of annihilation. He saw a preventive war in 1950 as preferable, not only for America but for mankind as a whole, to a war of annihilation later. I am not saying that he was right. I consider it unlikely that preventive war could have achieved its objective, either in 1936 or in 1950. I am only saying that to discuss von Neumann's advocacy of preventive war as Heims does, without mentioning the events of 1936 which dominated von Neumann's perception of the moral issues, is to miss the main point of the story.

Third and last, there is the question of freedom. The word "freedom" hardly appears at all in Heims's book. In Heims's view of the human situation, modern weapons and military establishments are instruments of enslavement, natural enemies of the independent rational soul. Wiener expressed this view eloquently in his writings and in his actions. Yet one cannot begin to understand the deep involvement of American scientists in military technology if one does not examine the contrary view, that freedom and military inventiveness are natural allies. Von Neumann's generation saw free societies obliterated all over Europe, not by internal forces of oppression but by Hitler's armies. Freedom survived in England in 1940 because the coastal radars and the fighter airplanes were there when they were needed. Many people at that time believed that freedom's survival was made possible by the willingness of British and American scientists to apply their skills wholeheartedly to the problems of war. Even Wiener shared this belief in the 1940s when he worked enthusiastically on the improvement of antiaircraft fire-control. After Hiroshima, Wiener changed his mind, but the majority of American scientists did not. The experience of World War 2 left behind it a widespread feeling that a permanent alliance between freedom and military science was right and proper. The alliance was evidently beneficial to both parties; a free society needed superior military technology to withstand the superior discipline of a totalitarian enemy, and the military establishment needed a free society to allow scientists and soldiers to work together in an informal and creative style that a totalitarian state could not match. In the context of the Soviet-American arms race, the free scientists of America would always carry a responsibility to stay ahead in the quality and variety of their inventions, so as to compensate for the larger military expenditures and the advantages of secrecy on the Soviet side. This doctrine may be naive and old-fashioned, but it was dominant in von Neumann's thinking. It still flourishes today in Israel and in the less sophisticated regions of America. When Heims writes of von Neumann and of the arms race without discussing the notion of "Fighting for Freedom," that grand illusion that lies at the root of the turmoil and tragedy of our times, he is plowing a shallow furrow in the rich soil of history.

I have criticized Heims harshly for undervaluing the moral impulses that drive the arms race. Let me end with praise for the two passages that I found most illuminating in his book. They show that Heims is aware of the importance of myths and symbols in human affairs. He tells us two old stories that von Neumann and Wiener frequently quoted. Each story is a literary archetype, a theme song illustrating one aspect of human destiny. Von Neumann's theme song was the Melian dialogue of Thucydides, the classic debate between an arrogantly oppressive empire and a defiant city resolved to defend itself to the death. Wiener's theme song was the W. W. Jacobs story of the monkey's paw, the magic talisman which fulfills human wishes but always in such a way as to bring grief to the wisher.

CHAPTER 24

Manin and Forman

.....

1 9 8 2

We are doubly lucky. A thoughtful and sensitive book, Yury Manin's *Mathematics and Physics,* has been thoughtfully and sensitively translated. Almost every one of its hundred small pages contains a sentence worth quoting. "The gyroscope that guides a rocket is an emissary from a six-dimensional symplectic world into our three-dimensional one; in its home world its behavior looks simple and natural." "Even those who see stars ask 'What is a star?', because to see merely with one's eyes is still very little." "The image of Plato's cave seems to me the best metaphor for the structure of modern scientific knowledge; we actually see only the shadows." "In a world of light there are neither points nor moments of time; beings woven from light would live nowhere and nowhen; only poetry and mathematics are capable of speaking meaningfully about such things." "The screws and gears of the great machine of the world, when their behavior is understood, can be assembled and joined in a new order; thus one obtains a bow, a loom or an integrated circuit." "Modern theoretical physics is a luxuriant, totally Rabelaisian, vigorous world of ideas, and a mathematician can find in it everything to satiate himself except the order to which he is accustomed."

Besides these verbal gems, Manin's book contains some equations and some technical exposition. His purpose was to make the thought processes of physics intelligible to mathematicians. He achieves this purpose by skillful selection of examples. Incidentally, by his style of writing and thinking, he makes the thought processes of a mathematician intelligible to physicists. He does not try to abolish or blur the distinction between mathematical and physical understanding. One of the many virtues of his book is that it leaves the central mystery, the miraculous effectiveness of mathematics as a tool for the understanding of nature, unexplained and unobscured.

Manin's book defies summary, because it already compresses into its small compass enough ideas to fill a dozen books of ordinary density. Each of its many topics is discussed without wastage of words. When I began trying to summarize it, I found myself willy-nilly selecting sentences and quoting them directly. The flavor of Manin's thinking is conveyed better by quotation than by paraphrase. I abandoned the attempt to describe the book in detail. Instead, I devote the rest of this review to the pursuit of a single question suggested by Manin's survey of contemporary science. Are we, or are we not, standing at the threshold of a new scientific revolution comparable with the historic revolutions of the past?

The two great conceptual revolutions of twentieth-century science, the overturning of classical physics by Heisenberg and the overturning of the foundations of mathematics by Gödel, occurred within six years of each other within the narrow boundaries of German-speaking Europe. Manin sees no causal connection between the two revolutions. He describes them as occurring independently: "Physicists were disturbed by the interrelation between thought and reality, while mathematicians were disturbed by the interrelation between thought and formulas. Both of these relations turned out to be more complicated than had previously been thought, and the models, self-portraits and self-images of the two disciplines have turned out to be very dissimilar." This lucid characterization emphasizes the differences between the Heisenberg and Gödel revolutions. But a study of the historical background of German intellectual life in the 1920s reveals strong links between them. Physicists and mathematicians were exposed simultaneously to external influences that pushed them along parallel paths. Seen in the perspective of history, the geographical and temporal propinquity of Heisenberg and Gödel no longer appears to be a coincidence.

The historical dimension of science is explored in another short and excellent book, *Weimar Culture, Causality, and Quantum Theory, 1918–1927: Adaptation by German Physicists and Mathematicians to a Hostile Intellectual Environment,* by Paul Forman. Forman is a historian, more familiar with physics than with mathematics. His book overlaps hardly at all with Manin. To arrive at a balanced picture of our scientific heritage, the two books should be read together. I now turn my attention to Forman and come back to Manin later.

Forman begins with Felix Klein, sixty-nine years old and approaching the end of his long career as grand seigneur of German mathematics. It is June 1918, the last summer of World War 1, and Klein is talking in Göttingen to an audience including leaders of German industry and of the Prussian government. He is addressing a formal session of the Göttingen Society for the Advancement of Applied Physics and Mathematics. He talks confidently of the coming victorious conclusion of the war, of the harmonious collaboration of German science with industry and the armed forces, and of the expected increase in support for mathematical education and research after the victory is won. Here in wartime Germany we see the first full flowering of the military-industrial complex in its modern style, soldiers and politicians sharing their dreams of glory with scientists and mathematicians. The Prussian minister of education responds to Klein with a generous grant of money for the foundation of a mathematical institute in Göttingen. Less than five months later, the dreams of glory have collapsed, the German empire is utterly defeated, the mathematical institute indefinitely postponed. In the new era of defeat and misery that begins in November 1918, the exact sciences are discredited together with the military-industrial complex that had sustained them. The Göttingen Mathematical Institute is ultimately built, after Klein's death, not with German government funds but with American dollars supplied by the Rockefeller Foundation.

Forman uses Klein's Göttingen speech to set the stage for a dramatic description of the intellectual crosscurrents of Weimar Germany. The dominant mood of the new era was doom and gloom. The theme song was *Der Untergang des Abendlandes* (Decline of the West), the title of the apocalyptic world history of Oswald Spengler. The first volume of Spengler's prophetic work was published in Munich in July 1918, the month in which the tide of war on the Western Front finally turned against Germany. After the November collapse the book took Germany by storm. It went through sixty editions in eight years. Everybody talked about it. Almost everybody read it. Forman demonstrates with ample documentation that mathematicians and physicists read it too. Even those who disagreed with Spengler were strongly influenced by his rhetoric. Spengler himself had been a student of science and mathematics before he became a historian. He had much to say about science. Not all of what he said was foolish. He said, among other things, that the decay of Western civilization must bring with it a collapse of the rigid structures of classical mathematics and physics. "Each culture has its own new possibilities of self-expression which arise, ripen, decay and never return. There is not one sculpture, one painting, one mathematics, one physics, but many, each in its deepest essence different from the other, each limited in duration and self-contained." "Western European physics—let no-one deceive himself—has reached the limit of its possibilities. This is the origin of the sudden and annihilating doubt that has arisen about things that even yesterday were the unchallenged foundation of physical theory, about the meaning of the energy principle, the concepts of mass, space, absolute time, and causal natural laws generally." "Today, in the sunset of the scientific epoch, in the stage of victorious skepsis, the clouds dissolve and the quiet landscape of the morning reappears in all distinctness. . . . Weary after its striving, the Western science returns to its spiritual home."

Two people who came early and strongly under the influence of Spengler's philosophy were the mathematician Hermann Weyl and the physicist Erwin Schrödinger. Both were writers with a deep feeling for the German language, and perhaps for that reason were easily seduced by Spengler's literary brilliance. Both became convinced that mathematics and physics had reached a state of crisis that left no road open except radical revolution. Weyl had been, even before 1918, a proponent of the doctrine of intuitionism, which denied the validity of a large part of classical mathematics and attempted to place what was left upon a foundation of intuition rather than formal logic. After 1918 he extended his revolutionary rhetoric from mathematics to physics, solemnly proclaiming the breakdown of the established order in both disciplines. In 1922, Schrödinger joined him in calling for radical reconstruction of the laws of physics. Weyl and Schrödinger agreed with Spengler that the coming revolution would sweep away the principle of physical causality. The erstwhile revolutionaries David Hilbert and Albert Einstein found themselves in the unaccustomed role of defenders of the status quo, Hilbert defending the primacy of formal logic in the foundations of mathematics, Einstein defending the primacy of causality in physics.

In the short run, Hilbert and Einstein were defeated and the Spenglerian ideology of revolution triumphed, both in physics and in mathematics. Heisenberg discovered the true limits of causality in atomic processes, and Gödel discovered the limits of formal deduction and proof in mathematics. And, as often happens in the history of intellectual revolutions, the achievement of revolutionary goals destroyed the revolutionary ideology that gave them birth. The visions of Spengler, having served their purpose, rapidly became irrelevant. The victorious revolutionaries were not irrational dreamers but rational scientists. The physics of Heisenberg, once it was understood, turned out to be as mundane and practical as the physics of Newton. Chemists who never heard of Spengler could successfully use quantum mechanics to calculate molecular binding energies. And in mathematics, the discoveries of Gödel did not lead to a victory of intuitionism but rather to a general recognition that no single scheme of mathematical foundations has a unique claim to legitimacy. After the revolutions were over, the new physics and the new mathematics became less and less concerned with ideology. In the long run, the value systems of physics and mathematics emerged from the revolutions essentially unchanged. Spengler's dream of a reborn, vitalistic, spiritualized science, "Western science returning to its spiritual home," was forgotten. The practical achievements of Hilbert and Einstein outlasted the fashionable despair of Spengler.

Now, fifty years later, the wheel has come full circle. The physics of quantum devices and the mathematics of effective computability have become everyday tools for engineers and industrialists to exploit. The new physics and the new mathematics are as friendly to the military-industrial complex of modern America as the old physics and the old mathematics were to the military-industrial complex of Germany in the days of Felix Klein. And once again we hear voices preaching revolution, a return to holistic thinking, a spiritualization of science. "Physics of Consciousness" is a fashionable slogan today, like the "*Lebensphilosophie*" of the 1920s. Fritjof Capra steps tentatively into the shoes of Oswald Spengler. Capra's *Tao of Physics* is selling, like Spengler's *Untergang* of old, in hundreds of thousands of copies. Are we heading toward a period of radical changes in science, comparable with the Heisenberg revolution of 1925 and the Gödel revolution of 1931? Who can tell? Forman's historical analysis may illuminate the past, but it cannot predict the future.

Forman and Manin represent two contrasting styles in the historiography of science. Forman looks at science from the outside, Manin from the inside. Forman sees science responding to external social and political pressures, Manin sees science growing autonomously by the logical interplay of its own concepts. Forman takes his evidence from what scientists say, in speeches and writings directed toward the general public. Manin takes his evidence from what scientists do, as they exchange methods and ideas with one another. Forman is concerned with the rituals of science, Manin with the substance.

Looking back on the events of the 1920s with the benefit of hindsight, we can see clearly that Heisenberg and Gödel did not need Oswald Spengler to tell them what they had to do. It is true, as Forman demonstrates, that Spengler created a mood of revolutionary expectation in German-speaking Europe, and that the existence of this mood helps to explain why young people in Germany and Austria were better prepared than young people elsewhere to make revolutionary discoveries. But the discoveries of quantum mechanics and mathematical undecidability would have been made within a few years, either in German-speaking Europe or somewhere else, even if Spengler had never existed. The time was ripe for these discoveries, and the internal development of physics and mathematics made them inevitable. An external mood of revolutionary expectation is neither a necessary nor a sufficient condition for the occurrence of a scientific revolution. If we wish to assess realistically the prospects of scientific revolutions in the future, we should study science itself and not the philosophical or political ambience of science. We should leave Forman aside and go back to Manin.

The picture of present-day physics and mathematics that Manin presents to us is far removed from the intellectual turmoil of the 1920s. Manin's picture is idyllic. He shows us physics and mathematics as two neighboring gardens, each growing luxuriantly with trees and flowers in great variety, while the busy physicists and mathematicians fly to and fro like bees carrying pollen for the cross-fertilization of one plant by another. In Manin's gardens there is growth and decay, sunshine and showers, but no hint of gloom and doom. Looking to the future from Manin's perspective, one sees no evidence of a coming cataclysm, no sign of that "craving for crisis" which was, according to Forman, the hallmark of a German academic in the 1920s. On the contrary, Manin's picture of science promises us a long period of fruitful and multifarious growth, with plenty of surprises and sudden illuminations but no radical changes of objective. In Manin's view, the present epoch is characterized by a growing willingness of physicists and mathematicians to learn from each other and to transfer tools and techniques from one branch of science to another. The increasing overlap between physics and mathematics provides opportunities for the continuing enrichment of both disciplines. The future of physics and mathematics lies in evolution rather than revolution. Manin sees Spengler's "quiet landscape of the morning" not as an end but a beginning.

The concluding paragraph of Manin's book gives us a glimpse of his vision of the future. "It is remarkable that the deepest ideas of number theory reveal a far-reaching resemblance to the ideas of modern theoretical physics. Like quantum mechanics, the theory of numbers furnishes completely non-obvious patterns of relationship between the continuous and the discrete, and emphasizes the role of hidden symmetries. One would like to hope that this resemblance is no accident, and that we are already hearing new words about the world in which we live, but we do not yet understand their meaning."

CHAPTER 25

Kennan

.....

1982

The Nuclear Delusion is a selection of George Kennan's writings extending over the years from 1950 to 1981, with a twenty-page introduction explaining how and why they came to be written. None of Kennan's work as a professional historian is included. The pieces here collected are concerned with current political issues and are mostly taken from lectures and speeches addressed to the general public. No matter how ephemeral the occasion of his writing, Kennan always writes for the ages. The early pieces have lost none of their cogency with the passage of the years. With astonishing foresight Kennan formulated and answered in the 1950s the questions that are still at the center of our concern in the 1980s. His writings are vibrant with an unresolved tension between his passionate faith in humanity and his exasperated despair over human foolishness.

There are two main themes, the nature of Soviet society and the nature of nuclear weapons. Kennan's view of Soviet society is based on long and intimate contact with Soviet bureaucracy and with ordinary Soviet citizens. He sees the individual human beings behind the facade of ideology. He is constantly fighting against the tendency of Americans to oversimplify and dehumanize their adversaries. For Kennan the Soviet Union is, first of all, a great and complicated assemblage of peoples burdened with a harsh historical heritage. Like other societies, it is more deeply concerned with its own internal problems than with the problems of the world outside. Like other societies, it sees itself as more threatened than threatening. Like other societies, it is struggling unsuccessfully to deal with the problems of alienated youth and rigid bureaucracy in a time of rapid economic change.

Kennan is well aware of the unpleasant characteristics of the Soviet state, the paranoid secretiveness, the intolerance of dissent, the self-righteous rhetoric, the casual cruelty, the glorification of military strength. Yet he bids us look behind these harsh realities and understand the human circumstances from which they arise. He sees the Soviet leaders as a group of elderly and conservative men, whose chief ambition is to push the Soviet Union along the path of economic progress which the Communist ideology promises to bring about. To accomplish this task, the leaders have only three tools, the authoritarian party apparatus, the overcentralized bureaucracy, and the armed forces. The party apparatus and the bureaucracy are clearly inadequate for the direction of a modern industrial economy. Of all the institutions of the Soviet state, the armed forces stand highest in technical competence, in morale, and in genuine contact with the masses of the Soviet population. The army in the Soviet Union is, as the French army was in the time of Napoleon, the poor man's university. It is no wonder that the armed forces command a disproportionate share of power and prestige, in the eyes of the ordinary Soviet citizen as well as in the secret corridors of the Kremlin. The massive accumulation of Soviet weaponry arises from this internal ascendancy of the armed forces, not from any plan of foreign conquest.

Kennan sees Soviet society as conservative but very far from static. He sees great historical changes occurring beneath the rigid surface of the system. A few months ago he said to me in the course of a casual conversation, "It is odd that I have been worrying for fifty years, for all of my professional life, about the strength of Soviet society. And now I am worrying about its weakness. I begin now to worry that the whole thing may disintegrate." He takes seriously the recent evidence of social decay in the Soviet Union, the rise in drunkenness and in infant mortality, the prevalence of bribery and corruption, the loss of a sense of purpose among the children of the elite. He sees great and possibly disastrous changes ahead if the processes of decay continue. He looks back at the events of 1917, when the American people joyfully welcomed the collapse of the tsarist empire and was surprised to see it replaced by the far more vicious tyranny of Lenin. He sees the American government now ignorantly harassing the present Soviet regime, careless of the possibility that this comparatively benign group of leaders will in their turn be replaced by something worse.

The other half of Kennan's argument concerns nuclear weapons. Here Kennan has been equally farsighted. Already in 1950 he formulated the view that he has steadily maintained ever since, that the decision of the American government to rely upon the first use of nuclear weapons as a defense against nonnuclear attack was a fundamental mistake. He predicted accurately that the first-use policy would stand in the way of any serious effort to bring the nuclear arms race under control, would prevent any military disengagement of Soviet and American forces in Europe, and would in the end deprive us of any possibility of using military strength to achieve reasonable political purposes. For many years he was a voice crying in the wilderness, alone in his consistent opposition to the first-use policy. Recently, a number of public figures have joined him. Both in America and in Europe, more and more people are coming to understand that the first-use policy is incompatible with any coherent strategy of national defense. It will be a long time before the policy is officially abandoned. Whatever progress we are making in that direction is due almost entirely to Kennan's leadership.

The nuclear delusion, the phrase that Kennan chose for the title of his book, means the belief that nuclear weapons are usable as other weapons are usable. This delusion is an essential part of the first-use policy. According to Kennan, as soon as the Soviet Union had acquired a substantial stockpile of nuclear weapons to balance the American stockpile, the weapons on both sides ceased to be usable for any rational purpose. They are no longer weapons but only instruments of suicide. Their existence poses a greater danger to our national security than any possible nonnuclear threat. The only rational strategy for the United States is therefore to deal with nonnuclear threats by means of nonnuclear weapons, and to seek agreement with the Soviet Union and other nuclear powers to do away with nuclear weapons altogether. Kennan is hopeful, and with good reason, that the Soviet government would be willing to go far in nuclear disarmament if the United States were sincerely committed to this course of action. Both in the official pronouncements of the Soviet government and in the private conversations of Soviet citizens, we find reiterated a desire for the complete abolition of nuclear weapons. Only if we negotiate seriously and in good faith can we find out whether this desire is genuine.

Kennan has no hope that much of value can emerge from arms-control negotiations conducted in the style of the SALT talks, with each side striving only to retain a maximum of weaponry for itself while putting its opponent to the maximum disadvantage. As he says, such negotiations "are not a way of escape from the weapons race; they are an integral part of it. Whoever does not understand that when it comes to nuclear weapons the whole concept of relative advantage is illusory—whoever does not understand that when you are talking about absurd and preposterous quantities of overkill the relative sizes of arsenals have no serious meaning—whoever does not understand that the danger lies, not in the possibility that someone else might have more missiles and warheads than we do, but in the very existence of these unconscionable quantities of highly poisonous explosives, and their existence, above all, in hands as weak and shaky and undependable as those of ourselves or our adversaries or any other mere human beings: whoever does not understand these things is never going to guide us out of this increasingly dark and menacing forest of bewilderments into which we have all wandered."

Underneath the melody of Kennan's flowing prose, we hear from time to time these deep organ tones of moral indignation, that moral indignation which is in the end the only human force strong enough to save us from our follies. For thirty-five years he has been telling us that our readiness to use nuclear weapons against other human beings is not merely a military miscalculation and a political mistake, but an insult to mankind and to God. Now, at long last, the world is beginning to listen to him.

CHAPTER 26

Oppenheimer Again

.....

1989

When Robert Oppenheimer went to England in 1953 to deliver the Reith Lectures, the lectures that make up the first half of *Atom and Void,* millions of listeners were baffled and disappointed. He was then, after Einstein, the second-most-famous living scientist. He had been a prime mover in the building of atomic bombs, in the effort to establish an international control of nuclear energy, and in the political struggles that raged around the building of hydrogen bombs. In 1953 the public already knew that he was involved in secret disputes that were to break out into the open with the denial of his security clearances a few months later.

The listeners in England expected hot news. They expected dramatic statements about the great events and great issues of the day. They expected a personal message from the man who in those days was widely proclaimed to be the conscience of humanity. Instead, they got these lectures. They got a scholarly and impersonal discussion of the history of science. They got a rarefied and philosophical view of the mysteries of quantum mechanics. They got a picture of the human predicament as it might be seen by an observer at an immense distance in space and time, totally detached from day-to-day events and practical details. Barely a word about the bomb. No answers to any of the urgent political questions of the 1950s. No glimpse of that inner world of action and power in which Oppenheimer had been living for the previous ten years. No wonder the listeners were scornful. One of my English friends who heard the lectures compared Oppenheimer unkindly with the poet Bunthorne in the Gilbert and Sullivan operetta *Patience:*

> *You walk down Piccadilly with a poppy or a lily in your*
> *   medieval hand . . .*
> *   And everyone will say,*
> *   As you walk your mystic way,*
> *   "If this young man expresses himself in terms too deep for me,*
> *   Why, what a very singularly deep young man this deep young*
> *   man must be."*

Now, thirty-five years later, we can see that Oppenheimer chose his subject matter wisely. He knew that any discussion of current events that attempted to be up-to-date would soon be out of date. He had no wish to give lectures that would cause a political sensation today and be obsolete tomorrow. He wanted to speak to the ages, to say something of permanent value. As a result, these lectures have stood well the test of time. They are as pertinent to our situation in 1989 as they were in 1953. The English listeners' loss is our gain. We can now see that Oppenheimer's sense of history, his awareness of the long past and the long future, are the most important part of his legacy to mankind. In these lectures, and especially in the quotations assembled in the appendix at the end, his sense of history shines like a beacon, guiding our footsteps into the unknown for centuries to come.

When he went to give the Whidden lectures in Canada, the lectures that make up the second half of *Atom and Void,* less was expected of him. Nine years after the Reith lectures and eight years after his fall from power, he had become a respected elder statesman of science, no longer a worker of miracles. Nobody expected political thunderbolts. He spoke, as before, quietly, mostly about the history of science. But he allowed himself, in the last lecture, to unbend a little, to tell some personal stories about his involvement with the bomb and its consequences. His listeners were grateful for that last lecture, and we may be grateful too.

To end this preface I would like to put on record a description of Robert Oppenheimer written by Lansing Hammond in a letter to me in 1979. Hammond was in charge of programs and placements for the Commonwealth Fund Fellows, young Britons who came to America to study at American universities with fund support, as I had come thirty years earlier. I replied to his letter, "It is sad that in the official memorials to Robert there was never anything said or written that gave such a fine impression of Robert in action. I hope there may still be a chance sometime to make your story public." Hammond died a few years later and this preface gives me the chance that he missed. Here is Hammond's story:

I'd just received copies of the application papers—sixty of them—for the 1949 awards. Among them were four or five in that, to me, shadowy borderline realm between theoretical physics and mathematics. I was in Princeton for a couple of days, asking for help on all sides. Summoning all the courage I could muster, I made an appointment to see Robert Oppenheimer the next morning, leaving the relevant papers with his secretary. I was greeted graciously, asked just enough questions about my academic background to put me at ease. One early comment amazed me: "You got your doctorate at Yale in 18th-century English literature—Age of Johnson. Was Tinker or Pottle your supervisor?" How did he know that?

Then we got down to business. In less than ten minutes I had enough facts to support trying to persuade candidate Z that Berkeley was more likely to satisfy his particular interests than Harvard; he would fare well at the Institute; would be welcome; but Berkeley was really the best choice. I was scribbling notes as fast as I could; occasionally a proper name produced wrinkles on my forehead. Oppenheimer would flash me an understanding grin and spell out the name for me: "That may save you some time and trouble."

As I was gathering up my papers, feeling I'd already taken up too much of the great man's time, he asked gently: "If you have a few minutes you can spare, I'd be interested in looking at some of your applications in other fields, to see what this year's group of young Britons are interested in pursuing over here?" I took him at his word, and was completely overwhelmed by what ensued: "Umm—indigenous American music—Roy Harris is just the person for him, he'll take an interest in his program. Roy was at Stanford last year but he's just moved to Peabody Teachers'

College in Nashville. Social psychology, he gives Michigan as first choice—Umm—he wants a general, overall experience. At Michigan he's likely to be put on a team and would learn a lot about one aspect. I'd suggest looking into Vanderbilt; smaller numbers; he'd have a better opportunity of getting what he wants." (The candidate was persuaded to try Vanderbilt for one term, with the option of transferring to Michigan if he wasn't satisfied. He spent two years at Vanderbilt, with profit and enthusiasm.) "Symbolic logic, that's Harvard, Princeton, Chicago or Berkeley; let's see where he wants to put the emphasis. Ha! Your field, 18th-century English Lit. Yale is an obvious choice, but don't rule out Bate at Harvard, he's a youngster but a person to be reckoned with." (My field, and I'd not yet even heard of Bate, but I took pains, the next time I was in Cambridge, to meet and talk with him.) We spent at least an hour, thumbing through all of the sixty applications. Robert Oppenheimer knew what he was talking about. He pleaded ignorance about two or three esoteric programs. Every positive comment or recommendation was right on target. And so, when it finally came time to leave, I couldn't resist saying that if I could only bribe him, once a year, to repeat what he'd just done, it would save me months of sweating. He really grinned at that. "That wouldn't be fair to you, Dr. Hammond. It would take away the satisfaction and excitement of talking with lots of other people and finding out for yourself." I left, walking on air, head a-buzz, most of my problems solved. Never before, never since have I talked with such a man. No suggestion of trying to impress. No need to. Robert Oppenheimer's was just genuine interest in all fields of the intellect; a fantastically up-to-date knowledge of what was going on in U.S. graduate schools and research centers; an intuitive understanding of where a given person with definite interests would best fit in; and taking pleasure in being of help to someone who badly needed it.

The Robert Oppenheimer that Hammond saw that morning in 1949 was the same Robert Oppenheimer who had mastered every detail of the bomb project at Los Alamos five years earlier, and had fitted the most appropriate task to each scientist and engineer in his army of subordinates. He was equally at home in the world of literature and the world of science, in the eighteenth century and the twentieth. His listeners in 1953 were surprised to hear a voice from the eighteenth century discussing the discoveries of the twentieth. Readers of *Atom and Void* need not be surprised to find that the continuity of human experience over the centuries is its central theme, defining both the style and the substance of Oppenheimer's discourse.

CHAPTER 27

Morson and Tolstoy

.....

1989

Two great spirits presided over the birth of modern science in the seventeenth century. Francis Bacon, the Englishman, said:

> All depends on keeping the eye steadily fixed on the facts of nature, and so receiving their images as they are. For God forbid that we should give out a dream of our own imagination for a pattern of the world.

René Descartes, the Frenchman, said:

> I showed what the laws of nature were, and without basing my arguments on any principle other than the infinite perfections of God, I tried to demonstrate all those laws about which we could have any doubt, and to show that they are such that, even if God created many worlds, there could not be any in which they failed to be observed.

In the history of science, from its beginnings to the present day, the Baconian and the Cartesian traditions have remained alive, Baconian science emphasizing empirical facts and details, Cartesian science emphasizing general ideas and principles. The healthy growth of science requires that both traditions be honored. Bacon without Descartes would reduce science to butterfly collecting; Descartes without Bacon would reduce science to pure mathematics.

What has the history of science to do with Gary Morson's book *Hidden in Plain View,* and with Leo Tolstoy's *War and Peace*? Since I am a scientist, I see Morson's dichotomy of literature into prosaics and poetics as analogous to the old dichotomy of science into Baconian and Cartesian. *War and Peace,* as Morson describes it, is a supreme example of Baconian literature. In his arrangement of incidents and characters, as well as in his historical interpretations, Tolstoy is following Bacon's dictum: "God forbid that we should give out a dream of our own imagination for a pattern of the world." Tolstoy's view of history is firmly Baconian. Strategic plans and theories are repeatedly shown to be illusory. The true cause of historical events lies in the innumerable and unpredictable details of human behavior. The aim of the novelist and historian should be to observe and describe the details of events, "receiving their images as they are," not to explain them with preconceived theories.

In opposition to Morson's concept of prosaics stands the Aristotelian notion of poetics. According to Aristotle, poetry and drama must be subject to strict rules. The doctrine of the *Poetics* decrees that the portrayal of human destiny be squeezed into a formal structure. To a greater or lesser extent, all of classical literature from Plutarch's *Lives* to Milton's *Paradise Lost* followed the Aristotelian pattern. Man's fate is deduced from general principles. Nothing happens by accident. Tolstoy consciously and deliberately violated the Aristotelian rules. He held that the imposition of Aristotelian patterns upon history led to nothing but falsehood and illusion. If Tolstoy had been a scientist, he would have rejected just as vehemently the attempt of Descartes to deduce the laws of nature from philosophical principles. If Bacon had been a novelist, he would have approved Tolstoy's method: "I was more interested to know in what way and under the influence of what feeling one soldier kills another, than to know how the armies were arranged at Austerlitz and Borodino."

Tolstoy failed to convert the majority of writers and historians to his way of thinking, just as Bacon failed to convert the majority of scientists. In science as in history, dogma dies hard. Deep in human nature is the desire to explain the cosmos with all-embracing schemes. In my own professional field of particle physics, the Cartesian spirit reigns supreme. The young explorers

are furiously engaged in the search for a "theory of everything."
Few of them are listening to the cautionary words of Bacon:

> The subtlety of nature is greater many times over than
> the subtlety of the senses and understanding, so that all
> those specious meditations, speculations, and glosses in
> which men indulge are quite from the purpose. . . . The
> logic now in use serves rather to fix and give stability to the
> errors which have their origin in commonly received no-
> tions than to help the search after truth.

Likewise, few of our contemporary historians and sociolo-
gists have chosen to follow the method of Tolstoy as Morson describes it:

> Tolstoy's uniqueness lies in his profound understanding
> of the ordinary, and in the very ordinariness of his pro-
> found understanding. In his view, truth is not buried but
> camouflaged. Unlike most thinkers of his time and ours,
> he rejected philosophy's prevailing impulse to locate mean-
> ing in the distance, in a concealed order. Tolstoy was in-
> stead a philosopher of the present, of the open present,
> with all its unrealized opportunities and wasteful care-
> lessness.

In my book *Infinite in All Directions*, I have described the history
of science as a dialogue between unifiers and diversifiers. Unifiers
are following the tradition of Descartes, diversifiers are following
the tradition of Bacon. Unifiers are trying to reduce the prodigal-
ity of nature to a few general laws and principles. Diversifiers are
exploring the details of things and events in their infinite variety.
Unifiers are in love with ideas and equations; diversifiers are in
love with birds and butterflies. My friend and colleague, the physicist Chen Ning Yang, told me once that when he was a boy of six
in China he looked up at the stars and asked what are the laws that
make them move across the sky. But when I was a boy of six in
England, I looked up at the stars and asked what are their names.
Yang was interested in stars in general; I was interested in stars as
individuals.

In the sphere of history, Karl Marx was the great unifier, believing that with his single key of dialectical materialism he could unlock the mysteries of the past and the future. Tolstoy was the great diversifier, believing that historical truth can only be found in details, in the actions of individual human beings. Yet Tolstoy understood, as the scientist studying birds and butterflies understands, that individuals are tied together in an infinitely complicated web of interdependence. Science is our exploration of the web that ties birds and butterflies together. History is our exploration of the web that ties human actions together.

Perhaps we may interpret the new revolution that Mikhail Gorbachev is trying to bring about in Russia as a move away from narrow Marxism toward a more Tolstoyan view of the human predicament. In many places in Gorbachev's book *Perestroika,* we hear echoes of the message that Tolstoy put at the end of *War and Peace.* Tolstoy was describing an analogy between the Copernican revolution in astronomy and the new view of history to which his study of war and peace had led him. Here is Tolstoy's final sentence, proclaiming the mutual interdependence which both East and West must learn to recognize:

> In astronomy we had to give up our illusion of fixity in space and accept an imperceptible motion; in exactly the same way, in history, we have to give up our illusion of freedom and accept an imperceptible dependence on one another.

PART VI

People

○○○○

LEAD YOUR LIFE WITH A GENTLE HAND AND BE READY

TO LEAVE WHENEVER YOU ARE CALLED.

> LEO SZILARD,
> "TEN COMMANDMENTS"

CHAPTER 28

Letter from Armenia

.....

1 9 7 1

I. THE COUNTRY

One day long ago God divided the Earth into countries and called together representatives of all nations to choose where they should live. The Englishman and the Frenchman came first and were given green and pleasant countries. The later arrivals got countries too hot or too cold for comfortable living. At the end of the day only the Armenian and the Georgian had not come. They had been busy playing dice. When the game was over they came to God and complained that He had not treated them fairly. After a long argument God said, "As a matter of fact, I do have one country left, but there is only one, and it is such a miserable place that I doubt whether anybody could live there. It is as hot as an oven in summer and as cold as a blizzard in winter, and it has hardly any water. But I suppose it is better than nothing. You two throw your dice once more and the winner shall have it." So they threw and the Armenian won. God gave him Armenia and he went off grumbling. Only the Georgian was left. God told the Georgian to go away and stop bothering Him. The Georgian still argued. Finally, God became angry and told the Georgian to go to hell. But the Georgian said, "You don't get rid of me so easily. I can see that You are hiding something under your apron. I think it is a country that you are hiding, and it rightfully belongs to me." God said, "All right, I may as well admit it. This was a little country I was keeping to live in Myself. But since you are such a pest, I suppose I have to give it to you." The Georgian received Georgia and God was left in peace.

This story is a piece of Armenian folklore, told to generations of Armenian children. It explains to them why they live in a land that is bleak and barren while their northern neighbors the Georgians live in fertile valleys sheltered by the Caucasus Mountains. The same story might have been invented by the inhabitants of the Mexican plateau looking north to the orchards of California.

Yerevan, capital of the Armenian Soviet Socialist Republic, is in many ways similar to Mexico City. It is a metropolis in a land of villages. It houses one third of the inhabitants of the republic, and is still growing rapidly. It has magnificent museums and public monuments recording the achievements of an ancient civilization. It has great expanses of dusty grey houses stretching out to the barren hills around it. And above the city, towering up from the horizon when the air is clear and floating in the sky when it is hazy, stands the huge snowcapped dome of Ararat, nearer and bigger than the cone of Popocatapetl over Mexico. The ancient kingdom of Armenia had ten times the area of the present republic, and extended far into what is now Turkey and Iran. Ararat was then in the middle of Armenia, and became a holy place and a symbol of Armenian national identity. Now the inhabitants of Soviet Armenia can see Ararat every day but can never set foot on it, for it stands in Turkey. Lest they forget, the dome of Ararat also appears on the flag of the Armenian republic.

After Ararat, the second natural wonder of Armenia is Lake Sevan, a five-hundred-square-mile expanse of blue water lying six thousand feet above sea level, surrounded by wind-swept and treeless hills. The lake presents to the Armenians a severe conflict between aesthetics and utility. The water in the lake can be of enormous economic value if it is used for irrigation. Being at such a high altitude, it can easily be channeled to the places where it is needed. It can convert thousands of square miles of arid plains into thriving farms and vineyards. But the lake in its natural state cannot be so used. Its area is so great and the air over it so dry that 92 percent of the total inflow is evaporated. An additional 4 percent disappears into underground streams, and 4 percent flows out into the Hrazdan River. So the natural lake wastes 96 percent of its water and offers only a variable and unreliable 4 percent for irrigation. If the lake had been an artificial reservoir rather than a gift of God, every right-thinking ecologist would have condemned it as a wasteful monstrosity.

The Soviet authorities of the period 1930 to 1960 were intent on rapid economic development and had no hesitations in using drastic methods to put the water to productive use. The only way to stop the evaporation of the water is to make the lake smaller. So a fifty-year plan was drawn up, at the end of which the lake would be reduced to one-seventh of its original size. The water level would be lowered 150 feet by deepening the channel of the Hrazdan River. The result of this would be that 60 instead of 4 percent of the inflow would exit through the Hrazdan. In addition to irrigation, large-scale hydroelectric power generation in the Hrazdan gorge was a part of the plan. During the 1950s many of the power stations were built and the shoreline of Lake Sevan began to recede.

About 1960 the Armenians, like people in other parts of the world, became acutely aware that the price of economic development could be too high. They did not enjoy watching their magnificent lake disappear. Heated arguments began between those who wished to restore the lake to its natural state and those who were committed to the fulfilment of the fifty-year plan. Complete restoration was hardly a practical possibility, since it would mean abandonment of much land already under irrigation. But complete fulfilment of the plan seemed less and less attractive to a people no longer preoccupied with the bare necessities of life. By the end of the 1960s a compromise had been reached. It was agreed to halt the emptying of the lake at the 1970 level. The lake will lie permanently fifty feet below its original level and will have 87 percent of its original area. After a few years the muddy "bathtub rim" effect produced by a lowering water level will have disappeared, and the lake will look almost as beautiful as it did before man laid his hand on it.

The compromise means that wastage of water by evaporation will remain extremely high. To save the existing irrigation and hydroelectric works, the inflow to Lake Sevan will be increased by an expensive diversion of a river underneath an intervening mountain. After this is done, the end result will be that 66 percent of the inflow will evaporate and 30 percent will be available for power and irrigation. Barely half of the original objectives of the fifty-year plan will be achieved. All in all, the compromise represents a considerable victory of sentiment over expediency.

Another victory of sentiment was achieved in 1965 in an event which the Armenians call "our little revolution." Nineteen sixty-five was the fiftieth anniversary of the great massacre of the Turkish Armenians. About half of all Armenians alive in 1915 were in the original homeland in eastern Turkey, near to the Russian border. On the pretext that Armenians were disloyal in the war then raging between Russia and Turkey, the Turks massacred over a million of them and drove the few survivors into exile. The 1915 massacre is as deeply rooted in the folk memory of Armenia as Auschwitz in the memory of Israel. However, the Soviet government, ever since it gained control of Russian Armenia in 1920, did its best to discourage public recognition of the massacre. From the point of view of the government in Moscow, Armenia is a military liability rather than an asset. It is a remote and vulnerable salient, hard to defend against a Turkish attack at times when the Soviet Union is preoccupied elsewhere, as it was during the initial phases of World War 2. The Moscow government maintained correct relations with Turkey and tried to convince the Armenians that it would be best to pretend that the massacre had never happened. In 1965 there was no public commemoration of the anniversary.

To the astonishment of the older generation of Armenians who had learned under Stalin to keep their feelings to themselves, a massive demonstration of young people occurred in 1965 in the main square of Yerevan. The demonstrators demanded that the authorities finally put an end to their policy of disowning the million of their people who had died. The authorities sent in the local Armenian police, who dispersed the demonstrations and bashed a few heads, but did not kill anybody. The authorities did not call in the Soviet army, which was readily available in its positions along the Turkish frontier a few miles away. A short time later, construction began on the brow of a hill where a public park overlooks the city of Yerevan. A monument went up, austere and abstract in style, beautiful in its proportions. It is composed of two parts, a building in the shape of a low pyramid, with beside it a high tapering spire. At last, the fifty-year official silence is broken.

In spite of massacres, barbarian conquests, and earthquakes, Armenia has a rich legacy of buildings and books surviving from ancient times. The kingdom of Armenia was the first officially Christian state, having adopted the Christian religion in A.D. 308, sixteen years before the Roman emperor Constantine. The Armenian church has maintained its continuity and autonomy ever since. In Yerevan a special library, the Matenadaran, houses a vast collection of books and illuminated manuscripts, many dating from the ninth and tenth centuries. Some of them are Byzantine in style, some of them Persian, some of them equal in color and brilliance to anything in Western Europe. The earliest texts are ecclesiastical, but there are many scientific and medical books written at the time of the Arab Renaissance. The language and script are Armenian.

The Armenian alphabet was invented by a monk named Mesrop in A.D. 405. Armenians had a great literature four hundred years before the Russians had even an alphabet. The shops and public buildings of Yerevan are adorned with neon signs in Armenian characters, elegant in appearance even if unhelpful to the Western visitor. After I had taken the trouble to decipher the alphabet, I discovered that the movie being shown at the local cinema on September 8, 1971, was *Oliver.*

The following day I visited an old monastery at Gegard. It was built in the thirteenth century when Armenia was under Mongol domination. A succession of churches was secretly excavated out of solid rock, one behind another in the side of a mountain. The site is remote and the surroundings spectacular. The churches are not only for tourists. Armenians from the village come there to pray, and there is a priest in attendance. While I was waiting to go in, a villager appeared in the courtyard in front of the monastery, carrying a live chicken. Taking a central position in the courtyard, he ceremonially pulled a sharp knife from his pocket and cut off the chicken's head. Blood spurted over the stones, the truncated bird flapped its wings ineffectually for some time, and the head noiselessly opened and closed its mouth. When all was still, the villager advanced toward the church and presented his bloody offering to the priest. I was not able to find out whether this per-

formance was an act of Christian charity or a survival from pagan
sacrificial rites of two thousand years ago. The priest accepted the
gift as a matter of course, without embarrassment.

2. THE OBSERVATORY

Fifteen miles from Yerevan, on the slopes of the twelve-thousand-
foot mountain Aragats, stand the village of Byurakan and the
Byurakan Astrophysical Observatory. The village is an old one,
taking its water from a natural mountain stream. Its beauty has
not been spoiled by contact with modern civilization. Sheep and
chickens roam the streets. In the yard in front of a cottage stands
a big stone water jar in the shape of a Greek amphora, its pointed
bottom stuck into the earth. The girls from the village who work
as waitresses in the cafeteria at the observatory do not understand
Russian.

The observatory is first-rate. The important thing in modern
astronomy is not the size of the instruments but the way they are
used. At Byurakan the main working instrument is a 1-meter telescope. With this modest instrument the observer Markaryan has
discovered a new class of galaxies. They are known in the astronomical community as "Markaryan objects." The trick was to attach a large spectrographic grating to the front end of the
telescope, and then to know what to look for on the resulting
photographs. It sounds simple, as big discoveries usually do after
they have been made. A bigger telescope is being installed in a
dome nearby. We expect that Markaryan will put it to good use.

On the roof of the laboratory building at Byurakan stands a
laser that can fire a narrow beam of light to a similar instrument
in Yerevan fifteen miles away. If you stand in front of the receiver
you can faintly see in the distance a tiny red dot, the beam coming
back from Yerevan. The dot dances and flickers in the turbulent
air over the sun-baked hills. The laser beams are connected to a
big black box full of electronics, which allows them to be used as
a telephone channel. They can carry twenty-four simultaneous
conversations. The chief engineer picks up the telephone and dials
his assistant in Yerevan. A rapid conversation in Armenian follows. He hands the phone to me. I make some feeble remarks in

ungrammatical Russian. The assistant laughs and replies with an undeserved compliment. The quality of the voice is astounding. The sound shows no trace of the visible flicker. How can that little dancing red dot do it?

The director of the Byurakan observatory is Academician Viktor Ambartsumyan, a man of immense energy and many-sided talents. He is equally outstanding as originator of astronomical theories, as administrator of large scientific enterprises, and as toastmaster at Armenian banquets. He talks easily and without formality in Armenian, Russian, or English. He lives in a large house near to the telescopes, and he has made the whole of the observatory grounds into a garden. Astronomers walk from one building to another along narrow paths bordered with flowers and overhung with fruit trees.

Fifteen years ago Ambartsumyan startled the astronomical world with a revolutionary theory of the origin and evolution of galaxies. The orthodox view is that galaxies begin as large diffuse gas clouds and evolve by gradual contraction. Gravity pulls the inner parts together, so that old galaxies develop bright, dense cores in their central regions. Ambartsumyan turned this picture inside out. He proposed that the cores were there to start with, and that the galaxies are merely debris shot out from the cores in titanic explosions. In his view the galaxies with the brightest and most active cores are the youngest. When this theory was first proposed, it seemed to be a wild speculation unsupported by any substantial evidence. Up to that time few people had looked carefully at galactic cores. The universe was considered to be a quiet place, and titanic explosions were regarded as figments of an overheated Armenian imagination. But Ambartsumyan constantly urged his colleagues, "Look at the galactic cores, and you will see that things are not as quiet as you think."

During the last fifteen years one major discovery after another has shown that the universe is indeed not a quiet place. Evidence of titanic explosions is all around us. Careful study of galactic cores has shown that many of them have exploded or are exploding. The Markaryan objects are the latest addition to the list of galaxies with active cores. All this does not mean that Ambartsumyan's theory of the birth of galaxies is right. Few astronomers agree with his ideas in detail. But all agree that his arguments helped to push observational astronomy into new directions that proved immensely fruitful.

3. THE CONFERENCE

Ambartsumyan was host to the First International Conference on Communication with Extraterrestrial Intelligences, held at Byurakan in September 1971. It was a gathering of about forty learned men, mostly from the United States and the Soviet Union. Astronomers were in the majority, but there were also some biologists, anthropologists, linguists, and historians. The purpose of the meeting was to exchange ideas and to arrive at some agreement concerning two practical questions. First, supposing that some intelligent societies exist elsewhere in the universe (whether our own society should be called intelligent is a moot point), what are the most promising and economical ways to find out where they are? Second, supposing that the search for intelligent societies is a reasonable activity for astronomers to engage in, whose time, whose money, and whose instruments are to be devoted to this task? The meeting lasted for five days and was sponsored by the national academies of science of the USSR and the United States.

Our communication with our earthling colleagues was enormously helped by the presence of Boris Belitsky. He is the finest scientific translator I have ever met. He is not a professional interpreter, being normally employed by Moscow radio and television as a scientific commentator. His job and his wide reading have made him familiar with the niceties of jargon in all fields of science in Russian and English. He can jump from electronic engineering to biology to extragalactic astronomy without a moment's hesitation. While translating rapid conversation he would frequently correct errors of fact or supply half-remembered names. He speaks an idiomatic American English. His only weakness is that he gets a little tired after four or five hours of two-way translation.

The importance of fine points of semantics was brought home to me forcibly by an episode on the third day of the meeting. I almost fell into a linguistic trap. The morning had been spent in a long and unprofitable discussion of the probability of existence of extraterrestrial civilizations. There is no satisfactory way to estimate this probability in the absence of tangible evidence. In the end, the conversation degenerated into a philosophical argument concerning the meaning of probability. After lunch I wanted to steer the meeting into a more practical direction, and so I prepared some remarks beginning with the words "To Hell with Philosophy!" To emphasize my point I wrote this on the blackboard in Russian: "K Chortu s Filosofiei!" Luckily, I checked it with a Russian friend before the meeting reconvened. He smiled and said cryptically, "I do not think that these words say exactly what you have in mind." He explained that *filosofia* in modern Russian does not mean "philosophy" in general, but means the particular brand of Marxist dogma that is taught to students under this label. The words that I had written on the blackboard had a strong political flavor that I had not intended. My friend found me a synonym for *filosofia* that is free from unwanted political associations. I had narrowly escaped breaking the first rule of etiquette of international scientific meetings, the rule that excludes political polemics of any kind from our discussions.

The subject of extraterrestrial intelligence (ETI) occupies a peculiar limbo on the borderline between science and science fiction. The vast amount of bad fiction that has been written about ETI makes serious scientists a little afraid of becoming involved with it. Only people with solidly established reputations in legitimate science feel free to talk about ETI without risk to their respectability. Our meeting of forty people included almost all the scientists who have made serious contributions to the theory and practice of searching for evidence of ETI.

So far, only two actual searches for artificial radio signals from the cosmos have been made. One was by Frank Drake of Cornell University, the other by Troitsky of the Soviet Radio Physics Institute in Gorky. Nothing was found. But the failure of these initial attempts surprised nobody. Both searches were brief and covered only a fraction of the sky. They were preliminary exercises to develop the technique of searching. If either of them had found a signal, it would have been an incredible piece of luck. Both Drake and Troitsky were at Byurakan and talked about what they had done and what they had learned from it.

The basic difficulty with searching for intelligent signals is that it demands the time of astronomers and telescopes that have other more urgent things to do. There are immense numbers of exciting and puzzling natural objects in the universe, and not enough people and instruments to look at them. Individual astronomers have a limited amount of telescope time available to them. If they have a month of time with a good telescope, they are lucky. If they use their month to look carefully at one or more of the natural puzzles, they are virtually certain to discover something interesting. If they use their month to look for artificial signals, they are virtually certain to discover nothing. Even though the discovery of an artificial signal would be one of the great events in human history, the chance of its happening to any one group of astronomers is too small to justify their gambling away much of their precious time on it. It is as if you asked people to give up half of their income for life for a thousand-to-one chance of winning a billion dollars. The bargain may be a favorable one if you calculate the mathematical expectations, but nobody who is not crazy would accept it. Both Drake and Troitsky are acutely aware of this dilemma.

What then is to be done? There are three schools of thought concerning the future of the search for ETI. The conservative school thinks that the search should be left as at present to the initiative of individual astronomers. This means that very little will happen. Perhaps a few more preliminary exercises, but nothing further. Naturally, this school of thought was poorly represented in Byurakan. The radical school thinks that a full-scale program of searches should be organized, using new large instruments specially built for the purpose. The cost of such a program would be comparable with the total cost of the resources now devoted by mankind to ground-based astronomy of all kinds, but substantially less than the cost of existing space programs. The search program would necessarily be funded by national governments, and perhaps directed by an international authority. Only a few people at Byurakan advocated the radical view. They argued that nothing less than a massive centralized program could give us a reasonable assurance of picking up whatever artificial signals may exist in our corner of the universe. However, the majority felt that we are still far too ignorant to embark on large and expensive programs. The general consensus at Byurakan belonged to an intermediate school of thought that one may call gradualist. The gradualists believe that an organized long-range program of searches for ETI should be begun, so that the costs and risks can be shared between many astronomers and institutions. But they envisage a program of modest scope, using only a small fraction of the time of any one telescope, and subordinated to the exploration of natural objects, which is the main business of astronomy.

The Byurakan meeting had two tangible results. The first and most important result is that we all got to know each other. Shklovsky and Kardashev are no longer mythical names on the title pages of books, but real people with whom one can exchange Armenian jokes. The second and lesser result is a formal agreed statement containing our recommendations to our respective national academies of science. The recommendations advocate a gradualist course of action and give detailed suggestions for developing the necessary instruments as we go along. Whether this statement will have any practical effect remains to be seen. We do not expect anything spectacular to come of it. We shall be satisfied if our meeting has helped even slightly to persuade our fellow human beings all over the earth that the search for extraterrestrial intelligence is a legitimate and hopeful activity for intelligent humans to pursue.

Like other scientific meetings, this one had its lighter moments. At one point an astronomer digressed into a rambling and improbable theory of mental creativity. He told us that our intellectual powers wax and wane with the eleven-year period of the sunspots. He illustrated his theory by enumerating the great discoveries of Newton and Einstein that were all made at times of maximum sunspot activity. Shklovsky leaned over to his neighbor and whispered loudly, "This theory was invented during a deep sunspot minimum."

CHAPTER 29

Brittle Silence

.....

1981

"A creative person is born, not made," say the skeptics. But I have a new argument to introduce into this old discussion. Even the skeptics ought to accept my argument. It is alive. It is, as people sometimes say, a miracle that proves the invincibility of the human spirit. The miracle happened at Zagorsk. You have probably heard of the striking results achieved at the Zagorsk children's home in studying, educating, and humanizing deaf-blind children. The teachers I. A. Sokolyansky and A. I. Meshcheryakov recently received a state prize for their work.

I have known Sasha Suvorov, Yura Lerner, Natasha Korneyeva, and Sergei Sirotkin for a long time, but now I work with them in the same institute. I deal with them as equals. Perhaps that is why I sometimes forget how their unusual lives began. Sasha Suvorov described it: "Ivan Afanasyevich Sokolyansky taught us to smile. He made masks of smiling faces and gave them to us to feel. Then the children tried to reproduce the same expressions on their own faces."

Sasha Suvorov's room is stacked up to the ceiling with books. Thick Braille volumes of Marx's *Capital*, Pushkin, Dostoyevsky, and favorite stories from his childhood. He would like to know so much, and he still does not have enough books. When Sasha once said to me that he would like to hear some wind-ensemble music of Wagner and Beethoven, I only sighed. But Sasha got hold of a tape deck and paid for it out of his own earnings (in addition to his scientific work he also writes articles for popular magazines), and now he is playing his tapes ten times a day, trying with his feeble vestiges of hearing to grasp the patterns of music, to distinguish a melody and even to sing along with it. He is convinced that if he can only master the notation he will be able to learn to read music from a score.

If you look into the apartment of Sasha's neighbor Yura Lerner, you see at once that he is addicted to sculpture. Figures in plaster, clay, papier-mâché, ceramic, and bronze are on his shelves and tables. All this is his own work.

Once a week we have something which we call a "Pavlov circle." We sit around a table hand in hand, so that Sasha and I can spell words into each other's hands on one side and Sasha and Yura on the other. Our favorite subject of discussion is "What is creativity?" We decided to talk about this in terms of real experiences, or as Sasha puts it, without ringing phrases. At the next session we discussed Yura's journal *My World,* which runs to five hundred pages in Braille. I ask Yura, "Why did you begin modeling?" "I wanted to make for myself the toys I was playing with." "And then?" "Then, when I couldn't communicate with other children, modeling became a substitute for playmates." "And then?" asks Sasha. "And then, it just got to be more and more interesting."

I am trying to understand why only Yura, out of the group of students at the Zagorsk children's home, was attracted to artistic sculpture. All of them learned to model. For deaf-blind children, modeling replaces drawing, and up to a certain age it replaces writing too. To express a true picture of their surroundings, the children have to copy with models the objects they come into contact with. An ordinary youngster may boldly draw a dog as big as a house, but the teacher cannot let a deaf-blind child do that. The students recall how Seryozha Sirotkin was asked in school to model a sparrow on a twig. His sparrow sat in human fashion with its feet dangling below the twig. The teacher scolded him. "Are you laughing? Are you laughing?" asks Sasha, touching my cheeks with his fingers. "No," say I, "I am furious. Does that mean that fantasy is forbidden to the children?" "Fantasy?" Sasha explodes (this is his scientific theme, and also his hobbyhorse). "In that case fantasy could not exist anymore. Only mistakes in the perception of reality." Then he was silent for a moment.

"Only then, how do you tell where mistakes end and fantasy begins?" "I don't know," answers Yura. I don't know either, I think to myself. If only I knew how to distinguish between the mistakes of ignorance and the "mistakes" of discovery, how to find the intangible nuance that separates creativity from mindless craftwork.

Our session lasts until late in the evening. I say goodbye and go out into the street. A frosty starlit night. Sasha loves nights like this because he can see stars. He has some perception of light. Silence. The snow crunches under my feet. Does it crunch or does it tinkle? Sasha once said it in a poem: "A silence as brittle as fine glass. Somebody squeezed it a little, and it crunched and tinkled as it died." He hears the silence and sees the stars. What more does a poet need?

Every time, after meeting with the students, you feel you are getting a second wind. Many details which you would not ordinarily notice suddenly begin to give you a feeling of joy and wonder. And at the same time, you become aware of your own clumsiness, you become ashamed of your own and other people's weakness, of your inability or unwillingness to be a human being. For us there are so many opportunities to be human.

[*Postscript, December 1991*] For ten years after this article was published, I heard nothing more about Sasha Suvorov. Then I received a letter from Joel Cunningham, president of Susquehanna University in Pennsylvania, telling me that Sasha received an honorary degree at Susquehanna University in May 1991 and gave a commencement address. Now in his middle thirties, Sasha has established himself in Russia as a poet and educator, and as a spokesman for deaf and blind people. Like Helen Keller, he combines phenomenal talent with phenomenal courage and strength of character. He also helps to run an enterprise with the name Oasis and Company, a craft workshop for deaf workers in Moscow. During his American tour he visited Gallaudet University in Washington and the Perkins School for the Blind in Boston.

CHAPTER 30

Helen Dukas

.....

1982

Helen Dukas had a fantastic memory. That was the most striking of her many excellent qualities. It is easy to understand why Einstein found her indispensable, faced as he was with constant demands on his time and attention, incessant correspondence and requests for interviews. Helen could remember infallibly who had written what when, who needed an answer and who didn't, who was an earnest seeker after truth and who was a journalistic pest. She remembered the precise dates of all the official events in Einstein's life, the names and faces of the people he met, even the clothes they had been wearing. What a marvelous gift it was that Helen brought to Einstein, to allow him to live the life of an absentminded professor; she kept to herself the tiresome details that he wanted to forget, and she reminded him of the important things that he wanted to remember.

Helen's phenomenal memory was equally indispensable in her second career as keeper and collector of the Einstein archive. For twenty-seven years, up to the week of her death, she conducted an enormous and worldwide correspondence. She was finding new Einstein documents in unexpected places and establishing their historical context. She was helping historians from all over the world to locate and interpret the documents already in the archive. There was nobody else who could pick up an Einstein postcard, the preferred mode of communication of his earlier years, and tell at a glance when it was written, what it said, and how it fitted into the story. There was nobody else who remembered even the names of all the people Einstein knew, let alone their dates, titles, jobs, and family connections.

Helen's professional work for Einstein was the most important thing in her life, but it was not the whole of her life. The second most important thing was family connections. She had a deep and enduring sense of family, including other people's families as well as her own. A good memory for names and faces goes together with a warm and genuine interest in people. She had grown up in a close-knit and lively family of seven children in Freiburg. Her mother died while Helen was still a child, and this loss bound the children together even more closely. The father was a wine merchant who seems to have presided as a tolerant and good-humored captain over his crew of seven individualists. After Hitler had scattered the family to the winds, Helen kept in close touch with all of them, regularly visiting her sisters and brothers, nephews and nieces, great-nephews and great-nieces, in Israel and in England and in various parts of America. Now, alas, only two of the original seven are left, but a whole crowd of the younger generations will remember Helen as a favorite aunt and great-aunt.

This is how my wife and I came to be friends of Helen. She became attached not so much to us as to our children. Although she had close ties to her sisters and brothers scattered around the world, she lacked a family of her own in Princeton. And our children lacked grandparents on this side of the ocean. So it happened that when Helen came for the first time to our house, twenty-one years ago, little one-year-old Dorothy grabbed hold of her hand and would not let go. Helen became our substitute grandmother and remained so for the rest of her life. Children need grandparents, and Helen needed grandchildren. So she kept on coming to our house, especially for the big events, Thanksgiving and Christmas. She liked to be there when all the children were home. She liked our family because it was big and noisy, with a whole lot of children. It reminded her of the warmth of her own childhood.

She loved to tell us stories about the old days in Freiburg and Berlin and Princeton. I wish I could remember these stories as vividly as she told them. Unfortunately, I never wrote them down. And nobody could persuade her to talk to a tape recorder. She had learned by hard experience to distrust people who came to her with tape recorders. She was a very private person, and she was determined not to see her private life published in the newspapers. I used to argue with her, telling her that future generations of scientists and historians would be cheated of their inheritance if she did not leave them a record of her memories. But she was not to be tempted. Once she made up her mind to say no, that was final.

Let me now tell one of her stories, one which happens to be fresh in my mind, since she told it a few days before she died. She was describing her first arrival in Princeton, when she came fresh off the boat with Einstein and his family in 1933. The first thing that happened after the Einsteins occupied their lodgings in Library Place was that Helen walked into town to buy some groceries. She stopped at Bamman's, a high-class old-fashioned grocery store which used to stand next to where the Wine-and-Game shop is now. She explained her needs in a thick German accent, and pulled out of her handbag a wad of old twenty-dollar bills which Frau Einstein had drawn from a bank in Europe. Mrs. Bamman looked at Helen strangely and said, "Just a moment," ran to the telephone, and called the Princeton police. In two minutes the police arrived with screaming sirens and the shop was surrounded in case Helen should try to escape. Helen, meanwhile, stood calmly wondering whether she had arrived by mistake in Hollywood instead of Princeton. "Anyway," she said as she told the story, "living with Professor Einstein, I was accustomed to things turning into a circus wherever we went." Mrs. Bamman then escorted her into an inner room where the chief of police questioned her and carefully examined her twenty-dollar bills. After a few minutes he politely said goodbye and told her she was free to go home. She walked back with the groceries, wondering whether this was going to happen every time she went shopping in Princeton. Several days later she found out the cause of the fuss. The ransom for the kidnapped Lindbergh baby had been paid in twenty-dollar bills of an old series no longer current in 1933, and the shopkeepers of New Jersey had been asked by the police to report immediately any suspicious characters who might be trying to pass the ransom money.

Now we are left with our memories of Helen, that warm and wonderful person who had learned from Einstein the art of laughing at the human comedy while remaining always aware of the background of tragedy against which the comedy is played. We also are treasuring a dozen letters which she wrote to us at odd moments during the years when we happened to be away in Europe. Her letters are like herself, easy and spontaneous and not intended for reading aloud on a public occasion like this. When we were in Freiburg, she wrote to us nostalgically about the Rheinstrasse, the street where she grew up, and of how it had changed out of all recognition when she went back to see it after the war. When we were in Munich, she wrote full of excitement about the newly discovered Einstein letters to Willem de Sitter which had turned up in an old laboratory in Holland. Another time she wrote joyfully about the letter from Einstein to Karl Schwarzschild which her friend Martin Schwarzschild had found among his papers here in Princeton, "all about the eclipse and Mercury, etcetera, four pages of it." And usually at the end of her letter Helen says something like this: "I miss you and the girls very much and am looking forward to your return eagerly. Kiss the babies for me. Will they still know me when they return?" Of course they did. They will not forget her, and neither will we.

CHAPTER 31

Paul Dirac

.....

1 9 8 6

Paul Adrien Maurice Dirac was the last survivor of the group of young men who in the three years from 1925 to 1928 created quantum mechanics. Together they overthrew the foundations of classical physics and established the new foundations on which all our modern understanding of atoms and particles, fields and interactions, chemistry and molecular biology is based. Dirac was at the age of twenty-three one of the leaders of the quantum revolution. At the age of twenty-five he made, alone, his most famous and original discovery, the Dirac equation, which describes the behavior of an electron with almost perfect accuracy. He won the Nobel Prize for physics in 1933. He continued thereafter to publish important and original contributions to physics, always in his personal and inimitable style. In this brief memoir I will not attempt to describe the substance of his discoveries but will concentrate on the question of style. The Dirac style has an importance transcending the particular field of science in which he worked.

To give to nonexperts a true impression of the Dirac style, it is best to use his own words. Here is Dirac, at the age of seventy, talking to a mixed audience at the University of Miami in Coral Gables. The title of his talk was "Basic Beliefs and Fundamental Research."

> There is one fairly obvious way of getting a new theory.
> Keep close to the experimental results, hear about all the

latest information that the experimenters obtain, and then proceed to set up a theory to account for them. That is a more or less straightforward procedure and there are many physicists working on such lines, competing with one another, and it might develop somewhat into a rat-race. Of course it needs rather intelligent rats to take part in it. But I don't want to speak about this method of procedure.

There is another way in which a theoretical physicist may work which is slower and more sedate and may lead to more profound results. It does not depend very closely on experimental work. This consists in having some basic beliefs and trying to incorporate them into one theory. Now why should one have basic beliefs? I don't know that I can explain that. It's just that one feels that nature is constructed in a certain way and one hangs onto the idea rather like one might hang onto a religious belief. One feels that things simply have to be on these lines and one must devise a mathematical theory for incorporating the basic belief.

These two styles of theorizing are well known in the history of science. Historians call the first style Baconian and the second Cartesian. Our young colleagues today, with less awareness of their place in history, are accustomed to call the two styles "bottom-up" and "top-down." Dirac in his talk went on to explain how the very greatest theoretical physicists, in particular Newton and Einstein, worked from the top down, deducing laws of nature from fundamental beliefs rather than inducing laws from the results of experiment. Dirac himself is in modern times the supreme example of a top-down physicist. Here is what he says about himself:

My own early work was very much influenced by Bohr orbits, and I had the basic belief that Bohr orbits would provide the clue to understanding atomic events. That was a mistaken belief . . . . I found out that my own basic belief was wrong and I had to go over to quite a new line of thinking. I had to have some more general basis for my work, and the only reliable basis I could think of, the only basis which was sufficiently general so as to secure me from making the same mistake again, was to set up a principle of mathematical beauty: to say that we don't really know what the basic equations of physics are, but they have to have great mathematical beauty. We must insist on this, and that is the only feature of the equations that we can have confidence in and insist on. . . . How can one make beauty a fundamental test for the correctness of a physical theory? Well, it is quite clear that beauty does depend on one's culture and upbringing for certain kinds of beauty, pictures, literature, poetry and so on. . . . But mathematical beauty is of rather a different kind. I should say perhaps it is of a completely different kind and transcends these personal factors. It is the same in all countries and at all periods of time. . . . Well, that is the essence of what I wanted to tell you. In fact one can feel so strongly about these things, that when an experimental result turns up which is not in agreement with one's beliefs, one may perhaps make the prediction that the experimental result is wrong and that the experimenters will correct it after a while. Of course one must not be too obstinate over these matters, but still one must sometimes be bold.

Dirac was bold. His confidence in his own instinct for mathematical beauty led him in succession to three fundamental discoveries: first, the general abstract formulation of quantum mechanics; second, the correct quantum description of electromagnetic radiation processes; and third, the Dirac equation for the electron. In each case he was led not merely to a new physical law but to a new style of mathematical description of nature. And in each case the experiments proved him right, although, as he hints in the Coral Gables lecture, there were initially some contradictory experimental results which he was bold enough to ignore.

Dirac's fundamental belief, the belief that the basic criterion for choosing a physical theory should be aesthetic, proved itself in his hands overwhelmingly successful. Nature agreed with his criterion. And this agreement between Nature's and Dirac's notions of beauty presents us with a new example of an old philosophical riddle. Why should Nature care about our feelings of beauty? Why should the electron prefer a beautiful equation to an ugly one? Why should the universe dance to Dirac's tune? These are deep questions which neither scientists nor philosophers know how to answer. Dirac, by his style of discovery, has posed these questions more sharply than anyone else. More even than Newton and Einstein he used the criterion of beauty consciously and directly as a way of finding truth.

Inevitably, it happened as Dirac grew older that his aesthetic judgment became less sure. He came to Princeton in 1950 when the new quantum electrodynamics of Schwinger and Feynman had achieved spectacular successes in explaining some fine details of experiments in atomic physics. The theories of Schwinger and Feynman were in essence nothing more than clarifications of the quantum theory of radiation invented by Dirac in 1927. Schwinger and Feynman left untouched the basic physical concepts of Dirac and added only new mathematical tricks and techniques of calculation. The new tricks were elegant and gave results confirmed by experiment. I was delighted that these technical advances had increased the power and scope of Dirac's theory. I confidently expected that Dirac would be equally delighted by the new triumphs of his twenty-three-year-old brainchild. I brashly approached Dirac and asked him, "Well, Professor Dirac, what do you think of these new developments in quantum electrodynamics?" He answered my question, as he always answered questions, quietly and precisely: "I might have thought that the new ideas were correct if they had not been so ugly." That was his verdict. There was nothing more to be said. Now, thirty-six years later, it appears that in the matter of quantum electrodynamics Nature disagrees with Dirac's aesthetic judgment and agrees with Schwinger and Feynman. But the last word has not been said. Quantum electrodynamics is not a closed and completed chapter of science. It could still happen, as Dirac surmised, that a wider perspective may ultimately make the tricks of Schwinger and Feynman superfluous.

Dirac's claim for the primacy of aesthetic judgment in physics has acquired a new immediacy in recent years with the advent of the theory of superstrings. Superstrings are enormously popular among theoretical physicists of the younger generation. The quest for mathematical beauty has led the devotees of superstrings to a world of abstraction far removed from mundane experiment. The superstring theory is not merely untested by existing experiments; it does not yet lead to any specific consequences that might be tested by experiment in the future. Faith in superstring theory rests upon an extreme form of Dirac's philosophy. The theory is put forward as a likely foundation for the whole of physics, simply by virtue of its incomparable beauty, and in spite of the fact that it is presently untestable. We must admire the courage and skill of the superstring fraternity, even if we do not share their faith. Perhaps Nature will in the end smile upon their efforts, as she smiled upon Dirac's electron.

Another area of science in which Dirac has been active is cosmology. Here too he was guided by his aesthetic principles rather than by the detailed observations of astronomers. His starting point was the notion that the fundamental laws of nature ought not to contain any arbitrary large numbers. In fact, we find one such large number conspicuously built into our existing physics, namely the ratio between the strengths of electric and gravitational forces. This ratio is a pure number independent of the units of measurement and has a value roughly equal to 10^{39}. Dirac considered it unacceptable for a number of this size to occur a priori in the basic laws of physics. He remarked that the present age of the universe measured in atomic units of time is a number of the same order of magnitude. Therefore, he said, it makes sense to assume that the two large numbers are equal, that the ratio between electrical and gravitational force is now as large as it is because we are observing it at a correspondingly large number of atomic units of time after the beginning of the universe. Upon this basis Dirac built an unorthodox cosmology. The main features of the Dirac cosmology are that space-time in the large has zero curvature and that the strength of gravitational forces decreases with time. Both these predictions of Dirac's theory are testable, and both are consistent with present-day observations. Within a few years, using precise data obtained from the tracking of planetary spacecraft, the hypothesis of a decreasing strength of gravity should be definitely confirmed or rejected.

I have no space here to enlarge upon Dirac's personal life, his character, his family, and his famous silences. Others who knew him better have written more substantial memoirs of his life. The memoirs abound with "Dirac stories," typically recording a conversation in which Dirac disposed of a large subject with few words. My favorite Dirac story comes from his brother-in-law, Eugene Wigner. Wigner was sitting with Dirac at a lunch table while heated arguments were going on. Dirac sat, as usual, silent. Finally, Wigner addressed him directly: "Well, Paul, everybody would like to hear what you think about this. Why don't you say something?" Dirac replied, "There are always more people wanting to talk than people wanting to listen."

CHAPTER 32

Beacons

.....

1 9 8 8

I. THE LEMON AND THE CREAM

The title of this section is taken from a story in the book *Surely You're Joking, Mr. Feynman*. The same story also provided the title for that book. All friends of Dick Feynman are indebted to Ralph Leighton for preserving Dick's stories on tape and collecting them into books. The lemon and the cream appeared at a tea party given by Mrs. Eisenhart in Princeton in 1939. Princeton is socially a stuffy place, and in the bad old days it was even stuffier than it is now. Mrs. Eisenhart was a legendary figure in the Princeton of 1939. She was the social director of Princeton high society. She decided what was done and what was not done in Princeton. The great German mathematician Carl Ludwig Siegel came to Princeton in 1934 to escape from Hitler, and then in 1935 he went back to Germany. He said to his friends when he went back that living under Hitler was bad but living under Mrs. Eisenhart was worse. That was, of course, a mistake. In 1940 he had to admit that he had made a mistake, and he came back to live in Princeton.

There were two people in Princeton that Mrs. Eisenhart was never able to bully. One was Einstein and the other was Dick Feynman. Einstein simply ignored her and refused to go to her parties and wear the proper clothes. He probably had Mrs. Eisenhart in mind when he wrote his classic description of Princeton in a letter to the queen of the Belgians: "Princeton is a quaint and ceremonious village, peopled by demigods on stilts." Dick Feynman was too young to ignore Mrs. Eisenhart, but he kept the upper hand by always speaking the truth. He met her for the first time when he had just arrived in Princeton, a young student from Far Rockaway on Long Island, without any training in correct formal behavior. He was invited to one of her tea parties. There she was, in full regalia, pouring the tea, when Feynman approached. She began with the customary ritual, "Would you like cream or lemon in your tea, Mr. Feynman." Feynman said innocently, "I'll have both, thank you." That completely flummoxed her. That had never happened before at one of her tea parties. All she could do was to fix Feynman with an icy stare and say, "Surely you're joking, Mr. Feynman."

Fortunately, the social snobbery that used to flourish in Princeton is now dead. Instead, we now have academic snobbery, the snobbery of people who think that just because they work at a university and have a Ph.D. after their name they are a superior breed and are entitled to despise others who don't have a Ph.D. and who have to work at intellectually inferior jobs in industry or business. Academic snobbery is a real problem in Princeton, even though Mrs. Eisenhart is no longer with us. We several times offered Dick Feynman a professorship at Princeton and he always turned us down because he could not stand the snobbery.

The reason why Dick Feynman had such a rich and exciting and useful life is that he began by saying yes to everything. That is what it means not to be a snob. A snob is somebody who is always saying no to things. A snob says no to things because they are not proper, or because they are vulgar, or because they are just not done, or because they are low-brow, or because they are beneath the dignity of an intellectually superior person. Dick Feynman said yes because he wanted to try everything. He said yes to the lemon and also to the cream. That is the story of his life. By saying yes to things he got into all kinds of trouble. He got into absurd and unnecessary disasters. But then, when he had tried something out and it ended badly, he had the strength of mind to say no. He was firm in saying no, after he had said yes and proved to himself by firsthand experience that something was no good. He said yes to Princeton when he came there as a student, and then, after he had tried the Princeton intellectual high society and decided it was a fake, he said no to Princeton for the rest of his life.

The book *Surely You're Joking, Mr. Feynman* is the best antidote against academic snobbery. It has a wonderful collection of stories, all true, about Feynman's undignified adventures. It has a highly uncomplimentary description, also true, of the Institute for Advanced Study in Princeton where I work, and of the reasons why Feynman never wanted to work there. And it has the best account ever written, also true, of what it was like to be working at Los Alamos during the time the first bombs were put together.

After Dick Feynman died last winter, his friend Ralph Leighton put together another book, with the title *What Do You Care What Other People Think?* The title is a quote from Feynman's first wife, Arline, who died in 1945. Feynman said yes to Arline, and married her, although they knew when they married that she had only a couple of years to live. Feynman said yes again, forty-four years later, when he was asked to serve on the Board of Enquiry investigating the Shuttle disaster, although he had barely survived his second big cancer operation and knew he had not many years to live. He saw the shuttle enquiry as a great chance to educate the American public, to show the public a little bit of real science in action. He grabbed the opportunity and made the enquiry into a moment of truth for the American people.

What Do You Care What Other People Think? is a second collection of conversations. The second collection is more serious than the first. The second book is half about Arline and half about the shuttle. This time Mr. Feynman is not joking. Arline's short life was a tragedy, and the shuttle disaster was also a tragedy. Feynman did not close his eyes to tragedy. He knew as well as anybody the bitterness of chronic illness and early death. But he also knew, as Shakespeare knew, that in every tragedy there are moments of comedy, moments when the tragic hero steps aside and lets his place on the stage be taken by the clown. To remain sane as Feynman did in the midst of tragedy, it helps to be a bit of a clown. Feynman said yes both to tragedy and to comedy. Even when he was most serious, nursing Arline through her last weeks in Albuquerque, or digging out the causes of the shuttle disaster in Florida, or struggling with the infinite self-energy of the electron in Ithaca, he was never solemn.

Dick Feynman was a great communicator. I never saw him give a lecture that did not make the audience laugh. And yet, I never heard him talking down to an audience. His lectures were serious,

full of scientific meat, often difficult. He was always more concerned with the scientific substance of his talk than with the jokes.
The jokes just came to him naturally. And the jokes gave his audience a feeling for the joy of doing science. Feynman was able to
convey to the public, better than anybody else, the simple no-
nonsense common sense that is at the heart of all good science.
His finest hour as a communicator came when, already mortally
ill, he performed an experiment at a televised session of the shuttle
enquiry. He demonstrated on camera the loss of resilience of a
piece of the shuttle O-ring after it was dunked in a glass of ice
water. The public saw with their own eyes how science is done,
how a great scientist thinks with his hands, how nature gives a
clear answer when a scientist asks her a clear question.

Feynman tells us, in his account of the shuttle enquiry, that the
staging of the O-ring experiment was not as easy as it appeared to
the audience. Like all good demonstration experiments, it needed
careful preparation and careful timing. Feynman had to fight hard
to make sure the experiment would actually work in the short
time it would be on camera.

The last time I went to see Feynman at his home in Pasadena, I
found him recovering from a typical Feynman disaster. He doesn't
mention this disaster in either of the two books. He had run into
trouble baby-sitting for a boa constrictor. His teenage daughter
had a friend, and the friend had a pet boa constrictor, and the
friend went away on vacation for a month, and so Feynman found
himself responsible for the care and feeding of the boa constrictor.
The boa constrictor was supposed to eat live white mice, but
when Feynman fed him the mice, he was too stupid or too lazy to
catch them. Instead of the boa constrictor eating the mice, the
mice began eating the boa constrictor. So Feynman had to sit up
at night to stop the mice from nibbling holes in the boa constrictor's skin. And then, when the owner of the boa constrictor came
back, she scolded Feynman for taking care of the animal so badly.
He said he had learned something from this experience. In future,
if anybody asked him to baby-sit for a boa constrictor, he would
say no. It was a no-win situation.

The story of Feynman's involvement with nuclear weapons was
like the story of the boa constrictor. He worked in the Manhattan
Project when he was a young man in his twenties. He started in

the isotope-separation part of the project at Princeton and then went to Los Alamos. He worked hard and was very good at it. This was before the days of electronic computers. All the detailed calculations of the hydrodynamics and the radiation in a nuclear explosion had to be done by hand. Feynman organized the human computers and infected them with his enthusiasm so that they got the numbers out in time. These were the first accurate calculations of what happens in a nuclear bomb when it goes off. Feynman at the age of twenty-seven had a big share of responsibility for the fact that the first bombs did what they were supposed to do when they were dropped.

The reason why Feynman said yes to the bombs, when he was asked to join the project at the beginning, was the same reason all the other physicists gave for working at Los Alamos. There was a war on, Hitler was still going strong, and people were scared of what Hitler might do if he had the bomb and we did not. They thought they were in a race against Hitler for the bomb, and it seemed a good idea to work as hard as possible to make sure America would not lose the race. Besides this patriotic reason, Feynman also had personal reasons for working hard at Los Alamos. The bomb was something real, it was an exciting scientific challenge, and it was a job he happened to be spectacularly good at. He naturally said yes because it was his nature to say yes to any new and unlikely adventure.

After the project succeeded, after the bombs were dropped on Hiroshima and Nagasaki and World War 2 was over, Feynman understood quickly that nuclear weapons were no good. He understood that we would be living in fear of nuclear weapons for the rest of our lives, and he decided to have nothing more to do with them. In 1946, when he left Los Alamos, he gave up his secret clearances and said no to any further involvement with military projects. He looked back at what he had done at Los Alamos, believing at the time that it would make the United States safer, and saw that it actually made the United States more unsafe than it had ever been before. He did not regret having been at Los Alamos, just as he did not regret his battle with the boa constrictor forty years later. The lesson of Los Alamos was the same as the lesson of the boa constrictor. It is all right to say yes once to a dumb idea, to try it out and see if it is any good. But you are a fool if you say yes twice to the same dumb idea. After things turn out badly the first time, you say no.

In a letter to my parents written before I had got to know Feynman well, I described him as "half genius and half buffoon." This was partly true, but it was not the whole truth. A truer description would have said that Feynman was all genius and all buffoon. The deep thinking and the joyful clowning were not separate parts of a split personality. He did not do his thinking on Monday and his clowning on Tuesday. He was thinking and clowning simultaneously. During the early years when I knew him best, he was thinking and clowning incessantly. He was at the same time gregarious and intensely private, banging away at his bongo drums and mourning his dead wife. He was adventurous and at the same time critical. He took the lemon and the cream of his life together.

2. FATHER OF E.T.

Another of my heroes is Philip Morrison. He is, like Dick Feynman, a lemon-and-cream character. Philip Morrison has done much, in many different ways, to bring human concerns into science and to bring science into the mainstream of humanistic culture. He has been active as a teacher, as a reformer of school curricula, as a writer, and as an incomparable reviewer of books, besides being a first-class scientist and an effective politician.

I remember vividly the first time I heard Phil talk to a public audience. It was in the winter of 1947, soon after I arrived in America as a graduate student. Phil was talking in Ithaca to the local chapter of the Federation of Atomic Scientists, which later changed its name to the Federation of American Scientists. He was describing the island of Tinian in the Marianas as he had seen it in the summer of 1945 when he was preparing equipment for the nuclear missions against Japan. Phil could make your flesh creep with the starkness of his language. He spoke of that island, bulldozed flat, turned into one vast airfield, five hundred heavy bombers landing and taking off with their great loads of high-explosive and incendiary bombs, the air constantly rumbling with the greatest concentration of military power ever seen on this planet up to the summer of 1945. That immense concentration of power was what it took to destroy a city, until Hiroshima. And then Phil described how he watched the *Enola Gay* take off, a single airplane taking off gently into the dark sky, attracting no attention, to outward appearance no different from her five hundred sisters on the island. And that single airplane, within a few days, changed the incessant roar and turmoil of the island into silence.

When I heard Phil speak in Ithaca, it was not the first time he had told that story. He had told it to bigger and more important audiences in Washington. He had told it in testimony before congressional committees. Everywhere he went, he left behind him a profound impression. Of all the scientists who were then trying to teach mankind the facts of our nuclear predicament, Phil was the one who spoke most clearly, most simply, and most effectively.

Then again, twelve years later, it was Philip Morrison and his friend Giuseppe Cocconi who invented E.T. They demonstrated, with simple scientific arguments, that humans could search for radio signals transmitted by extraterrestrial civilizations in the sky, using radio telescopes of feasible size and sensitivity. This demonstration led to the start of observational programs searching for extraterrestrial radio signals, programs that are now after thirty years rapidly becoming more sophisticated and more cost-effective. And in the meantime the idea of E.T. has become firmly rooted in the imagination of people all over the world. Of all Phil Morrison's great contributions to public education, E.T. is probably the one that will be remembered longest.

3. COMMUNISTS AND EMPIRE BUILDERS

I happen to be a naturalized American who was originally English, and I am proud of both my countries. Both England and America have done well by being adventurous and critical at the same time. The British Empire was an absurd adventure for most of the people who built it. I come from a family of empire builders and I used to have uncles and aunts scattered all around Africa. My favorite uncle was Oliver Atkey, a medical doctor who spent his life in the Sudan training Sudanese doctors and building up from nothing a public health administration for a country twice as big as Texas. The colonial medical service was like the Peace Corps, except that it allowed people to stay in one place for thirty years and gave them the chance to create something permanent. Uncle Oliver loved the Sudanese and had many Sudanese friends. After he retired, his apartment in London was constantly full of Sudanese friends who came to see him when they were visiting England. The empire gave him a wide horizon and let him practice his trade on a scale he never could have imagined if he had remained an ordinary physician in England. It was absurd to think that a little island like England could run the affairs of half the world, but the absurdity of it didn't stop Uncle Oliver and his friends from doing it rather well most of the time. The empire was in many ways a good thing while it lasted. And when it started to fall apart, we succeeded in dismantling it quickly and leaving behind some vigorously independent countries such as the one of which we are now citizens. Uncle Oliver was a socialist, and his wife, Aunt Dulcibella, was a member of the British Communist Party, pledged to demolish the empire which they loyally served.

I am not denying the dark side of the empire, the many grievous mistakes and crimes that were committed in the course of its history. The Sudan today, with chronic civil war and famine in the southern provinces, has hardly fulfilled the high hopes that Oliver and Dulcibella held for its future. But the empire also had a bright side. The bright side was the opportunities it gave to people like Oliver and Dulcibella who were both adventurous and critical. They were adventurous enough to take on the impossible job of organizing and molding whole continents of alien people in their own image. And they were critical enough to understand when the time had come to quit and go home.

My aunt Dulcibella was perhaps an extreme case. She was the first woman in England to take out a license to pilot an airplane. She persuaded Oliver to buy an airplane in the 1920s, when airplanes were hardly a reliable means of transport. Oliver used his airplane to descend unexpectedly on medical stations in distant parts of the Sudan, so that he could check what kind of a job his trainees were doing in the villages. When Oliver and Dulcibella had vacations, they flew crazy trips in their airplane all over Africa. Once they looked out of the window of the airplane over some remote part of Africa and saw a man in a field below being mauled by a lion. They landed in the field, scared away the lion, rescued the man, bundled him into the airplane, took off and flew him to hospital and saved his life. I know this story is true because I met the rescued man in London afterward. He had lost a piece of his nose but was otherwise in good shape.

Another of my African cousins, likewise adept in saying yes to lemon and cream, settled in Rhodesia and remained a staunch supporter of white supremacy throughout the years of Rhodesian independence, and now continues to live there peacefully as a citizen of Zimbabwe. At the time of the transfer of power he wrote to me, "Of course we will get along all right with the blacks. If we hadn't been able to get along with the blacks, we wouldn't have lasted six weeks." He wrote more recently that he went on a vacation to Victoria Falls, the great tourist attraction of Zimbabwe, and was happy to see there the statue of the Scottish doctor David Livingstone still standing where he stood when he discovered the falls in 1855, and under the statue the original inscription still proclaiming to the tourists: EXPLORER, MISSIONARY, LIBERATOR. The word LIBERATOR records the fact that Livingstone was engaged in putting an end to slavery in Africa at the same time as his contemporary Lincoln was putting an end to it in America. If we are wise, we may hope to be remembered with words like these, a hundred years after we are dead.

I am hoping that Los Alamos, and the whole nuclear weapons enterprise of which it is a part, will have a history like the history of the British Empire. Los Alamos was a great adventure for people like Dick Feynman who went there at the beginning. Most of them would probably have gone there and said yes to the challenge of building a nuclear bomb, even if Hitler had not given them a political excuse for it. It was inevitable that human beings in various countries would rush into the excitement of building bombs when the possibility of it was first discovered. It is a grand thing for young scientists to do something new and extraordinary, to bring down to earth the energy that fuels the stars. The first generation of bomb builders was like the first generation of empire builders, young and enthusiastic and intoxicated with success. But then it happened with nuclear weapons just as it happened with the empire, that the pioneers settled down and became bureaucrats. Or the pioneers moved on somewhere else and the bureaucrats took over the enterprise. The nuclear weapons enterprise became a stodgy political establishment with a superstructure of dogmatic belief to justify its existence. In the later phases of the British Empire, we had the theorists justifying it with their dogmas of manifest destiny and the white man's burden. In the later phases of nuclear weaponry, we have the theorists justifying it with their dogmas of stable deterrence and invulnerable second-strike capabilities. In both cases, as the dogmas become more arcane and elaborate, the absurdity of the whole enterprise becomes more obvious. It was absurd to have ever imagined that a small island could permanently rule half the world, and it was absurd to have ever imagined that nuclear weapons could permanently keep the world at peace. The time has now come to say no to nuclear weapons just as we said no to the empire. Dick Feynman understood this and said his no when he left Los Alamos forty years ago.

The question now before us is how to begin the dismantling of the nuclear weapons empire. To dismantle an empire is not easy. It takes a long time and has to be done carefully. Even with the best of care it is not painless. When empires crash, people get hurt. It took us thirty years to dismantle the British Empire, and the job is not finished. There are still some tough little problems remaining in such places as Ireland and Hong Kong and the Falkland Islands. But on the whole we can look back on the dismantling with pride. It was done for the most part peacefully and in such a way as to hurt as few people as possible. If we go at the job of dismantling the nuclear weapons empire with courage and determination, there is a good chance we may see that job done in thirty years too. There may be some untidy ends left over, but it should be possible at least to get rid of the major nuclear weapons deployments all over the world within the lifetime of our children.

I have written about four people who acted for me as beacons, drawing me out of my narrow concentration upon science into a wider involvement with the great problems of human society. When I was a teenager in England, Uncle Oliver and Aunt Dulcibella filled my bookshelves with the flaming red monthly selections of the Left Book Club. When I came to America, Phil

Morrison and Dick Feynman continued my political education with their stories of Los Alamos. All four of them were role models, showing me how an uncompromising pursuit of excellence in a demanding professional discipline could be combined with joyful adventures in the world outside. Each of them was at heart a revolutionary. Each of them retained the respect of the professional establishment. All of them knew how to enjoy the lemon and the cream and make the best of both.

CHAPTER 33

Kennan Again

.....

1 9 8 8

I do not attempt to compile a list of George Kennan's qualities and achievements. Instead, I tell a little story taken from a novel by the Soviet writer Chingiz Aitmatov. Aitmatov is a Kazakh who divides his time between an apartment in Moscow and his home in Central Asia. His novel describes a people torn between their old culture based on religion and family and their new culture based on work and the Party. The novel is full of old Kazakh legends, the most striking of which concerns Queen Naiman-Ana and her son Zholaman. The novel was published in 1980 by the magazine *Novy Mir,* before the days of glasnost. Aitmatov is a mainstream writer, not a dissident. The two heroes of the novel are the railway worker Yedigei and his camel Karanar.

The queen's son Zholaman is captured in battle by the Zhuan-Zhuan, the ancient enemies of the Kazakhs. The Zhuan-Zhuan have a frightful way of treating their captives. They shave Zholaman's head and stretch over it an udder freshly cut from a young nursing camel. They tie him to a stake and leave him exposed for many days to the hot desert sun. The udder dries and shrinks until Zholaman becomes a Mankurt, an obedient slave of the Zhuan-Zhuan, his shrunken head retaining no memory of his previous existence. Too late, the queen rides out alone on her white camel into the desert to rescue him. She finds him, but he is now a Mankurt and does not recognize her. He tells his Zhuan-Zhuan masters of her visit and they arrange a trap for her. She comes a second time to rescue Zholaman, but this time he is armed with a bow and arrow and, obedient to his masters' instructions, shoots her dead.

The image of the Mankurt runs all the way through Aitmatov's bitter story. The old railway worker's son, taken away from his village and educated in a Soviet boarding school, is a Mankurt with no knowledge or respect for the old traditions, making his career in the city and getting drunk at his father's funeral. The hero's best friend is picked up by two Mankurt agents of the KGB and dies under their interrogation. The crime for which he is arrested is writing for his own children a truthful diary of his wartime experiences. The friend is also a collector of Kazakh legends. He dies because he is trying to save his young sons from becoming Mankurts.

What has this image of the Mankurt to do with George Kennan? I hope Kennan will agree with me that one of the great themes of his life has been the fight against the deliberate obliteration of the past. Why else did he become a historian? For Kennan as for Aitmatov, the deliberate obliteration of the past is the chief root of human folly, the chief cause of the evil that has been done in our century. To make a man into a Mankurt is a worse crime than murder. To make a whole people into Mankurts is the first step on the road to genocide.

George Kennan knows well that the tragedy of the Mankurt is a universal human problem, not merely a Soviet problem. The image of the Mankurt fits Germans and Americans as well as Kazakhs and Russians. Kennan has seen it most tragically in Germany during his Berlin years, when his friends of the old German aristocracy watched helplessly while Hitler led their Mankurt sons to disaster. He has seen Mankurts in action in America too, in the era of Joseph McCarthy, when wise old heads were purged from the State Department and the diplomatic service, and again in the 1960s when a generation of radical students seemed to be more intent upon destroying the past than building the future. All through his long life, wherever he happened to be, George Kennan has stood resolutely against the Mankurts and their masters. He has been saying for fifty years that the fundamental flaw in Soviet society is the inability of the regime to allow an honest accounting of its past. And he has taught us by his life and work that in the long run the most powerful weapon against tyranny and folly is the pen of the historian.

CHAPTER 34

Feynman in 1948

.....

1 9 8 9

I lived in the same town as Feynman for only one year, the academic year 1947–48, when he was a professor at Cornell and I was a graduate student. He was then thirty and I was twenty-four. I had the good luck to know him when he was at the height of his creative powers, struggling to complete the theory that he called the "space-time approach," which afterward became the standard approach for everybody doing calculations in particle physics. I walked by accident into the delivery room where Feynman's new way of doing particle physics was born.

When I was asked to give a talk in commemoration of Feynman, I thought at first I would recall memories of forty years ago and describe him as he was then. But forty-year-old memories are hopelessly unreliable. I can't be sure whether I really remember something or only remember the story I told thirty years later. Often, when I check memories against written records, I find that I remembered things completely wrong. I don't just forget things; I remember things that never happened. As every historian knows, reminiscences of politicians unsupported by written evidence are worthless. In this respect, scientists are no better than politicians. If I tried to describe the young Feynman from memory, the portrait would be a fake. Old memories are buried and overlaid with forty years of varnish.

Fortunately, written records of Feynman in 1948 exist. Being a dutiful son, I wrote home to my parents in England a weekly letter recording my adventures in America. My parents preserved the letters and I have them now in my hands. Instead of writing fake recollections of Feynman, I decided to quote directly from the letters. The letters are fragmentary and do not tell us much about Feynman's inner thoughts. Their virtue is that they are authentic, written within a few days of the events they describe, without editing and without hindsight. I include a few passages not involving Feynman directly but describing the context within which he was living and working. I arrived in America in September 1947 to do graduate work in physics under the direction of Hans Bethe. So far as I can tell from the records, I had never heard of Feynman before I came to Cornell. It took me a while to discover what a great man he was.

I begin with the letter in which Feynman makes his first entrance, written two months after my arrival in America.

CORNELL UNIVERSITY—NOVEMBER 19, 1947

Just a brief letter before we go off to Rochester. We have every Wednesday a seminar at which somebody talks about some item of research, and from time to time this is made a joint seminar with Rochester University. To-day is the first time this term that we are going over there for it. It is a magnificent day, and it should be a lovely trip; Rochester is due north of here, on the shores of Lake Erie, and we go through some wild country. I am being taken in Feynman's car, which will be great fun if we survive. Feynman is a man for whom I am developing a considerable admiration; he is the brightest of the young theoreticians here, and is the first example I have met of that rare species, the native American scientist. He has developed a private version of the quantum theory, which is generally agreed to be a good piece of work and may be more helpful than the orthodox version for some problems; in general he is always sizzling with new ideas, most of which are more spectacular than helpful, and hardly any of which get very far before some newer inspiration eclipses them. His most valuable contribution to physics is as a sustainer of morale; when he bursts into the room with his latest brainwave and proceeds to expound it with the most lavish sound effects and waving about of the arms, life at least is not dull.

On Monday night the Bethes gave a party to which most of the young theoreticians were invited. When we arrived we were introduced to Henry Bethe, who is now 5 years old, but he was not at all impressed, in fact the only thing he would say was "I want Dick. You told me Dick was coming," and finally he had to be sent off to bed, since Dick (alias Feynman) did not materialise.

About half an hour later, Feynman burst into the room, just had time to say "so sorry I'm late. Had a brilliant idea just as I was coming over," and then dashed upstairs to console Henry. Conversation then ceased while the company listened to the joyful sounds above, sometimes taking the form of a duet and sometimes of a one-man percussion band.

The new and lavishly built Nuclear Laboratory will be opened formally with a party on Saturday. Feynman remarked that it was a pity to think that after all the work that the builders had put into building it, so little would probably be done by the people who lived in it; and Bethe said that only because of the steel shortage is any nuclear physics worth mentioning done in the United States. This may well be true; at any rate the most outstanding experiments in the world are at present being done at Bristol by Powell with no apparatus more elaborate than a microscope and a photographic plate.

Next a brief item one week later. Leonard Eyges was another graduate student working with Bethe. Trudy was his wife.

NOVEMBER 27, 1947

The trip to Rochester last week was a great success, although we did not have time to see Lake Ontario (not Erie as I said in my last letter). I went there and back in Dick Feynman's car with Philip Morrison, and we talked about everything from cosmic rays downward.

On Saturday we had our great inaugural party for the Synchrotron Building. It was a great success; I played my first game of poker and found I was rather good at it; I won 35 cents. The synchrotron itself does not arrive for some time yet, so the building is still empty. The party consisted chiefly of dancing and eating; Bethe and Trudy Eyges danced together for about an hour, very beautifully, while Rose Bethe and Leonard Eyges exchanged disapproving glances.

Now we jump three months. During the winter I was working hard on the problem that Bethe gave me when I arrived at Cornell. As long as I was busy calculating for Bethe, I did not have much time for anything else. By March 1948 I was looking around for a new problem and beginning to pay more attention to Feynman.

There have recently been a number of articles on political topics in the "Bulletin of the Atomic Scientists" by Oppenheimer. They are remarkable not only for the breadth of view but for the excellent prose in which they are written, and this stimulated my curiosity so that one day I got Phil Morrison talking about Oppenheimer as a personality. Morrison has known him well since he started working under him at Pasadena, their ages being then approximately twenty and thirty. He said that at that time Oppenheimer was still an exceedingly intense and aesthetic young man, and divided his leisure between reading St. Thomas Aquinas in Latin and writing poetry in the style of Eliot. He came of a wealthy American family, but went to Göttingen to study and became thoroughly Europeanised; for a long time he contemplated becoming a Roman Catholic but finally didn't; and to furnish his mind he learned to read fluently in French, German, Italian, Russian, Latin, Greek and Sanscrit. So this to some extent explains the sensitivity of his prose, and the awe in which he is held by even such close friends as Bethe.

Yesterday I went for a long walk in the spring sunshine with Trudy Eyges and Richard Feynman. Feynman is the young American professor, half genius and half buffoon, who keeps all physicists and their children amused with his effervescent vitality. He has, however, as I have recently learned, a great deal more to him than that, and you may be interested in his story. The part of it with which I am concerned began when he arrived at Los Alamos; there he found and fell in love with a brilliant and beautiful girl, who was tubercular and had been exiled to New Mexico in the hope of stopping the disease. When Feynman arrived, things had got so bad that the doctors gave her only a year to live, but he determined to marry her and marry her he did; and for a year and a half, while working at full pressure on the Project, he nursed her and made her days cheerful. She died just before the end of the war.

As Feynman says, anyone who has been happily married once cannot long remain single, and so yesterday we were discussing his new problem, this time again a girl in New Mexico with whom he is desperately in love. This time the problem is not tuberculosis, but the girl is a Catholic. You can imagine all the troubles this raises, and if there is one thing Feynman could not do to save his soul it is to become a Catholic himself. So we talked and talked, and sent the sun down the sky, and went on talking in the darkness. I am afraid that at the end of it poor Feynman was no nearer to the solution of his problems, but at least it must have done him good to get them off his chest. I think myself that he will marry the girl, and that it will be a success, but far be it from me to give advice to anybody on such a subject.

Then, a week later, the shape of things to come begins to emerge.

MARCH 15, 1948

My own work has taken a fresh turn as a result of the new Schwinger quantum theory which Schwinger had not finished when he spoke at New York. This new theory is a magnificent piece of work, difficult to digest but with some highly original and undoubtedly correct ideas; so at the moment I am working through it and trying to understand it thoroughly. After this I shall be in a very good position, able to attack various important special problems in physics with a correct theory while most other people are still groping. One other very interesting thing has happened recently; our Richard Feynman, who always works on his own and has his own private version of quantum theory, has been attacking the same problem as Schwinger from a different direction, and has now come out with a roughly equivalent theory, reaching many of the same ideas independently; this makes it pretty clear that the theory is right. Feynman is a man whose ideas are as difficult to make contact with as Bethe's are easy; for this reason I have so far learnt much more from Bethe, but I think if I stayed here much longer I should begin to find that it was Feynman with whom I was working more.

Three more months go by without any mention of Feynman. He reappears only in the last letter from Cornell.

JUNE 11, 1948

Although our society is breaking up and many old friends have already departed, these last days are not at all lonely; the experimentalists here are still hard at work on their synchrotron, and in the last week we have had one supper-picnic, one swimming expedition and one sailing expedition, all of which were very enjoyable. However, this week I start out for the West, and no doubt that will be great fun too. Incidentally, the American "picnic" is not exactly what we understand by the term; it starts out with fried steak and salads, cooked on an open-air grille, and served with plates, forks, and other paraphernalia; this sort of thing, like the elegance of the average American home and of the women's clothes, seems to me rather a rebirth of the Victorian era, flourishing over here by virtue of the same conditions that nourished it in England. Not only in manners, but also in politics and international affairs, I often feel that Victorian England and modern America would understand each other better than either understands its contemporaries.

I don't remember how much I have told you about my plans; they were greatly helped by an offer of a ride across the country by Feynman, the bright young professor of whom I have often spoken. He is going to visit his (catholic) sweetheart at Albuquerque, New Mexico, and is driving across the country starting this week; I am to go to keep him company on the way out, and I shall leave him and make my own way to Ann Arbor as soon as I (or we) feel I have had enough. It should be a fine trip, and we shall have the whole world to talk about. On this visit Feynman intends to make up his mind either to marry the girl or to agree to part; most people are prepared to wager for the former alternative.

Two weeks later comes the next extract, written from Santa Fe, New Mexico.

JUNE 25, 1948

Feynman originally planned to take me out West in a leisurely style, stopping and sightseeing en route and not driving too fast. However, I was never particularly hopeful that he would stick to this plan, with his sweetheart waiting for him in Albuquerque. As it turned out, we did the 1800 miles from Cleveland to Albuquerque in 3½ days, and this in spite of some troubles; Feynman drove all the way, and he drives well, never taking risks but still keeping up an average of 65 mph outside towns. It was a most enjoyable drive, and one could see most of what was to be seen of the scenery without stopping to explore; the only regret I have is that in this way I saw less of Feynman than I might have done.

At St. Louis we joined Highway U.S. 66, the so-called "Main Street of America" which runs from Chicago to Los Angeles via Albuquerque. We thought that from there on would be plain sailing, as this is one of the best marked and maintained roads there is. However, at the end of the second day we ran into a traffic jam, and some boys told us that there were floods over the road ahead and no way through. We retreated to a town called Vinita [Oklahoma], where with great difficulty we found lodging for the night, the town being jammed with stranded travellers. We ended up in what Feynman called a "dive," viz. a hotel of the cheapest and most disreputable character, and with a notice posted in the corridor saying "This Hotel is under New Management, so if you're drunk you've come to the wrong place." During the night it rained continuously, and the natives said it had been raining most of the time for more than a week.

In the morning we went on our way, the floods having subsided, until we reached a place called Sapulpa. Here we were again stopped, and when we tried to make a detour we arrived actually at the water's edge, where the road disappeared into a huge lake. Returning to Sapulpa we were fortunate in picking up a Cherokee Indian and his wife (all the way we were giving lifts to hitchhikers, many of them interesting people who decided to go West for a lark or to find jobs, without much in the way of money or possessions; such people were usually young (16–20) and forthcoming with intelligent conversation). [The two Cherokees] were the most exciting of the hitch-hikers we encountered. They said they lived on an oil-field construction camp at a place called Shawnee, and had moved over for the week-end to visit some friends who had managed to secure 5 quarts of hooch whiskey. (In this country it is illegal to sell liquor of any sort to Indians.) Having spent a happy week-end getting through the whiskey, they were now on their way back to the job at Shawnee. They were able to direct us to an unpaved and indescribably muddy road, which however kept to high ground and so clear of the floods. In this way we came out onto a main road running westward north of U.S. 66. After a time this road too was blocked, and we had to detour still further to the North. Here the Indians left us, approximately as far from Shawnee as they were when they started.

Later on we had the bright idea of turning on the car radio, and we then picked up broadcasts from Oklahoma City and other places giving detailed stories of the floods. In this way we were able to mark on our map all the places that were under water, and plan our route accordingly. It turned out that the worst disaster was on U.S. 66 itself west of Oklahoma City, where many cars were trapped and the occupants rescued by boat, a few also being drowned. We were able finally to thread our way back to U.S. 66 a good deal further west than that.

The fourth day we drove the last 300 miles to Albuquerque before 1 p.m. This was the most beautiful part of the trip, though I was surprised to find how little of it was typical New Mexico mountains; the prairie actually extends half-way across New Mexico, and only the last 20 miles of our journey were in mountains, the Sandia range immediately East of the Rio Grande valley in which Albuquerque lies. As we advanced into New Mexico the prairie grew drier and drier, until a fair proportion of the vegetation was cactus, carrying at this time of year a profusion of large blood-red flowers. Coming down into Albuquerque, Feynman said he hardly recognized the place, so much has it been built up since he was there 3 years ago. It is a fine, spacious town of the usual American type; very little of the Spanish surviving.

Sailing into Albuquerque at the end of this Odyssey, we had the misfortune to be picked up for speeding; Feynman was so excited that he did not notice the speed limit signs. So our first appointment in this romantic city of home-coming was an interview with the Justice of the Peace; he was a pleasant enough fellow, completely informal, and ended up by fining us $10 with $4.50 costs, while chatting amiably about the way the South-West was developing. After this Feynman went off to meet his lady, and I came up by bus to Santa Fe.

All the way, Feynman talked a great deal about this sweetheart, his wife who died at Albuquerque in 1945, and marriage in general. Also about Los Alamos, and life and philosophy in general. I came to the conclusion that he is an exceptionally well-balanced person, whose opinions are always his own and not other people's. He is very good at getting on with people, and as we came West he altered his voice and expressions unconsciously to fit his surroundings, until he was saying "I don't know noth'n'" like the rest of them.

In Santa Fe we are not entirely cut off from the outside world. In the hotel is a radio, and on it we heard yesterday the voices of state delegates in Philadelphia unanimously balloting for Dewey, to-day also in Philadelphia an exciting commentary on the Louis-Walcott fight for the Heavy-weight championship. I myself had judged from the newspapers some time ago that Dewey would be elected; on the whole I think he will do well in what is likely to be a quiet and prosperous 4 years; his great virtue is not getting excited, and that makes up nowadays for a lot of virtues he lacks.

My success as a prognosticator of the 1948 election was no better than anyone else's. After leaving Feynman in Albuquerque, I spent the summer at Ann Arbor and Berkeley, and succeeded in understanding how the Schwinger and Feynman versions of electrodynamics fitted together. In September I arrived at the Institute for Advanced Study in Princeton. The next extract is written from Princeton, in response to my father's request for an explanation of what I had been doing. My father had called attention to a clause in the Athanasian Creed where it says: "There is the Father incomprehensible, and the Son incomprehensible, and the Holy Ghost incomprehensible, yet there are not three incomprehensibles but one incomprehensible." He remarked that this sounded a bit like Schwinger, Feynman, and Dyson. Here is my reply:

OCTOBER 4, 1948

To-day came a fat letter from you. Concerning your remarks about the Athanasian Creed, I think what you say is very much to the point; but I must disappoint any hopes that Dyson-Schwinger-Feynman might prove an effective substitute. Seriously, I should like some time, now that I understand these theories properly, to try to write some intelligible semi-popular account of them; but it would be a difficult job, not to be undertaken in one afternoon. The central idea of the theories, in any case, is to give a correct account of experimental facts while deliberately ignoring certain mathematical inconsistencies which come in when you discuss things that cannot be directly measured; in this there is a close similarity to the Athanasian Creed. However, there is the important difference that these theories are expected to last only about as long as no fresh experiments are thought up, so they will hardly do as a basis for a Weltanschauung.

Here I interject an editorial comment. This letter shows that in 1948 we all thought of the new quantum electrodynamics as a ramshackle and temporary structure, soon to be replaced by something better. We would never have believed it if anyone had told us then that our theory would still be around forty years later, the calculated effects of radiative reactions still agreeing with experiments to an accuracy of ten or eleven significant figures. We would have been even more surprised to learn that the ugliest and most awkward features of our theory, the tricky renormalizations of mass and charge, would remain as key features when the theory was eventually incorporated, first into the Weinberg-Salam unified theory of electromagnetic and weak interactions, and later into the grand unified theories of weak and strong interactions. For Feynman, renormalization was not something to be proud of but something to be got rid of. He spent a lot of his time trying to construct a finite electron theory that would make renormalization unnecessary. After that interruption I continue with the October 4 letter.

On Friday I went to New York and was welcomed by Bethe, who was as friendly and informal as ever. Bethe and I went for a walk in the park along the bank of the Hudson River, which was very lovely and peaceful with the evening air and the sun going down beyond it. We spoke of future developments in physics, and of the personal problems involved in the publication of my paper. Bethe is a man of tremendous common-sense and knows how to deal with such questions; I was very glad to have his advice. It happens that neither Schwinger nor Feynman has ever published any moderately intelligible account of his work. So it has been necessary for me in my paper to present the gist of both theories. I am reversing the tactics of Mark Antony, and saying very loud at various points in my paper, "I come to praise Schwinger, not to bury him." I only hope he won't see through it.

After the walk, Bethe took me to dine in a very good Chinese restaurant, and I got back here finally at midnight, very much the worse for wear. In all this day, the thing that bowled me over was Bethe's complete generosity and unselfishness. I wish my pursuit of truth was as disinterested as his; perhaps it will be by the time I am his age.

Another editorial comment belongs here. My fear that Schwinger might take amiss my stealing of his thunder turned out to be groundless. Schwinger was as friendly and as generous to me as Feynman. Neither of them ever grumbled at me for publishing their ideas. I was delighted to discover that both these great men, instead of resenting my intrusion, greeted me as a colleague and friend.

In the next letter a great woman appears, also a physicist, whose name was then Cécile Morette and is now Cécile DeWitt. She was in 1948 a member of the Institute for Advanced Study, having arrived from France via Dublin and Copenhagen. She was the first of the younger generation to grasp the full scope and power of the Feynman path-integral approach to physics. While I was concerned with applying Feynman's methods to detailed calculations, she was thinking of larger issues, extending the path-integral idea to everything in the universe, including gravitation and curved space-times.

BOSTON—NOVEMBER 1, 1948

After my last letter to you I decided that what I needed was a long week-end away from Princeton, and so I persuaded Cécile Morette to come with me to see Feynman at Ithaca. This was a bold step on my part, but it could not have been more successful and the week-end was just deliriously happy. Feynman himself came to meet us at the station, after our 10-hour train journey, and was in tremendous form, bubbling over with ideas and stories and entertaining us with performances on Indian drums from New Mexico until 1 a.m.

The next day, Saturday, we spent in conclave discussing physics. Feynman gave a masterly account of his theory, which kept Cécile in fits of laughter and made my talk at Princeton a pale shadow by comparison. He said he had given his copy of my paper to a graduate student to read, then asked the student if he himself ought to read it. The student said "No" and Feynman accordingly wasted no time on it and continued chasing his own ideas. Feynman and I really understand each other; I know that he is the one person in the world who has nothing to learn from what I have written; and he doesn't mind telling me so. That afternoon, Feynman produced more brilliant ideas per square minute than I have ever seen anywhere before or since.

In the evening I mentioned that there were just two problems for which the finiteness of the theory remained to be established; both problems are well-known and feared by physicists, since many long and difficult papers running to 50 pages and more have been written about them, trying unsuccessfully to make the older theories give sensible answers to them. When I mentioned this fact, Feynman said "We'll see about this," and proceeded to sit down and in two hours, before our eyes, obtain finite and sensible answers to both problems. It was the most amazing piece of lightning calculation I have ever witnessed, and the results prove, apart from some unforeseen complication, the consistency of the whole theory. The two problems were, the scattering of light by an electric field, and the scattering of light by light. After supper Feynman was working until 3 a.m. He has had a complete summer of vacation, and has returned with unbelievable stores of suppressed energy.

On the Sunday Feynman was up at his usual hour (9 a.m.) and we went down to the physics building, where he gave me another 2-hour lecture on miscellaneous discoveries of his. One of these was a deduction of Clerk Maxwell's equations of the electromagnetic field from the basic principles of quantum theory, a thing which baffles everybody including Feynman, because it ought not to be possible. At 12 on the Sunday we started our journey home, arriving finally at 2 a.m. and thoroughly refreshed. Cécile assured me she had enjoyed it as much as I had.

The next letter gives us another brief glimpse of Cécile Morette.

NOVEMBER 14, 1948

Cécile amused us all yesterday by bringing down a French millionaire to see the Institute (an industrial magnate of some kind). She said she hinted to him fairly strongly that France could do with an Institute of a similar sort; she said if she were made Director of the French Institute she would invite all of us to come and lecture there. It will be interesting to see if anything comes of it.

The man Cécile brought to see the Princeton Institute was Léon Motchane. Motchane later became the founder and first director of the Institut des Hautes Etudes Scientifiques at Bures-sur-Yvette in France. The IHES is a flourishing institution which has made a major contribution to the support of mathematics and theoretical physics in France. Cécile was twenty-six when she brought Motchane to Princeton and planted the seed that grew into IHES. A few years later she founded the Les Houches summer school, which is also a flourishing institution and has been a training ground for generations of European students.

The next extract describes the Winter meeting of the American Physical Society in New York.

JANUARY 30, 1949

All my friends from Cornell, Ann Arbor and Princeton were there, besides many others, and it was a continual social gathering from morning till night. On the first day the real fun began; I was sitting in the middle of the hall and in the front, with Feynman beside me, and there rose to the platform to speak a young man from Columbia whom I know dimly. The young man had done some calculations using methods of Feynman and me, and he did not confine himself to stating this fact, but referred again and again to "the beautiful theory of Feynman-Dyson" in gushing tones. After he said this the first time, Feynman turned to me and remarked in a loud voice, "Well, Doc, you're in." Then, as the young man went on, Feynman continued to make irreverent comments, much to the entertainment of the audience near him. Later on Feynman himself spoke on his own work, and created so much uproar with his clowning that the audience voted him twice the usual time for his talk.

My last extract from that year describes a visit of Feynman to the Institute at Princeton. Those who have read Surely You're Joking, Mr. Feynman, *will know that Feynman considered the Institute to be snobbish, stuffy, and scientifically sterile. He was invited many times to visit, but he almost never came. He did come once, as the next extract records.*

CHICAGO—FEBRUARY 28, 1949

On Thursday we had Feynman down to Princeton, and he stayed till I left on Sunday. He gave in 3 days about 8 hours of seminars, besides long private discussions. This was a magnificent effort, and I believe all the people at the Institute began to understand what he is doing. I at least learnt a great deal. He was as usual in enthusiastic mood, waving his arms about a lot and making everybody laugh. Even Oppenheimer began to get the spirit of the thing, and said some things less sceptical than is his habit. Feynman was obviously anxious to talk, and would have gone on quite indefinitely if he had been allowed; he must have been suffering from the same bottled-up feeling that I had when I was full of ideas last autumn. The trouble with him, of course, is that he never will publish what he does; I sometimes feel a little guilty for having cut in in front of him with his own ideas. However, he is now at last writing up two big papers, which will display his genius to the world.

That is the end of my meager record of the young Feynman. The next encounter with Feynman in the letters is thirty years later.

PRINCETON—DECEMBER 21, 1979

The best thing that happened was a supper with Dick Feynman at his home in Pasadena. The first time we had met for about 12 years. He had in the meantime had a big cancer operation 1½ years ago. Rumour had said he was dying but I found him in bouncing health and spirits. He is still the same old Feynman that drove with me to Albuquerque 30 years ago. He said they took a 6-pound lump out of him but since it was all fatty tissue (Liposarcoma) there is a good chance it was contained and will not recur.

Feynman has been married for about 20 years to an English wife called Gweneth. He enjoys the domestic life and they have a menagerie very much like ours, 1 horse (for the 12-year-old daughter), 2 dogs, 1 cat, 5 rabbits. But they have temporarily outdone us, for the next few months, by taking on a boa-constrictor who belongs to some neighbours on a leave of absence.

I heard later from Feynman that the affair with the boa constrictor ended badly, as recorded in chapter 32. Now comes the last letter in my collection, written to Sara Courant. Sara had been at Cornell in 1948 when her husband Ernest was a postdoctoral fellow.

URBANA, ILLINOIS—APRIL 9, 1981

I just spent a marvelous three days with Dick Feynman and wished you had been there to share him with us. Sixty years and a big cancer operation have not blunted him. He is still the same Feynman that we knew in the old days at Cornell.

We were together at a small meeting of physicists organized by John Wheeler at the University of Texas. For some reason Wheeler decided to hold the meeting at a grotesque place called World of Tennis, a country club where Texas oil-millionaires go to relax. So there we were. We all grumbled at the high prices and the extravagant ugliness of our rooms. But there was nowhere else to go. Or so we thought. But Dick thought otherwise. Dick just said: "To hell with it. I am not going to sleep in this place," picked up his suitcase, and walked off alone into the woods. In the morning he reappeared, looking none the worse for his night under the stars. He said he did not sleep much, but it was worth it.

We had many conversations about science and history, just like in the old days. But now he had something new to talk about, his children. He said: "I always thought I would be a specially good father because I wouldn't try to push my kids into any particular direction. I wouldn't try to turn them into scientists or intellectuals if they didn't want it. I would be just as happy with them if they decided to be truck-drivers or guitar-players. In fact I would even like it better if they went out in the world and did something real instead of being professors like me. But they always find a way to hit back at you. My boy Carl for instance. There he is in his second year at MIT, and all he wants to do with his life is to become a god-damned philosopher!"

As we sat in the airport waiting for our planes, Dick pulled out a pad of paper and a pencil and started to draw faces of people sitting in the lounge. He drew them amazingly well. I said I was sorry I have no talent for drawing. He said: "I always thought I have no talent either. But you don't need any talent to do stuff like this. Just a few years ago I made friends with an artist and we had an agreement. I would teach him quantum mechanics and he would teach me drawing. We both did quite well, but he was a better teacher than I was."

So I left him there in the airport at Austin, Texas, happily talking about Michelangelo and Raphael and Giotto with all the enthusiasm of a teen-ager. He said, "You know, I went in there to look at the Sistine chapel in Rome, and I could see at once that one of those panels wasn't as good as the others. It just wasn't good. And then afterwards I looked in the guide-book and it said that particular one was painted by somebody else. That made me feel good. I always thought Art Appreciation was a lot of hokum, but now I found out I can do it myself."

That was not the last time I saw Feynman, but it is the last glimpse of him recorded in my letters. Fortunately, we have a much more complete picture of Feynman in his own words, recorded and published by Ralph Leighton. The chapter "Hotel City" in the second Leighton book contains Feynman's version of the night he and I spent together in the hotel in Vinita in 1948. His version is different from the version I wrote to my parents. In deference to my parents' Victorian sensibilities, I left out the best part of the story. Feynman's version is better. Feynman always remembered what his first wife Arline had written to him from her hospital bed before he went to Los Alamos, the question that Leighton used as title for his second book, "What do you care what other people think?" Arline's spirit stayed with him all his life and helped to make him what he was, a great scientist and a great human being.

CHAPTER 35

The Face of Gaia

.....

1 9 8 9

My story begins in the year 1978. I am lying on my back under some bushes on C Street, between the Department of the Interior and the statue of Simón Bolívar, in the city of Washington. It is two o'clock on a Saturday afternoon in June. All I can see is the brilliant green of sunlit leaves and the deep blue of the sky. Two friendly bandits have fractured my skull and jaw and relieved me of my wallet. I am expecting that one of them may shortly put a bullet into me to make sure I will not talk. And now, at this un-likely moment, my spirit is filled with peace. The green leaves and the blue sky are beautiful. Everything else fades into insignifi-cance. This life is good and this death is good also. I am a leaf like the others. I am ready to float away on the blue wave of eternity.

This experience, which came to me as I walked, briefcase in hand, to a committee meeting of the National Academy of Sci-ences, ended happily for all concerned. My assailants escaped un-harmed with seventy-five dollars in cash and some photographs of my daughters. I made my entrance into the National Academy building, dramatically dripping blood upon the marble floor. Time healed my wounds, and the efficient Washington police re-trieved my unbroken bifocal glasses from the bushes. Life re-turned quickly to its ordinary routines. But I have not forgotten that moment of illumination when the glory of earth and heaven was revealed to me.

What is one to make of such a revelation? It is not an uncom-mon experience among people who have come face-to-face with death. Tolstoy in *War and Peace* describes how Prince Andrei lies wounded on the battlefield of Austerlitz, one among thousands of soldiers, mostly dead, left behind after the battle is over. The prince, like me, gazes into the blue sky, unconcerned about his fate, conscious only of the beauty and greatness of that overarching sky. Tolstoy himself fought in the battles of the Crimean War. His description of Prince Andrei's state of mind was probably derived from experiences of men wounded beside him in the Crimea, if not from his own experience. The prince's peaceful contemplation of the sky is interrupted by the arrival of Napoleon, strutting over the scene of his famous victory. Napoleon, until that day, had been the prince's hero. But now, seeing his idol face-to-face, the prince is unimpressed. The prince sees only the littleness of the emperor under the greatness of the sky. When the emperor notices that he is not dead and addresses some friendly words to him, the prince does not bother to answer. The prince only wants Napoleon to move out of the way so that his view of the sky will be unobstructed.

My view of the sky was blocked not by Napoleon but by a passing motorist on C Street who kindly stopped and pulled me out of the bushes. I gladly accepted his offer of a ride to the National Academy three blocks away. I came back fast from the empyrean to the world of people and committees.

Quite apart from their possible religious significance, about which I am as skeptical as Tolstoy's prince, these revelations tell us something important about human nature. They tell us that we are better equipped for handling violence, mentally as well as physically, than we suppose. Nature designed human beings for living in a world of violence. We are designed to function well in good times and in bad. As Ecclesiastes said long ago, there is a time to be born and a time to die. When fear of death assails me, as it assails everyone from time to time, I take courage from that memory of green leaves and blue sky. Perhaps, when death comes, he will once again come as a friend.

The three most important things in my life have been, in this order, family, friends, and work. When I think of family, I recall another happy moment when I am lying sprawled under a blue sky. This time I am not laid low by muggers but by my own incompetence. I came to grief skiing down an easy, wide-open snowfield in Austria. I went head over heels, scattering poles and skis in all directions. As I lie like a rag doll in the snow, I hear a raucous peal of laughter. My beloved youngest daughter, seven years old, comes by me at top speed, her laughter ringing across the mountain. Into my head comes a favorite pair of lines from Shakespeare:

This is to be new born when thou art old,
To see thy blood warm when thou feel'st it cold.

With six healthy children, I have plenty of opportunities to see my blood warm. I am sorry for those of my contemporaries who grow old alone, without children to keep them young.

When I think of friendship, I am reminded of a third story. The worst indignity that can happen to a scientist has happened to me. I have published a paper in a leading scientific journal. After it is published, it turns out to be completely, irreparably, wrong. I am overcome with misery. A scientist who publishes worthless papers must himself be worthless. I can expect nothing from my colleagues but ridicule and contempt. Then, while I am hiding my face in shame, my friend Res Jost, a Swiss physicist for whom I have a deep respect, comes to visit. "Cheer up," says Res. "There is nothing in the world more indestructible than a scientific reputation." And so I cheer up. I quickly discover that Res is right. My friends are still friends. Nobody cares about my wrong paper. I am still in good standing as a member of the scientific club.

Family is older than the human species, work is younger, friendship is about as old as we are. It is friendship that marks us as human. The biologist Lewis Thomas wrote an essay comparing human beings with termites. Termites build nests as elaborate and as well designed as our cathedrals. Every termite nest is an architectural wonder, with arches, vaults, galleries, ventilators, storerooms, and nurseries. But no single termite carries the architectural plan in her head. The building of the nest is a collective process. Each termite rolls little balls of mud and sticks them onto other little balls rolled by her neighbors. Out of this collective rolling and sticking the cathedral grows. Thomas is saying that human societies grow in the same fashion. Instead of rolling mud balls we play with words. Instead of sticking mud balls together to make arches, we stick words together to make conversations. Instead of piling arch upon arch to make a nest, we pile conversation upon conversation to make a culture. Just as no single termite knows how to build a nest, no single human knows how to build a culture. A single termite alone cannot survive, and a single human being alone is not human. Termite societies are glued together with mud and saliva; human societies are glued together with conversation and friendship. Conversation is the natural and characteristic activity of human beings. Friendship is the milieu within which we function.

Work came later in human history than conversation. We invented work when we became civilized. Unlike friendship, work is a mixed blessing. At its worst, work is slavery. At its best, work is a sustained and lifelong conversation. The more satisfying and enjoyable work is, the more it partakes of the nature of conversation. Science at the working level is mostly conversation. The building where I work has twenty people in twenty rooms. Most of the doors are open. From morning till night the buzz of conversation seldom ceases. That is the way science is done. When I am not talking with friends down the hall, I am writing papers for friends around the world. Without the friends, my activity would be pointless. Scientists are as gregarious a species as termites. If the lives of scientists are on the whole joyful, it is because our friendships are deep and lasting. Our friendships are lasting because we are engaged in a collective enterprise. Our enterprise, the exploration of nature's secrets, had no beginning and will have no end. Exploration is as natural an activity for human beings as conversation. Our friends the explorers are scattered over the centuries, from Archimedes and Euclid to the unborn genius who will one day understand the mystery of how our exploring minds work.

The destiny of our species is shaped by the imperatives of survival on six distinct time scales. To survive means to compete successfully on all six time scales. But the unit of survival is different at each of the six time scales. On a time scale of years, the unit is the individual. On a time scale of decades, the unit is the family. On a time scale of centuries, the unit is the tribe or nation. On a time scale of millennia, the unit is the culture. On a time scale of tens of millennia, the unit is the species. On a time scale of eons, the unit is the whole web of life on our planet. Every human being is the product of adaptation to the demands of all six time scales. That is why conflicting loyalties are deep in our nature. In order to survive, we have needed to be loyal to ourselves, to our families, to our tribes, to our cultures, to our species, to our planet. If our psychological impulses are complicated, it is because they were shaped by complicated and conflicting demands.

The central conflict in our nature is the conflict between the selfish individual and the group. Nature gave us greed, a robust desire to maximize our personal winnings. Without greed we would not have survived at the individual level. But Nature also gave us love in its many varieties, love of wife and husband and children to help us survive at the family level, love of friends to help us survive at the tribal level, love of conversation to help us survive at the cultural level, love of people in general to help us survive at the species level, love of nature to help us survive at the planetary level. Human beings cannot be human without a generous endowment of greed and love.

I turn now from the past to the future. The future of human evolution will be radically different from the past. For better or for worse we shall have the power to steer our own evolution. Each generation will have the means, limited only by law and custom, to modify the genetic endowment of its children. As soon as this power is in our hands, we shall be facing deep and heavy problems. To what ends shall the means be used? Shall we use our mastery of science to make our children happier, or healthier, or cleverer, or gentler, or more loving than their parents? We would like to make them wiser, but wisdom is of all virtues the most difficult to calibrate. The parents of the future, writing the specifications for the genetic endowment of their wonder child, will be dealing with the same problem that God faced in George Herbert's poem "The Pulley" three hundred years ago:

> When God at first made man,
> Having a glasse of blessings standing by,
> "Let us," said He, "poure on him all we can;
> Let the world's riches, which dispersèd lie,
> Contract into a span."
> So strength first made a way,

Then beautie flow'd, then wisdome, honour, pleasure;
When almost all was out, God made a stay,
Perceiving that, alone of all His treasure,
    Rest in the bottome lay.
    "For if I should," said He,
"Bestow this jewell also on My creature,
He would adore My gifts in stead of Me,
And rest in Nature, not the God of Nature:
    So both should losers be.
    Yet let him keep the rest,
But keep them with repining restlessnesse;
Let him be rich and wearie, that at least,
If goodnesse leade him not, yet wearinesse
    May tosse him to My breast."

Given freedom of choice in the endowment of a child, most of us will choose qualities of individual excellence. We want a child that will fill our hearts with parental pride when she graduates summa cum laude or wins first place at the track meet. If parents have free choice, the evolution of the species will be driven hard in the direction of individual competitiveness. In the short run, the results of such an evolution may be gratifying: young people more competent and more self-confident than their parents, a golden age of creativity in art and science. But in the longer run, we risk destroying the emotional balance that Nature built into us over tens of thousands of years. An accelerated evolution at the individual level may leave us less fit to survive at the species level. Nature made us a balanced mixture of greed and love. If we take Nature's power into our hands, we risk a fatal tilt of the balance—growth of greed and dying away of love. We risk a harsh intensification of class distinctions, a splitting of humanity into genetically divergent and emotionally estranged subspecies. Where is the pulley that can pull us back to Nature's breast?

The central complexity of human nature lies in our emotions, not in our intelligence. Intellectual skills are means to an end. Emotions determine what our ends shall be. Intelligence belongs to individual human beings. Emotions belong to the group, to the family, to the tribe, to the species, or to Nature. Emotions have a longer history and deeper roots than intelligence. The limbic structures of our brain, where emotions are supposed to reside, are more ancient than the cerebral cortex that carries our intelligence. Emotions must be our pulley. Somehow or other, when we begin to improve artificially the physical and intellectual capacities of our children, we must learn to leave their emotional roots uncut.

To cut emotional roots is fatally easy. A drug addict is a person whose emotions have been deranged by a chemical acting on the limbic structures. Addiction is a vicious cycle because the deranged value system brings a continued craving for the drug. Any change in our natural value system carries the danger of running into such a vicious cycle. Any short circuit of the value system is a form of insanity. Any genetic modification of our inherited emotions brings danger that our whole society may become insane. To be sane means to possess a value system that allows us to survive on all time scales in harmony with Nature.

One hopeful sign of sanity in modern society is the popularity of the idea of Gaia, invented by James Lovelock to personify our living planet. Respect for Gaia is the beginning of wisdom. And the love of Gaia carries with it a love of trees. The town of Princeton where I live is full of trees. If you go up to the top of a tower in Princeton in summer, the town is almost invisible. You see then that the inhabitants of Princeton are actually living in a forest. All these bankers and stockbrokers, wealthy enough to choose where they want to live, chose to live in a forest. The love of trees is rooted deep in our value system, planted in us during the hundreds of thousands of years we spent hunting and gathering on a largely forested planet.

The climatic equilibrium of our planet is now threatened by the greenhouse effect of carbon dioxide accumulating in the atmosphere. The carbon dioxide comes partly from burning of coal and oil and partly from destruction of forests. Fortunately, there is a remedy. The quantity of carbon in the atmosphere is about equal to the quantity in living trees. This means that the problem of the greenhouse is essentially a problem of forest management. A large-scale international program of reforestation could hold the greenhouse in check, besides producing many other economic and environmental benefits. The cost of growing enough trees to nullify the greenhouse is not prohibitive. Only the will and the international consensus required to do the job are at present lacking. But we shall probably see the will and the consensus emerge, as soon as the climatic effects of the greenhouse become obvious and severe. When that happens, the whole world will begin planting trees. In China and in Brazil, in Nepal and in California, people will be planting trees and feeling an old familiar joy as they see the planet turning green. At that point we may say that Gaia is using us once again as her tools, using the love of trees that she implanted in us long ago as the means to keep herself alive.

As humanity moves into the future and takes control of its evolution, our first priority must be to preserve our emotional bond to Gaia. This bond must be our pulley. If it stays intact, then our species will remain fundamentally sane. If Gaia survives, then human complexity will survive too. Perhaps, when I was lying under the bushes on C Street, the revelation which came to me was just Gaia showing me her face.

Bibliographical Notes

These notes explain how the various chapters originated, and give references to a small fraction of the relevant literature.

I have generally refrained from correcting mistakes in the older writings in the light of later events. Published pieces are mostly reproduced in their original form, except for the chopping out of needless words and redundant sections. Unpublished lectures have been brought up to date where this seemed appropriate.

PREFACE

Daisy Ashford, *The Young Visiters, or Mr. Salteena's Plan* (New York: George H. Doran Co., 1919).

PART TITLES

Leo Szilard's "Ten Commandments" were written in German in October 1940 and first published in *Die Stimme der Delphine* (Rowolt Taschenbuch Verlag, 1963). The English translation by Jacob Bronowsky did not satisfy Szilard and could not be published while Szilard was alive. It appears together with the German original as a frontispiece to the second volume of Szilard's collected works, *Leo Szilard: His Version of the Facts: Selected Recollections and Correspondence,* ed. Spencer R. Weart and Gertrud Weiss Szilard (Cambridge, Mass.: MIT Press, 1978), pp. vi–vii.

CHAPTER 1. SIR PHILLIP ROBERTS'S EROLUNAR COLLISION

The vocabulary of this piece is taken from Jules Verne, *From the Earth to the Moon and a Trip Around It,* trans. L. Mercier and E. C. King (London: Sampson Low, Marston and Co., 1873). The

French original was published in two parts in 1865 and 1870. "Columbiad" is Verne's word for a giant cannon. For a modern and technically feasible version of Verne's idea, see A. P. Bruckner and A. Hertzberg, "Ram Accelerator Direct Launch System for Space Cargo," *Proceedings of the 38th Congress, International Astronautical Federation,* Brighton, U.K., 1987, Document IAF-87–211. A working model of the ram accelerator has been built by Hertzberg and two students at the University of Washington in Seattle. It works beautifully.

In the last sentence the word "celestial" should be "terrestrial." The author's attention was evidently distracted at this point. The estimated length of two miles for the terrestrial columbiad came remarkably close to the length of 3.15 kilometers calculated by Bruckner and Hertzberg for their ram accelerator.

CHAPTER 2. ON BEING THE RIGHT SIZE

This chapter is a general introduction to the series of three Danz lectures given at the University of Washington in April 1988. The lectures are chapters 3 through 5.

J. B. S. Haldane, *Possible Worlds and Other Essays* (London: Chatto & Windus, 1927), pp. 18–26.

CHAPTER 3. SIX CAUTIONARY TALES FOR SCIENTISTS

Danz Lecture 1. Mia Dyson, "The Office of Community Development in Cameroun" (unpublished, 1986). I am grateful to Mia Dyson for permission to use facts from this document.

"Astronomy and Astrophysics for the 1980's," vol. 1, Report of the Astronomy Survey Committee (Field Committee Report) (Washington, D.C., National Academy Press, 1982).

Jesse L. Greenstein, "An Astronomical Life," *Annual Reviews of Astronomy and Astrophysics* 22 (1984): 1–35. See pp. 25–27 for the history of the Greenstein report.

Mapping and Sequencing the Human Genome, report of the Board on Basic Biology, National Research Council (the Alberts report) (Washington, D.C.: National Academy Press, 1988).

For a technical discussion of the problems of designing a particle accelerator radically different from the Superconducting Supercollider, see Andrew M. Sessler, "New Particle Accelerator Techniques," *Physics Today* 41 (January 1988): 26–34.

CHAPTER 4. TELESCOPES AND ACCELERATORS

Danz Lecture 2. F. Zwicky, *Discovery, Invention, Research Through the Morphological Approach* (New York: Macmillan, 1969), is not a conventional autobiography. Zwicky believed that his morphological method was a universal key to unlock the secrets of nature and to "overcome the aberrations of the human mind." His book is a collection of stories illustrating the triumphs of the morphological method, together with polemics against people whose aberrations he was unable to overcome. It was originally published in German in 1966. The quotations here are from pp. 91–92, 225–226, of the English edition.

W. Baade and F. Zwicky, "Cosmic Rays from Supernovae," *Proceedings of the National Academy of Sciences* (USA) 20 (1934): 259–63.

CHAPTER 5. SIXTY YEARS OF SPACE SCIENCE, 1958–2018

Danz Lecture 3. Wernher von Braun, *The Mars Project* (Urbana: University of Illinois Press, 1953).

Alan Morehead, *Darwin and the Beagle* (London: Hamish Hamilton, 1969).

Eric Linklater, *The Voyage of the Challenger* (London: John Murray, 1972).

Yoji Kondo, ed., *Exploring the Universe with the IUE Satellite* (Dordrecht: D. Riedel Publishing Co., 1987).

K. Eric Drexler, *Engines of Creation* (Garden City, N.Y.: Anchor Press, 1986).

CHAPTER 6. THE IMPORTANCE OF BEING UNPREDICTABLE

This chapter was written for the Britannica Award ceremony in New York, February 28, 1990. I am grateful to the Encyclopaedia

Britannica for the award and for permission to publish my remarks.

CHAPTER 7. STRATEGIC BOMBING IN
WORLD WAR 2 AND TODAY

Lecture given on March 1, 1990, in the series "The Legacy of Strategic Bombing" at the National Air and Space Museum, Washington, D.C. I am grateful to Martin Harwit, director of the museum, for inviting me to lecture and for encouraging a departure from the traditionally jingoistic tone of the museum.

The official history of British bombing operations in World War 2 is Sir Charles Webster and Noble Frankland, *The Strategic Air Offensive Against Germany, 1939–1945,* 4 vols. (London: H. M. Stationery Office, 1961). For Wing-Commander Tait's operations, see vol. 3, pp. 181–82, 191–96.

Robert C. Mikesh and Osamu Tagaya, *Moonlight Interceptor: Japan's Irving Night Fighter,* vol. 8 in the series *Famous Aircraft of the National Air and Space Museum* (Washington, D.C.: Smithsonian Institution Press, 1985). See p. 57 for details of the battle between Irvings and B-29s over Tokyo on May 25–26, 1945.

CHAPTER 8. FIELD THEORY

Published in *Scientific American* 188, no. 4 (April 1953): 57–64. When this article was written, field theory was in the ascendant. Ten years later field theory was almost abandoned as a failed enterprise while other fashions prevailed. Now the wheel of fashion has turned full circle, field theory is restored to favor, and the views expressed here are again orthodox.

CHAPTER 9. INNOVATION IN PHYSICS

Published in *Scientific American* 199, no. 3 (September 1958): 74–82. Five years after chapter 8, we see a more skeptical mood displayed. In the final paragraphs I am arguing against the view, already becoming popular in 1958, that field theory is moribund and radical alternatives are needed. The prognostications that I made of the future turned out to be reasonably accurate.

For the reference to Pupin, see chapter 21.

CHAPTER 10. TOMONAGA, SCHWINGER, AND FEYNMAN AWARDED NOBEL PRIZE FOR PHYSICS

Published in *Science* 150 (October 29, 1965): 588–89. The unnamed "unkind critic" was Robert Oppenheimer.

CHAPTER 11. ENERGY IN THE UNIVERSE

Published in *Scientific American* 225, no. 3 (September 1971): 51–59. This was an introductory chapter written for a special issue of *Scientific American* devoted to the subject of energy.

CHAPTER 12. CARBON DIOXIDE IN THE ATMOSPHERE AND THE BIOSPHERE

Radcliffe Lecture, given at Green College, Oxford, on October 11, 1990. This is a summary of conclusions reached after fifteen years of part-time work on the greenhouse problem. I am grateful to Alvin Weinberg for arousing my interest in the problem fifteen years ago, and for inviting me many times to Oak Ridge for discussions with him, Ralph Rotty, and Gregg Marland. The following references cover an infinitesimal part of the literature on this subject.

C. Tickell, *Climatic Change and World Affairs,* rev. ed. (Cambridge, Mass.: Harvard Center for International Affairs, University Press of America, 1986). The first edition was published, also at Harvard, in 1977.

F. J. Dyson, "Can We Control the Carbon Dioxide in the Atmosphere?" *Energy* 2 (1978): 287–91.

C. Keeling, "Overview of Scripps Program to Observe Atmospheric Carbon Dioxide," Scripps Institution of Oceanography preprint, January 2, 1989.

G. Marland, "The Role of U.S. Forestry in Addressing the CO_2 Greenhouse Problem," remarks before the Senate Committee on Energy and Natural Resources, September 19, 1988, Oak Ridge National Laboratory preprint.

D. L. Regehr, F. A. Bazzaz, and W. R. Boggess, "Photosynthesis, Transpiration and Leaf Conductance of Populus Deltoides in Relation to Flooding and Drought," *Photosynthetica* 9 (1975): 52–61.

351

P. P. Tans, I. Y. Fung, and T. Takahashi, "Observational Constraints on the Global Atmospheric CO_2 Budget," *Science* 247 (1990): 1431–38.

M. C. Trexler, P. E. Faeth, and J. M. Kramer, *Forestry as a Response to Global Warming: An Analysis of the Guatemala Agroforestry and Carbon Sequestration Project,* report published by World Resources Institute, Washington, D.C., June 1989.

CHAPTER 13. THE FUTURE OF PHYSICS

Lecture given at the dedication of Jadwin and Fine halls, Princeton University, March 17, 1970. I was invited to prognosticate, but my prognostications did not turn out so well as those recorded in chapter 9. It is lucky that prognosticators, like astrologers, are not held responsible for the accuracy of their predictions. I emphasized two directions for physicists to follow, cosmic-ray research and the sequencing of biological molecules by physical methods. Neither direction has yet proved popular or fruitful. The cosmic-ray proposal is no longer of interest and is here omitted. I still have hopes that the sequencing proposal may come to fruition, as did Haldane's 1924 predictions of biotechnology, after a longer time than I expected. The recent invention of the scanning tunneling electron microscope may cause a revival of interest in physical methods of biological sequencing.

CHAPTER 14. UNFASHIONABLE PURSUITS

Published in the *Mathematical Intelligencer* 5, no. 3 (1983): 47–54. This was a lecture given on August 24, 1981, at the Institute for Advanced Study in Princeton, to a conference sponsored by the Alexander von Humboldt Foundation. The published version has a number of references to technical mathematical literature which I omit here. I also eliminated some mathematical jargon from the text.

J. H. Conway, "Monsters and Moonshine," *Mathematical Intelligencer* 2, no. 4 (1980): 165–71, gives a semitechnical account of the monster group.

CHAPTER 15. ASTRONOMY IN A PRIVATE SPHERE

Published in the *American Scholar* 53, no. 2 (Spring 1984): 169–82. This piece originated in a lecture given at the University of Pennsylvania in 1981.

The Chicago newspaper cartoon is reproduced on p. 30 of H. Wright, J. N. Warnow, and C. Weiner, eds., *The Legacy of George Ellery Hale* (Cambridge, Mass.: MIT Press, 1972). Other quotes concerning Hale are taken from the same source, with references in the bibliography, pp. 110–11.

For the Ebert quote, *Carnegie Institution of Washington Year Book*, vol. 77 (Baltimore: Port City Press, 1978), p. 6.

For the life and times of Bernhard Schmidt, see the memoir by Paul C. Hodges, M.D., reprinted in A. G. Ingalls, ed., *Amateur Telescope Making, Book 3* (New York: Scientific American, 1961), pp. 365–75.

For Humason, see N. U. Mayall, "Milton M. Humason, Some Personal Reminiscences," *Mercury* 2, no. 1 (1973): 3–8.

For Hubble, see the memoir by N. U. Mayall, *National Academy of Sciences Biographical Memoirs* 41 (1970): 174–207.

CHAPTER 16. TO TEACH OR NOT TO TEACH

Published in *American Journal of Physics* 59 (1991): 491–95. This is a talk given at San Antonio, Texas, in January 1991, to the American Association of Physics Teachers. Parts of it are taken from an earlier talk with the title "Willard Gibbs and the Teaching of Science," published in G. D. Mostow and D. G. Caldi, eds., *Proceedings of the Gibbs Symposium, Yale University, May 15–17, 1989* (American Mathematical Society, 1990), pp. 269–76.

For the Russian women scientists, see Ann H. Koblitz, "Science, Women, and the Russian Intelligentsia: the Generation of the 1860's," *Isis* 79 (1988): 208–26.

C. R. Nappi, "On Mathematics and Science Education in the U.S. and Europe," *Physics Today*, May 1990, pp. 77–79. A longer version, with the title "On Women in Math and Science," is available as an Institute for Advanced Study preprint, IASSNS-HEP-90/43, dated April 26, 1990.

N. Bohr, "Discussion with Einstein on Epistemological Problems in Atomic Physics," in P. A. Schilpp, ed., *Albert Einstein, Philosopher-Scientist* (Library of Living Philosophers, vol. 7, 1949), p. 240.

S. Coyle, "The Long Haul to a Doctorate," preprint dated Sept. 9, 1990 (National Research Council, Washington, D.C.).

The traces of Bohr in Frost's poems were described by John Coletta at the San Antonio meeting of the AAPT, January 1991.

Chandler Davis, "The Purge," in Peter Duren, ed., *A Century of Mathematics in America, Part I* (Providence, R.I.: American Mathematical Society, 1988), pp. 413–28.

For further reading on science education at the college level, I recommend Sheila Tobias, *They're Not Dumb, They're Different* (Tucson, Ariz.: Research Corporation, 1990). I am grateful to Tobias for a copy of her book.

CHAPTER 17. PUGWASH 1962

Published in *Physics Today* 15 (November 1962) no. 11, 24–26. With hindsight one may say that the most immediately useful discussions at the 1962 Pugwash meeting occurred in working group 3, which dealt with test-ban problems and helped to bring about the Partial Test-Ban Treaty of 1963. Leo Szilard, as usual, looked further ahead than other people. He joined working group 4 because it dealt with things that he regarded as more important in the long run. Now, in 1990, Western and Eastern Europe have emerged into a situation where the concerns of working group 4 have practical relevance, but Leo Szilard's farsighted spirit is no longer here to guide us.

CHAPTER 18. DEATH OF A PROJECT

Published in *Science* 149 (1965): 141–44. A more personal account of Project Orion is contained in chapter 10 of F. J. Dyson, *Disturbing the Universe* (New York: Harper & Row, 1979). An excellent analysis of Orion and various later projects has been published by Anthony R. Martin and Alan Bond, "Nuclear Pulse Propulsion: A Historical Review of an Advanced Propulsion Concept," *Journal of the British Interplanetary Society* 32 (1979): 283–310. Martin and Bond did a thorough job of digging out obscure documents. Their bibliography is the best available.

The nostalgic view of Orion recorded in this 1965 article does not imply that I would now wish to revive the project, if by some miracle the necessary funding and political support for it should become available. We now have better, cleaner, and less clumsy systems of space propulsion waiting to be developed. One such system is mentioned in the notes to chapter 1. For others, see chapter 9 of F. J. Dyson, *Infinite in All Directions* (New York: Harper & Row, 1988).

CHAPTER 19. HUMAN CONSEQUENCES OF THE EXPLORATION OF SPACE

Carlson Memorial Lecture, given at Iowa State University in April 1968. Most of it was published in the *Bulletin of the Atomic Scientists* 25, no. 7 (September 1969): 8–13.

Wells's *When the Sleeper Wakes* (originally published 1899; reprinted in *Three Prophetic Novels* [New York: Dover, 1960]), was made into the Woody Allen movie *Sleeper* without any credit to Wells for the story.

For the economics of space operations, T. B. Taylor, "Propulsion of Space Vehicles," chapter 39 of R. E. Marshak, ed., *Perspectives in Modern Physics* (New York: Interscience, 1966).

CHAPTER 20. THE HIDDEN COSTS OF SAYING NO

Published in the *Bulletin of the Atomic Scientists* 31, no. 6 (June 1975): 23–27. This was a lecture given at the International Meeting on Scientific Research and Energy Problems, Madrid, Spain, in October 1974.

Carl Djerassi, "Prognosis for the Development of New Chemical Birth-Control Agents," *Science* 166 (1969): 468; and "Birth Control after 1984," *Science* 169 (1970): 941. The economic and political obstacles to the development of new birth-control agents remain as formidable in 1990 as they were in 1970, but some new agents have recently become available in spite of the obstacles.

Paul Berg et al., "Potential Biohazards of Recombinant DNA Molecules," *Science* 185 (1974): 303. This was the statement that launched the movement to establish international guidelines for the regulation of experiments using recombinant DNA. At a meeting convened by Berg and others at Asilomar, California, in

1975, guidelines were proposed which governmental regulatory authorities have followed ever since. On the whole, the regulations have been successful in avoiding biohazards while allowing the development of science and technology to go forward rapidly.

Leon Cooper, lecture at the Naval Research Laboratory Fiftieth Anniversary Celebration, Alexandria, Virginia, October 1973.

CHAPTER 21. PUPIN

Preface written for a new edition of Michael I. Pupin, *From Immigrant to Inventor* (New York: Scribner's, 1960; orig. ed. pub. 1922).

For Pupin and the Pupin building, see the booklet *Celebration of the Fiftieth Anniversary of the Pupin Laboratories* (New York: Columbia University, 1977).

CHAPTER 22. OPPENHEIMER

Review of Alice Kimball Smith and Charles Weiner, eds., *Robert Oppenheimer, Letters and Recollections* (Cambridge, Mass.: Harvard University Press, 1980), published in the *New Republic,* May 24, 1980.

I received a letter from Frank Oppenheimer dated February 6, 1981, correcting some of the statements in the review. Here are the relevant passages from his letter:

> I found the letters to Herbert Smith interesting because they, along with the others to me and his contemporaries, illustrated how as a late adolescent he became the person that he thought he was supposed to be, with his family, with his mentor and his friend, each a different version of himself. Because he wrote so well, this aspect of growing up was more evident and even charming than is apparent with most of us.
>
> It is difficult to write books in which the details of history do not become distorted. My brother did not persuade Edith Warner to set up her restaurant on the Rio Grande. She had done so many years before. My friend Roger Lewis and I had first encountered her wonder after a long, long day of riding up the river from Cochiti. We took my

brother there after a somewhat shorter ride from Frijoles Canyon a couple of years later. He was as taken with her, her spirit and her style, as Roger and I had been.

The final quote in the review is from a letter by Ursula Niebuhr, dated August 16, 1979. Ursula and Reinhold Niebuhr were guests of the Institute for Advanced Study for the academic year 1957–58, invited by Robert Oppenheimer. For "The Pulley," see note to chapter 35.

CHAPTER 23. HEIMS

Review of Steve J. Heims, *John von Neumann and Norbert Wiener: From Mathematics to the Technologies of Life and Death* (Cambridge, Mass.: MIT Press, 1980), published in *Technology Review,* February–March 1981, pp. 17–19.

Robert J. C. Butow, *Japan's Decision to Surrender* (Stanford, Calif.: Stanford University Press, 1954).

CHAPTER 24. MANIN AND FORMAN

Review of Yury I. Manin, *Mathematics and Physics,* trans. by Ann and Neal Koblitz (Boston: Birkhäuser, 1981), published in the *Mathematical Intelligencer* 5, no. 2 (1983): 54–57. The Russian original was no. 12 in the series *Novoye v Zhizne* (Moscow: Znaniya, 1979).

Paul Forman, *Weimar Culture, Causality and Quantum Theory, 1918–1927: Adaptation by German Physicists and Mathematicians to a Hostile Intellectual Environment,* vol. 3 of *Historical Studies in the Physical Sciences,* (Philadelphia: University of Pennsylvania Press, 1971).

Oswald Spengler, *The Decline of the West,* trans. by Charles F. Atkinson, 2 vols. in 1 (New York: Knopf, 1939), pp. 418, 427–28.

CHAPTER 25. KENNAN

Review of George F. Kennan, *The Nuclear Delusion: Soviet-American Relations in the Atomic Age* (New York: Pantheon Books, 1982), published in the *Christian Science Monitor,* October 5, 1982.

CHAPTER 26. OPPENHEIMER AGAIN

Preface written for J. Robert Oppenheimer, *Atom and Void: Essays on Science and Community* (Princeton, N.J.: Princeton University Press, 1989). This collection is a combination of two earlier books by Oppenheimer: *Science and the Common Understanding* (New York: Simon & Schuster, 1954), and *The Flying Trapeze: Three Crises for Physicists* (New York: Oxford University Press, 1964).

The Hammond letter is dated October 1979. Lansing Hammond died in December 1980.

CHAPTER 27. MORSON AND TOLSTOY

Review of Gary Saul Morson, *Hidden in Plain View: Narrative and Creative Potentials in "War and Peace"* (Stanford, Calif.: Stanford University Press, 1987), published in *Tolstoy Studies Journal* 2 (1989): 1–3. This issue of *TSJ* contains my review together with four others, followed by a long reply, "The Potentials and Hazards of Prosaics," by Morson.

James Spedding et al., eds., *The Works of Francis Bacon* (London: Longman & Co., 1860). Vol. 4 contains a translation of *The Great Instauration,* an unfinished work of which the "Novum Organum" was a part. The quotes are taken from pp. 32 and 48. The Latin original was published in 1620.

René Descartes, *A Discourse on Method* (Everyman's Library; London: Dent & Sons, 1912), pp. 34–35. The French original was published in Leyden in 1637.

CHAPTER 28. LETTER FROM ARMENIA

Published in the *New Yorker,* November 6, 1971, pp. 126–37.

For the hydrology of Lake Sevan, see S. V. Shaginyan, *Lake Sevan* (in Russian) with photographs by O. I. Gladun (Leningrad: Gidrometeoizdat, 1970).

The proceedings of the Conference on Communication with Extraterrestrial Intelligence, held at Byurakan Observatory, September 5–11, 1971, were published in a book, *Communication with Extraterrestrial Intelligence,* edited by Carl Sagan (Cambridge, Mass.: MIT Press, 1973). The book contains a lecture by me (Appendix D, pp. 371–89) which is not reprinted here. Pieces of it were incorporated into *Disturbing the Universe* (New York: Harper & Row, 1979).

CHAPTER 29. BRITTLE SILENCE

Published in *Outlook,* no. 40 (Summer 1981), pp. 17–19. Translated from the Russian of A. Tsirulnikov, "Khrupkaya Tishina" *Literaturnaya Gazeta,* December 3, 1980. I am grateful to Professor Yury Manin (author of the book reviewed in chapter 24) for bringing this article to my attention. *Outlook* was a quarterly magazine edited by Tony Kallet and published by the Mountain View Publishing Company, Boulder, Colorado. It was the only magazine that I regularly enjoyed reading cover-to-cover. Unfortunately, it is defunct. The last issue was no. 59 (Spring 1986).

CHAPTER 30. HELEN DUKAS

Contribution to the memorial ceremony for Helen Dukas at the Institute for Advanced Study on March 15, 1982. Helen Dukas (1896–1982) became Einstein's secretary in 1928 and remained with him, first in Berlin and then in Princeton, until the end of his life. From the time of his death until her own, she worked at the Institute as curator of the Einstein archive. The closest she came to a personal statement about her life's work is the book *Einstein: The Human Side* (Princeton, N.J.: Princeton University Press, 1979), in which she published an assortment of items from her *Zettelkästchen,* a little box containing scraps that she had copied from the archive because she enjoyed sharing them with her friends. Abraham Pais, who had known her longer and worked with her more closely than I, also spoke at the ceremony. A copy of his remarks is preserved in the Princeton Physics Department (Fine Hall) library.

CHAPTER 31. PAUL DIRAC

Obituary notice of Paul A. M. Dirac, published in the *Yearbook of the American Philosophical Society,* 1986, pp. 101–5.

For the Dirac lecture from which I quoted, see CTS Bulletin

VI-6 (Coral Gables, Fla.: University of Miami Center for Theoretical Studies, December-January 1972-73), pp. 6-12.

The recent evidence of the constancy of gravitational forces makes it unlikely that Dirac's cosmology can be correct.

For the Wigner story, see B. Kursunoglu and E. Wigner, eds., *Reminiscences About a Great Physicist: Paul Adrien Maurice Dirac* (Cambridge: Cambridge University Press, 1987), p. 64.

CHAPTER 32. BEACONS

Lecture given at IBM Watson Research Center in October 1988, responding to the Gemant Award given by the American Institute of Physics for "creative work in the arts and humanities that derived from a deep knowledge of and love for physics." The previous winner of the award was Philip Morrison.

Richard P. Feynman, *Surely You're Joking, Mr. Feynman: Adventures of a Curious Character,* ed. Ralph Leighton (New York: Norton, 1985), p. 60. Richard P. Feynman, *What Do You Care What Other People Think? Further Adventures of a Curious Character,* ed. Ralph Leighton (New York: Norton, 1988).

For Einstein's letter to the queen, see Otto Nathan and Heinz Norden, eds., *Einstein on Peace* (New York: Simon & Schuster, 1960), p. 245.

Letter from Robert Armstrong of Mutare, Zimbabwe, dated June 17, 1984.

CHAPTER 33. KENNAN AGAIN

Speech at a banquet given by Physicians for Social Responsibility in honor of George Kennan, March 5, 1988.

Chingiz Aitmatov, *The Day Lasts More than a Hundred Years,* trans. John French (London: Macdonald & Co., 1983). The Russian original was published under the title *Buranny Junction,* with the English title as subtitle (Moscow: Novy Mir, 1980). For the story of Naiman-Ana and her Mankurt son Zholaman, see pp. 124-46 of the English ed.

CHAPTER 34. FEYNMAN IN 1948

An abridged version of this chapter was published in *Physics Today* 42, no. 2 (1989): 32-38, with the title "Feynman at Cornell." That issue of *Physics Today* is a commemoration of Feynman and contains eight talks, of which this is one, given at the memorial session of the American Physical Society in San Francisco, January 18, 1989.

The extracts printed here are taken from my letters, without marking where phrases, sentences, or paragraphs have been omitted. Nothing has been added.

CHAPTER 35. THE FACE OF GAIA

This chapter was published in an anthology: Clifton Fadiman, ed., *Living Philosophies: The Reflections of Some Eminent Men and Women of Our Time* (Garden City, N.Y.: Doubleday, 1990), pp. 7–15.

Res Jost, for many years professor of theoretical physics at the Federal Institute of Technology (ETH) in Zürich, died in October 1990. My wrong paper was published in the *Physical Review* 111 (1958): 1717–18.

Lewis Thomas, *The Lives of a Cell* (New York: Bantam, 1975). The comparison between termite and human societies is in the chapters "Social Talk" and "Living Language," pp. 102–6 and 156–64.

The Poems of George Herbert (World's Classics ed.; Oxford: Oxford University Press, 1907), p. 144. "The Pulley" was first published in 1633.

James Lovelock, *The Ages of Gaia: A Biography of Our Living Earth* (New York: Norton, 1988).

INDEX

371